Oscar F Reed

WRESTLING WITH LUTHER

WRESTLING
WITH
luther

An Introduction to the Study of His Thought

John R. Loeschen

Publishing House
St. Louis

Quotations from

Luther: Lectures on Romans, the Library of Christian Classics, Volume XV, newly translated and edited by Wilhelm Pauck. Copyright © MCMLXI W. L. Jenkins. The Westminster Press, Philadelphia;

Luther: Early Theological Works, the Library of Christian Classics, Volume XVI, edited and translated by James Atkinson. Published in the U.S.A. by The Westminster Press, Philadelphia, 1962. Copyright © S.C.M. Press, LTD., London, 1962;

Luther and Erasmus: Free Will and Salvation, the Library of Christian Classics, Volume XVII, translated and edited by E. Gordon Rupp, Philip S. Watson, A. N. Marlow, and B. Drewery. Copyright © MCMLXIX, The Westminister Press;

are used by permission of The Westminster Press, Philadelphia, Pa. 19107

Concordia Publishing House, St. Louis, Missouri
Copyright © 1976 Concordia Publishing House
MANUFACTURED IN THE UNITED STATES OF AMERICA

Library of Congress Cataloging in Publication Data
Loeschen, John R   1940-
    Wrestling with Luther.

    A revision of the author's thesis, Graduate Theological
Union, 1968.
        Bibliography: p.
        Includes index.
        1. Luther, Martin, 1483-1546—Theology. I. Title.
BR333.2.L56 1976   230'.4'10924   75-33815
ISBN 0-570-03256-3

This book is dedicated to that small band of graduate students who found themselves in the crucible that was the Graduate Theological Union during its first years in Berkeley.

And the Word became flesh and dwelt among us, full of grace and truth.

—John 1:14 RSV

For even if it [philosophy] seems to think and say that God is omnipotent, nevertheless, it cannot understand and establish that God was made man because the infinite would be contained in the finite.

—Martin Luther
The Disputation on "The Word Was Made Flesh" 38, p.262.

"That religion will conquer which can render clear to popular understanding some eternal greatness incarnate in the passage of temporal fact."

—Alfred North Whitehead
Adventures of Ideas
(New York: Mentor Books, 1955), p.40.

CONTENTS

Preface   9

Introduction
Essay I *Coram Deo - Coram Mundo*   15

Part One
God's Address   41
Essay II *Homo Incurvatus - Homo Ingressus*   43
Essay III *Lex et Fides*   59

Part Two
God's Futurity   81
Essay IV *Promissio et Fides*   83
Essay V *Initium Novae Creaturae*   104

Part Three
God's Body   121
Essay VI *Ubiquitas Carnalis Christi*   123
Essay VII *Larvae Dei*   138

Conclusion
Essay VIII *Regnum Dei - Regnum Mundi*   159
Notes   178
Bibliography   188
Index   192

PREFACE

For one who was born and raised in the Lutheran church, there is often a bias against Luther studies as a choice for academic specialization. It was thus without intending to, and with initial kicking against the pricks, that I fell into the fatal fascination during the summer of my first year at Chicago Theological Seminary. I had been working through Luther's *Commentary on Romans* in connection with an interest in the history of the interpretation of that epistle. At the same time I was reading Dietrich Bonhoeffer's *Ethics*. It began to occur to me that Bonhoeffer had developed, particularly in the third and fourth chapters of his work, a model which beautifully captured the Luther of the *Romans* commentary—a Luther that I had not seen in most secondary presentations.

I began to work in Luther more intently, trying to ascertain the degree to which his thinking did and did not support Bonhoeffer's model. This study resulted in a B.D. thesis in 1965. I owe a great deal to Otto Betz of CTS, whose initial skepticism changed to warm support; to Ragnar Bring, then lecturing at the University of Chicago, whose *jawohl* to the basic ideas gave me the first technical confirmation that I was at least in the ball park; and to W. W. Schroeder of CTS, whose incorrigibly analytical mind and ruthlessly intimate questioning of his students taught me how to read.

I continued to pursue Luther at the Graduate Theological Union in Berkeley, and the thesis blossomed into a doctoral dissertation in Medieval and Reformation studies in 1968. This book is a considerably humanized translation of the dissertation. A project of this scope and in this form is not normally acceptable as a dissertation. Once again a debt of gratitude is owed to three men: to John von Rohr and Robert Goeser of the GTU, who supported the actual content of the work, and especially to John Dillenberger, then dean of the GTU, who not only gave me his complete personal support for the project, but who almost singlehandedly piloted it—and me—through the difficult struggle for academic acceptance.

I have thus been wrestling with Luther for 15 years—as a ministerial student, a graduate student, and as a teacher. During that time there has been much personal pain, due in part to the fact that when you get caught up in Luther many other needs and obligations go unmet. But I see no end to it. I have tried to describe my own experience of studying Luther in the book along with the results of the study to date. I did not do this as a personal advertisement but rather because of a completely objective fact of life. Luther, like Thomas and Augustine, completely captures anyone who ventures too close. You will become charmed with Augustine; you will be seduced by Thomas; Luther will assault you. I think it is of value, therefore, to convey to the prospective student something of what he can expect when he enters into this existential meaning of the "Luther affair." For those already deeply involved the book is an indication that their experiences are shared.

The book is intended to illustrate the characteristic issues and patterns of thought which every student will meet in his study, and to suggest what I feel are the best approaches and the best tools for interpreting Luther. The eight essays provide detailed outlines, not exhaustive analyses, of their respective subjects. Each essay is both independent of and dependent on all the others. The particular subject is not a *part*, to be supplemented by other parts, but is a *perspective* on the *whole* of Luther's theology. In general each essay begins with an empirical reconnoiter of the issue, moves to a more systematic and occasionally speculative abstraction from the data, and concludes with a reinterpretation of empirical material, assisted by whatever advance has been made and by relevant conclusions from preceding essays. A variety of methodological approaches is evident. Occasionally an exhaustive analysis of a particular text will dominate the form and content of an essay; sometimes a more synthetic accumulation from a wide range of material. Sometimes it's a matter of sticking very stubbornly to the literal substance of what Luther says; sometimes it is the verbal associations and the puns that give insight. The decision in each case is made simply on the basis of what feels right. If this suggests methodological sloppiness or subjectivism, and if any defense is needed, I can only offer the following.

Luther is a figure who is new and arresting to every generation in part because he provides an occasion for expressing the sensitivities and interests of one's own time. Every secondary work on Luther ever written is thus the product of an encounter: the Luther text in all its variety with the quite distinct mind that takes it up. The phrase *so sagt Luther* must be the beginning of the discussion, not the end of it. There is simply no such thing as "assured results." Anyone who has studied the history of Luther interpretation learns that—and usually forgets the lesson when it comes to his own conclusions. Technical accuracy is of course the paramount ideal and the critical test of all work. Yet we simply have got to learn to live with the social relativity of knowledge. The best ways to do this are first to resist the temptation to reject everything in alternate interpretations, past or present, while absolutizing one's own claims; and second, to become conscious of the biases and assumptions which one brings to the study. Ideally these biases and assumptions should also be clearly indicated to the reader—and in the first chapter. But perhaps that is too much to ask of sinful men with aspirations unto God.

I don't think you will have much difficulty uncovering at least some of my own commitments. In a few instances the task of personal decision in the face of ambiguous data is itself part of the discussion, as I suggested above. Beyond every particular commitment, however, stands one's basic philosophical commitment. Whether or not it is directly relevant to the study, it is always better if the reader knows who it is he is allowing to lead him into a subject. I am persuaded by the philosophy of organism, of which A.N. Whitehead, Charles Hartshorne, and H.N. Wieman are the seminal figures. Anyone who is familiar with process metaphysics will recognize its effects in this study. It is, of course, methodologically and historically unsound to attempt to interpret Luther as a process theologian. It could not be pulled off in any case. I do not think that any data was perverted, any conclusions rendered invalid, due to an improper intrusion of an independently derived philosophical position. What the commitment to process philosophy has done, however, is to sensitize the eye to features of Luther's theology which have been overlooked, underestimated, or found embarrassing to students with quite different though equally obvious philosophical commitments. The Kantian epistemology so predominant in the tradition of Luther scholarship is at least as alien to Luther as is process metaphysics. That tradition and its accuracies is at present in no danger of being replaced. But a commitment to process philosophy allows the student to exercise at least a corrective function. At best it enables him to enter sympathetically into the study of the Luther who speculates daringly, who assumes the epistemological continuity of man, nature, and, with some qualifications, God, and whose theological writing is as dynamic, teleological, and value-laden as the universe it presents. These characteristics are not always easily associated with the stubborn old dogmatician from Wittenberg. If this study has no other effect than to persuade the reader that Luther's theology is a living, growing, open-ended, and adventurous enterprise, I will consider it well worth the effort of its publication.

The selection and use of sources must now be explicated. The Luther corpus is so large that a systematic selection must be made in order to entertain the possibility of making headway. As this study is concerned with Luther's theology in the restricted sense and not primarily with either his own history or that of the Reformation, exclusion of the correspondence, table talk, liturgical materials, and the German Bible was possible. For the most part, the sermons and tracts have been excluded because everything of importance in them is usually said better, more exactly, fully, and reliably elsewhere. The key is degree of confidence: one can always find confirmation in the sermon of what is said in the commentary, but not vice versa.

Luther's only self-acknowledged title was "lecturer in Bible." His major theological form is the commentary, a genre including such a diverse group of materials as marginal notes, sermon collections, and the important subsidiary form of the theological treatise on a specified subject. It is the commentaries and treatises which provide the basic material for the study. The material represents the whole of Luther's historical journey. Three works are most important. As it happens they divide Luther's career in three decades: 1515–24, 1525–34, and 1535–44. The *Commentary on Romans* of 1515–16 (LCC 15) is the first major writing during the evangelical breakthrough; it serves as the touchstone for assessing subsequent development. At the beginning of the second period stands *De servo arbitrio* of 1525 (LCC 17). Not only is it important because it is Luther's major effort against the humanists and enthusiasts, but it is his most sustained and intense treatment of a single theme. At the beginning of the third period, when Luther was beginning to engage the antinomians, stands the *Lectures on Galatians* of 1535 (26, 27), a work which, with the possible exception of *De servo arbitrio,* is Luther's most famous and consequential technical theological exercise. The primacy of these three works functions in this way: any position taken *must* be documented in these sources and *should* be supported elsewhere. Any position taken from other material, no matter how well documented, remains suspect if it is not found in these three sources.

The second and supporting group of sources tends to fall towards the middle of the periods marked by the primary sources. In the first period are the *Operationes in Psalmos* (W 5), the full expression of the "theology of the cross"; the *Assertio omnium articulorum* (W 7), a distillation and watershed of Luther's progress; and the famous treatises of 1520 (31, 36). In the second period are the 1527 and 1528 works on the Sacrament (36, 37), most germane to Part Three of the study. In the third period, the *Antinomian Disputations* (W 39) are important, especially to Part One.

The third group of sources fills in the gaps and enriches the basic materials. The school disputations of 1517 and 1518 (31), the lectures on *Hebrews* (LCC 16) and *Galatians* (27), and the treatise against Latomus (LCC 16) fill in the first period. The commentary on *Jonah* (W 19), and especially a great number of individual commentaries on single psalms, make up the data of the second period. For the balance of the third period there is the *Genesis* commentary (1–8), and the disputations of the late 1530s.

I have not usually taken account of the temporal order of the writings discussed or cited in the study. The titles and dates of the major documents discussed will be noted where it is not clear from the text. There is possibly a slightly greater use of the *Romans* commentary in the first half of the study and of the *Galatians* commentary in the second half. I am almost always discussing Luther's "mature" position on a topic. This study assumes the general agreement on most issues of the "young" and the "old" Luther. Most of the changes are shifts in perspective or interest, and are not substantive alterations of a previous position. Luther, however, did not reach a mature position on all fronts at once. His full presentation of the "theology of the Word" is not represented until *Galatians*. His full understanding of Law and its relation to human nature is not represented until the *Antinomian Disputations;* his sacramental theory not until the writings of 1528. His epistemology is not fully developed until the "letter-spirit" polarization drops out around 1520 to be replaced by "faith by hearing" and "the theology of the cross." For all of these matters one can find adumbrations in the pre-1520 works. On most matters I have used the pre-1520 material only where it is directly confirmed in a later source or where it reveals a preliminary attempt to formulate a matter that Luther will handle more satisfactorily later. The major exception to this rule is the early *Lectures on Romans,* which I use as a definitive source for Luther's anthropology.

I said above that most of the changes in Luther's thought reflect shifts of perspective. Specific shifts on individual topics will be manifested in the comparison of sources. The shift indicated in the comparison of the first and last essays is more basic. This shift is, as the titles indicate, from the *coram* to the *regnum* motif. The former is a formal, relational perspective, and I think it best represents Luther's thought at the beginning of his career. The latter is a more empirical, substantive perspective, and I think it best represents Luther's mature position. The question is merely one of relative dominance and not of substitution. There is no one place where the shift is to be clearly established. Perhaps the slight shift toward what Luther called the "objective" grounds for faith in the Lord's Supper, coming in the early 1520s, is as clear an indicator as one can find. This study itself, as it runs its changing course from first essay to last, reflects this shift. In addition it embodies the basic reality of Luther's direction of thought: from form to matter, spirit to flesh, from God to the world. The reader will appreciate the dimensions of this process of thought only after having concluded his reading.

JRL

Introduction

Essay I: *Coram Deo - Coram Mundo*

A Way In

The Weimar edition of Luther's works, over 100 volumes at present and still growing, must nearly overwhelm the beginning student. But Luther did not write a *Summa Theologiae,* an *Institutes,* or a *Systematic Theology* in three neat volumes bound in different colors, to help guide the student through this sea of words. If the student is still not defeated in the face of the awesome task thus set before him, a look at the equally large library of secondary works on Luther will often provide the finishing touch.

But if he survives this scholarly baptism, the student may begin to see the Luther library in all its possibilities. And now the student is no longer a novice; for he has started to experience for himself the quiet despair, the exciting and vigorous hope, that has characterized generations of Luther scholars.

Both the despair and the hope emerge from the simply unavoidable task of presenting Luther's theology in some more or less cogent order. In spite of first appearances it must be assumed that Luther's thinking has its rules, its reasons—that it has a form and structure which, moreover, this most brilliant of linguists was able to communicate to his readers. If one only had the eyes to see. But to speak of the "structure" of Luther's theology is to be confronted with a rather formidable problem. It does not take very much reading of Luther to realize that his theology has neither parts nor sequence. It is a cardinal sin to presume to study Luther topically, as though one could expect to master one subject in relative independence of any and every other subject. You must rather grasp the whole of it rather intimately before you can say much about anything with any degree of confidence.

And once a rough and preliminary comprehensiveness has been achieved and you begin to prepare to speak on Luther, the problem of sequence arises. There seems to be no compelling reason for beginning the presentation at one place or in one way rather than another. This problem is a reflection of the same characteristic of Luther's writing that the student discovered to his frustration in reading him. You begin by studying, for example, Luther's understanding of theological knowledge, and are confronted by a pair of likely looking terms, "faith" and "reason." But soon you discover that these terms not only are used in the most varied of contexts for the most different of purposes, but also that in order to begin to understand them you must master another set of terms, "nature" and "grace," for example. Now this progression of study never ends. Luther leads you like a will-o'-the-wisp from one thing to another until you are back where you began. In the process you discover that while one brace of terms has led to the next with an internal necessity, the brace itself is not a unit. The contrast to "faith" could just as easily have been "nature," and that to "grace" could have been "reason." To sum up this capsule history, the experience of which is the first and daily baptism of a Luther scholar, let me say that most sets of terms define perspectives on the whole of Luther's theology, and thus implicate every other set. The one explicates the many, and the many the one. Luther's theology is holistic and extraordinarily systematic.

Each topic falls into a brace of terms which involve the whole; it leads therefore to other sets, which are themselves somewhat interchangeable in composition. This is a situation which reflects what I shall describe more fully below as the *dialectical* character of Luther's theology. "Dialectical" is an adjective that can be applied to Luther's theology at every level of discourse and at every degree of generalization. An appreciation of the importance of this characteristic is the first step in the making of a Luther scholar, if such a creature is made rather than born. While the meaning of "dialectical" will accrue as the study advances, we already have before us an essential dialectical feature which can provide us a way into the study of Luther's theology: he almost invariably spoke in twos. "Law and Gospel," "wrath and grace," "flesh and spirit," "faith and works"— every brace of terms coming to mind when you think of Luther's themes—are of course terms overflowing with the hard-won content of Luther's experience. Yet one can't escape the impression, increasingly vivid in his writings from the 1520s onward, that Luther also used the dialectical pairs as a kind of linguistic or intellectual shorthand to guide both himself and his students through an otherwise unmanageable complex of ideas. It seems odd to suggest in full view of those long library shelves, that Luther was parsimonious about anything. But it would be more implausible for just the same reason to assume he did not develop these pairs of terms into signs which at once generalized a wealth of concrete experience and located a perspective on that experience.

In any case Luther did speak in twos, and at the beginning of our study it will be helpful to start with that fact, concentrating interest on Luther's dialectical language in its formal interrelations rather than on content. This introductory essay accordingly may seem more of an abstract, linguistic exercise than would ordinarily be acceptable. The initial tasks are those of learning how to read Luther's writing and of developing a language for organizing and interpreting that writing. The content will come later. First, it is necessary quite literally "to come to terms" with Luther.

1

The Subject of Theology

One of the first linguistic impressions on the eyes of a beginning reader of Luther is the reformer's apparently promiscuous use of a recurrent series of terms which very soon become *theologoumena,* sign-words for an assumed content or perspective. These terms usually occur in pairs, and even when one member is not expressed, it must be kept in mind in order to understand the implications of its contrasting term correctly. Often the terms on one side of the hyphen are piled up serially and contrasted with those on the other side. This is especially the case when Luther is holding forth on Christ's atoning work, a subject which many scholars think is the living center of his theology. The presentation of this work, for example in Luther's astonishing commentary of 1535 on Gal. 3:13 ff., reveals this massing of terms with particular intensity. Law, sin, death, curse, world, devil, flesh, wrath, are overcome on the cross by faith, grace, Gospel, Christ, Spirit. The impression one gets from reading such passages is that substantively the terms on each side of the hyphen are nearly interchangeable and that the only bases for their verbal distinction are connotative differences reflecting shifts in perspective on the subject.

A second and complicating feature of Luther's language is the fact that most of the paired terms can be used both *disjunctively* and *conjunctively.* In some contexts Luther spoke, for example, of flesh *or* spirit, works or faith, reason or grace, even of Law or Gospel, although we shall have to consider the last example more carefully later. At the same time, and often enough in the same passage,[1] Luther used the terms conjunctively, for example, flesh *and* spirit, Law and Gospel, sinner and saved. Again the bases for the difference in phrasing seem to lie in shifts in perspective on the subject.

I have spoken of "contrast" and "perspective" in opening the

17

consideration of Luther's language. Both terms are important if we are to get a feeling for Luther's pattern of thought. The use of a pair of terms in both disjunctive and conjunctive senses is due to the fact that the terms express a relationship of *contrast*. By a "relationship of contrast" I mean, first, that there are perspectives from which one can see both an *identity* and a *difference* of the terms contrasted. Thus in the polarization "flesh — spirit," for example, "flesh *or* spirit" expresses the apartness or opposition, "flesh *and* spirit" the togetherness of the contrasted terms. Which sense of the contrast Luther developed in a given passage depended on his perspective.

Second, it is very important not to mistake the relationship of contrast as static. One can get this impression rather easily from Luther's use of his pairs as sign language. But in the real order of things the contrast is a very dynamic, vectorial, or even eschatological one. This means that properly distinguishing and identifying the realities named in the contrast is a process, in fact a task which always has to be accomplished. The task of distinguishing flesh from spirit, Law from Gospel, God's grace from His wrath, is a task which every Christian, and especially the theologian, must undertake every day. The task is as difficult as it is necessary. Time and again Luther defined a good theologian as one who could distinguish properly, and no less often did he remark that even after years of experience the task was unusually difficult for him. So difficult is the business of theology both in life and in thought that in fact it cannot be accomplished by the Christian at all, but is rather done by God Himself. The same situation obtains for the other side of the contrast. *Overcoming* the distinction is similarly a task, a process of becoming which characterizes the whole of Christian life and thought. God's wrath is meant to lead to His grace, which in turn excludes wrath. The "proper" or theological use of the Law is that which leads to the Gospel. And the Christian is in the process of becoming transformed from flesh into spirit. This task is also one which must be entered into anew everyday, like Baptism, and it is similarly to be accomplished not by man, but by God in man.

Luther's habit of expressing his meaning in pairs of terms whose relationship is a contrast is only the most obvious indication of the dialectical character of his theology. So profound and insistent is this form of thinking that Dietrich Bonhoeffer, here as elsewhere showing himself one of Luther's best interpreters, was moved to term his theology a *theologia relationis*,[2] a theology of relationships. Our preliminary discussion has already implicated us in the task of pursuing Luther's dialectical relationships at a more profound or original level. This deepening of the question is made necessary just because Luther used his pairs now in a conjunctive, now in a disjunctive sense, and even in both senses at once. I suggested "changes in perspective" as the reason for such changes of expression. By a "perspective" I mean a viewpoint from which Luther judged the whole of his subject. This judgment then comes to expression in a conjunctive, disjunctive, or mixed contrast. If we can discover these perspectives, we will have taken a big first step toward organizing and interpreting Luther's theology.

What we are after, when it comes right down to it, is the answer to the question, what distinguishes a viewpoint or perspective as theological? As usual Luther himself is the best guide to Luther. Whether the subject is the created world, the nature of man, or the revelation of God, Luther usually gives us clear indications of the characteristics of theological discourse. In his 1516 commentary on Rom. 8:19, for example, he says that Paul, instead of defining the creation "metaphysically" or in terms of "substance," defines it rather in terms of *relation,* in this case in terms of its "expectancy"—a new and strange theological word."[3] Consistently Luther argues that Scripture defines man not metaphysically but theologically, meaning by this "in the eyes of God." He constantly says that man is, becomes, and always remains *coram deo* ("in the presence of, before, God") — a phrase which not only can be an alternate expression for *regnum dei* ("kingdom of God") but also is a good definition of man's conscience.[4] The law of God has a use which Luther differentiates as theological: that of leading man to Christ, setting man in God's sight.

These examples suggest that the answer to our question is that a perspective is "theological" which relates to Christ or the God or the kingdom of God. The fact that these perspectives appear to be developed in opposition to other perspectives—"theological" in contrast to "metaphysical," for example—suggests that they too are dialectical in character. The question of the meaning of "theological" is like the medieval question, "What is the subject of theology?" Here and there in the Luther corpus one finds a passage which brings together all of Luther's ideas in a particularly concentrated fashion. Luther's introduction to his 1538 commentary on Ps. 51 is one such passage. A detailed analysis of it is appropriate at this juncture not only because it concerns the subject of theology but also because of the many verbal associations Luther makes in presenting his case. From these verbal associations we will gain the names, the functions, and the interrelations of the perspectives we are seeking.

Every Man a Theologian

1. Toward the end of his introduction to the commentary[5] Luther

summarizes by saying that the content of the psalm is "the theological knowledge of man and also the theological knowledge of God." With this phrase Luther exemplifies a rule which brooks no exceptions, i.e., that man and God always be considered together. The two sides of this most basic dialectic are not meant to be taken as supplemental. The relationship is given classic expression by Calvin in the opening pages of the *Institutes:* true knowledge of man depends on true knowledge of God and *vice versa.* The interesting feature of Luther's statement, otherwise a common enough principle for theology, is his application of the adjective "theological" to the subjects of the knowledge of man and the knowledge of God. Luther thereby indicates that there is an alternate way of approaching the issues, a perspective which not only produces a different estimation of the two subjects but also a denial of their interdependence.

The conflict over the best approach to the subjects of man and God emerges right from the beginning of Luther's text. True knowledge of Christian doctrines, he says, is not something which can be formed in terms of human wisdom and grounded in the human heart, but is both given and revealed from heaven. Throughout his introduction Luther constantly opposes the approach of the scholastic doctors, lawyers, physicians, and other sinners (!) to the true approach. The difference between "science" and "theology" is in the first place a difference of perspective. With the former the attitude of approach can be characterized as *coram mundo*—man and God as seen from the world, by the world, for, and before the world. In theology the subjects are approached instead *coram deo*—from God's point of view, in His terms, and for His purposes. We thus must work with a fourfold differentiation of the subject of theology: man *coram mundo* and *coram deo:* and God *coram mundo* and *coram deo.*

Luther never once simply claims that the "scientific" view of man is wrong within its own confines. Even when that science is brought into the "theological circle" in the form of scholastic theology, Luther argues not that it is wrong, but rather that it is superficial, inept, and useless. The "theology of reason without the Word of God," such as Luther feels is practiced by his Catholic opponents, seems concerned only with human acts of sin and the acts whereby God is placated. Reason does not get to the root of human sin and thereby fails miserably to comprehend both its power and the nature of God's grace. The consequence is an overestimation of man's ability, a *coram mundo* overestimation which not only fails to comfort the troubled conscience but is also at odds with what the conscience experiences about itself.

And it is the consideration of man as he is in his conscience, that is, of man *coram deo,* which is the truly theological perspective. The knowledge the conscience has of itself is a true knowledge gained in the serious struggle of feeling and experience. King David's confession is a good example for the conscience of human sin and God's grace. From the psalm we learn that man is completely turned away from God, that he is, in other words, nothing but sin. The conscience, far from escaping God by this turning away, becomes a haunted, guilty, evil conscience. There is no escape from conscience; every man is a theologian. David's testimony teaches his fellow-consciences that there are two kinds of sin: the original sin that is the fatal corruption of human nature, and the actual sins against God's law.

Inseparably joined to the "scientific" or *coram mundo* misunderstanding of man is a misunderstanding of God. When man and his works are overestimated, God and His work is underestimated. If you assume that human nature is sound, Luther says, you obscure the knowledge of grace. By assuming God is moved by works and observances, you fail to recognize that God searches out the heart, the conscience. You fail to see that death is not a natural necessity, but rather a punishment for sin. Worst of all, the nature of God Himself is monstrously perverted. With the fall, Luther argues, human nature became so corrupted and diverted by sin that man "lost his correct judgment before God." Man in his own sinful judgment did not see Him as God. He appeared as an idol to be appeased, and since this is never possible, as an implacable judge and tyrant.

It is only *coram deo,* in the conscience which is led by God's Word, that the true knowledge of God, or rather the knowledge of the true God, is possible. There God is seen, not simply as a judge but also as merciful and good. And accordingly we also learn that true repentance is composed of two elements: the recognition of sin and the recognition of grace. Or to put it in more familiar terms, says Luther, the fear of God and the trust in His mercy.

At this point in the analysis another way of expressing the pattern of Luther's thinking is beginning to emerge. "God *coram deo*" seems an ungainly phrase. Discovering the knowledge of man and of God is a task common to all men. True knowledge, however, comes only through the conscience led by the Word of God, as we have seen. But "conscience" and "Word of God" in themselves are not sufficiently specific ideas. All men possess a conscience and all men think they possess the Word of God. For Luther, however, God's true nature as good and merciful can be discovered only in Christ the Word. It is only through Christ that man can be free of guilt, hopelessness, and despair, can find himself both judged and justified, convicted and redeemed. The new experience, the true knowledge of God and man, cannot be achieved by man, but is accomplished by Christ. It does not happen through the application of reason or through conscience simply as conscience, but rather through faith. What differentiates the *coram deo* perspective from the *coram mundo* perspective on the knowledge of God and man is just the appeal of the former to Christ and to faith. Thus we must now consider what could be called the root of Luther's *coram* pattern. The grounds or locus of the appeal for the truth of that pattern can be expressed in the dialectic, "Christ and faith."

2. In the preceding subsection I have sketched Luther's argument with "science" over how God and man are known. The *coram* dialectic is a basic methodological feature of Luther's thinking. It expresses the structure or pattern of everything Luther presents as evangelical truth. But in order to validate this form of thinking, Luther appeals to Christ and to faith. The dialectic "Christ and faith" is thus basically epistemological in character. It expresses *where* God and man are known in the *way* Luther describes. Christ and faith are not to be seen as one case or element, even the most important one, of a truth complex whose foundation in reality is elsewhere. The reference to Christ at the beginning of Luther's introduction is not indifferent, as we shall see.

The scholastics go wrong right from the start, Luther says, by taking the psalm only in reference to the actual sins of David. Rather one must see it in reference to Christ and take it as a good example of Christian repentance for all sin. Otherwise the psalm is superficial and irrelevant. Luther's religious and professional criticism of scholastic theology was that it was conceptually unable to reflect the experience of the depth of human sin and the power of God's grace.

Luther's central theological concern is most clearly expressed as he moves into the heart of his discourse on the subject of theology. The view that "the natural powers [of man] are unimpaired" is the assumption underlying the *coram mundo* evaluation of man, and leads to a position more serious than a greater or lesser overestimation of human ability. "If the natural powers are unimpaired," asks Luther, "what need is there of Christ?"[6] And here we see Luther's essential objection to scholastic thought on the nature of man. The question preserves the *coram* dialectic, but now gives it the more concrete appeal that the dialectic itself required. This appeal to Christ is not an appeal which simply opposes the view of God and man that is maintained by the world. As I noted above, Luther does not claim the *coram mundo* interpretation is materially wrong. Rather it is by itself incomplete, too simple and superficial. It only becomes wrong, as we shall see in the next section, because it asserts it is the whole truth. Luther's appeal to Christ is a concrete appeal which will view *both* God *and* man in a dialectical fashion, i.e., according to Christ.

Having introduced this concretization into the discussion, Luther first indicates the disjunctive character of the relation "sinner—Christ." With the loss of knowledge of God, man began to trust his own power. The quest for human autonomy becomes an attack on God. Human nature now persecutes the Word by responding to God against and beyond the Word. So far the relation "sinner—Christ" has the same "either—or" character as that of "reason—revelation" discussed earlier. But it also has a conjunctive side. For Luther it is the ground for the conjunction that is the heart of the Gospel, and this ground illustrates the necessity for the appeal to Christ and faith. The second part to theological knowledge is the knowledge of grace and justification, man's restoration through Christ. Christ is called the "Justifier" because He belongs to sinners and was sent for sinners. Then Luther gives a capsule definition of the subject of theology which says it all.

> The proper subject of theology is man guilty of sin and condemned, and God the Justifier and Savior of man the sinner. Whatever is asked or discussed in theology outside this subject, is error and poison. All Scripture points to this, that God commends His kindness to us and in His Son restores to righteousness and life the nature that has fallen into sin and condemnation.[7]

This knowledge is discovered only in faith. The conscience by itself convinces man of his sinfulness; but that man knows himself as *both* sinner *and* saved—this is knowledge that only faith provides.

We now see the reason Luther does not condemn outright the *coram mundo* knowledge of God and man. In that view the relation between God and man was univocal. God was understood as the Giver of laws, man as the doer of works. Such a simple view of things did not, according to Luther, appreciate the depths of God's judgment or the nature of His grace. Moreover, that view ignored the insistent experience of the conscience that it could not ever fulfill the Law. When that experience is admitted to consciousness, the result is that man is driven to despair of self and hatred of God.

The knowledge of God and man that is gained in Christ and in faith, however, preserves the truth that God is the Judge of man the sinner. But it also gains the other side of the contrast and so becomes a truly dialectical knowledge. For by the appeal to Christ the statements about God and man become *bivocal.* God is both the Judge and the Savior, man is both the sinner and the saved. Such a dialectical understanding of man and God is not possible except in Christ and in faith. And it is because of this dialectical perspective that Christian theology can and must say both a "yes" and a "no" to the world and its theology.

I have used the term "concretization" to describe the grounds which make it possible to speak of God and man in this two-sided fashion. Were Christian theology simply to condemn the knowledge of God and man developed by the world, there would be no point of contact between the two. The difference would resolve to a difference of subjective attitude. The *coram mundo* and *coram deo* perspectives could be set side by side and viewed as interesting alternatives. The question of reality would never arise, or if it did, each side could view its "reality" as a separate province, a complement to the reality of the other.

By the appeal to Christ and to faith, however, Luther indicates that "reality" is very much at issue. Christian theology does not restrict itself to the "spiritual realm" but engages the *coram mundo* approach with the *coram deo* approach in a single dialectical perspective. Asserting the intrinsic connection between these attitudes is already a denial of the world's own self-understanding. By incorporating the world's self-understanding into its discourse, Christian theology is able to subject that self-understanding to an *internal* and not merely external criticism. It challenges the "worldly realm" on its own ground, on its own terms.

It is the dialectical character of theology which thus initiates a serious conflict with the world over the nature of reality. It is no mere game of words, but rather a life-or-death struggle for dominance, for the loyalties and energies of men. It is in reference to this struggle that Luther's dialectical language finds both its most concrete and its most generalized expression. The distinction Luther uses to describe this aspect of the knowledge of God and of man is in fact one of his most famous distinctions, the dialectic *regnum dei—regnum mundi*.

3. By introducing the term *regnum* I have shifted focus to an aspect of Luther's presentation which first appeared as an incidental qualification of the *coram* pattern, and then in the preceding section emerged as a substantial characteristic of his discussion of Christ and faith. This aspect is the *struggle* involved between the two perspectives on the knowledge of God and man. *Regnum* connotes "rule," or "power." The fact that the Christian is able, on the basis of Christ and faith, to affirm both the *coram mundo* and *coram deo* perspectives on man and God, means that he recognizes *two* realms or powers. And because Christian theology actively engages worldly theology in

a real dispute over the nature of reality, the Christian finds himself engaged in a power struggle between the two realms.

Luther begins his introduction with a reference to his exposition of Ps. 2, in which he described the struggle and triumph of the kingdom of Christ over the kings and peoples of the world. He then moves without further ado in Ps. 51, which he says concerns repentance. It is hard to see at first the connections Luther has in mind. Soon enough, however, they begin to emerge. The standard interpretation of this psalm of repentance, Luther begins, vastly underestimates the *power* of human sin, and is thus without the power to console the conscience. By failing to look at sin in its root the scholastic doctors have missed the whole import of the psalm. David's actual sins against the Second Table of the Law are relatively beside the point. The chief matter is that David, like Saul, wanted to appear holy, fell into smugness and impenitence, and thus broke the First Table of the Law. David was guilty of blasphemy. He had set himself up as god, could not therefore let God be God, and the battle was on. The attempt to appease God with works and observances is not only slanderous but is also a not-so-subtle attempt to control God, to turn Him into an idol. This attempt, so natural to man, is based on the assumption, equally natural, that "the natural powers are unimpaired." And it is this assumption that Luther attacks by his appeal to Christ. The assumption is itself blasphemy, for if it is held to be correct, then what need is there of Christ? The answer to Luther's somewhat rhetorical question is that there is no need for Christ if the natural powers are unimpaired. To the extent that nature, or more specifically the human community, is seen as capable and autonomous, as a *regnum mundi,* the power and reality of the *regnum Christi* is obscured and its meaning perverted. In fact, Luther argues, the natural powers are so corrupt that man has lost his correct judgment *coram deo.* Once the world has rather absurdly constituted itself a *regnum,* its view of God changes. It is in such a situation that God is seen functioning in roles appropriate to a competing, threatening power, i.e., as judge and tyrant.

The stake involved in the world's constitution of itself as a *regnum,* and in God's opposition to this *regnum,* is glory, the eternal struggle over the First Commandment. Luther says that with the loss of knowledge of God we no longer seek "the glory of God but our own glory in God and in all creatures." *"Regnum mundi"* is properly speaking a contradiction in terms.[8] It describes the creation denying its createdness. The self-contradiction is expressed in the fact that in trying to escape its subjection to its Creator, the creation—now become a *regnum*—finds itself in subjection to itself, unable to control

25

itself, unable to evade its own facticity as creature. The essential nature of man turned away from God, says Luther, is a "nature corrupted by sin and subject to eternal death." But the *regnum mundi* denies the *regnum dei* and thereby denies its own self-contradiction, its own absurd pretentions to aseity. It prefers to view death, which is the eminent sign of its contingency, not *coram deo* as a punishment for sin, but as a natural necessity. Luther gives the examples of a lawyer speaking of man as an owner and master, and of a physician speaking of man as healthy or sick. When these examples are noted again somewhat later, the competitive powers of the two *regna* are clearly in evidence.

> Let no one, therefore, ponder the Divine Majesty, what God has done and how mighty He is: or think of man as the master of his property, the way a lawyer does; or of his health, the way a physician does.[9]

It is only in Christ that man can see the futility of this approach, can recognize *both* the *regnum dei and* the contradiction of the *regnum mundi.* For now comes the summarizing passage on the subject of theology which I quoted above. The alternate to viewing man and God in terms of their respective powers is to view man as sinner and saved, God as Justifier and Savior. It is the consideration of Christ and faith that now provides the correct understanding of man's relation to the Creator and the rest of creation. Physical life, Luther goes on, was created before man, and for man. Man's rule over it is not self-derived. Rather it is given to him as both a gift and a task by God, who is the Creator and true master. Thereby all thought of a *regnum mundi* is excluded. What man has regarding the world, which can now remain "creation" rather than *"regnum,"* is a *mandate.* And this mandate can be carried out faithfully only by the Christian who sustains the double interpretation of himself as "guilty of sin and subject to death" and of God as "the Justifier and Redeemer of a man who knows himself this way." As for those men who refuse to recognize their true creatureliness, preferring instead to listen to lawyers, physicians—and parents (!): "Let them go," Luther says in closing his introduction to the psalm. The care of such people is not a theological concern.

2

With a Little Help from His Friends

In the preceding section nearly all the subjects we shall be concerned with have been introduced. I have suggested three dialectical perspectives which I think are very useful in organizing Luther's theology. It would be only a small exaggeration to say that the *coram deo—coram mundo* perspective appears explicitly on nearly every page of Luther. Clearly it does not have a content of its own, but rather indicates the characteristic attitude from which Luther approaches all his subjects. Its presence serves first of all to point up how completely dialectical Luther's thinking is. Second—and this is less apparent but I think no less true—Luther seems to use the *coram* dialectic as basically an analytical tool. He uses it to differentiate, to point up the disjunctive side of his contrasts.

The perspective I have termed *in fide—in Christo,* is at least as ubiquitous as the *coram* language, but does not in Luther's writing have the character of a formula or sign-word. Early in his career Luther was very self-conscious of a hermeneutical distinction he developed. This was the conjunction of the Christological meaning of a passage in Scripture with it's "tropological" or "faith and morals" meaning. The dialectic "Christ—faith" soon drops out of Luther's writing as an *explicit* hermeneutical device. But its effects are so profound that one could say it is the axis on which the considerable girth of Luther turns. The phrases "in," "to," or "for faith," and "in," or "according to Christ" do of course differentiate contents. But their association, and more importantly Luther's use of this dialectic more frequently than any other to organize his descriptions of the Christian life and experience, suggest the dialectic functions for Luther primarily as a synthesizing instrument or as a way of emphasizing the conjunctive side of his contrasts.

The function of our third perspective, *regnum dei—regnum mundi,* is more difficult to put into words. Beside the Scriptural warrant for its inclusion in Luther's vocabulary, he seems to use it most frequently to generalize his other two perspectives. He always connotes by it the struggle of God with the world, thus incorporating the *coram* perspective. And he always connotes by it the reality of the struggle, or the struggle over reality. It is the real God enfleshed in Christ and in faith who struggles with the flesh of the world over the reality of God and the world. This aspect is then an incorporation of his second perspective.

In this essay the task we have set for ourselves is that of developing organizing and interpretive tools for the study of Luther. We are now at a critical point. So far we have focused attention on the diadic form of Luther's writing and have come up with three dialectical perspectives, each with distinctive connotations, each utilized for different purposes. But these perspectives all occur together in Luther's text. While we are now in a position to make a little better sense out of the way Luther uses the language he does in a given passage, we still have no answer to a question asked at the beginning of the essay. How are we to arrange and interpret Luther's *subjects?* In such a way, moreover, that they will faithfully reflect the dialectical perspectives we have been examining? In a word what is the order of the order, the relation of the relations?

The decision on this matter is about the most consequential one a student must make. On such a decision rests the whole complexion of Luther's theology, its impression as static, eschatological, critical, constructive, or all of these—or no "theology" at all. Merely exegesis or polemics. Fortunately or un-, Luther himself gives almost no help here. Just when we need him most, there is that gaping hole: Luther wrote no systematic theology, did not even give us the beginnings of one. His own occasional summaries of the faith follow a creedal form, but otherwise there appears to be no intrinsic reason for adopting this arrangement.

This situation forces the student to develop his *own* model for organizing and interpreting Luther. Such a procedure is in fact taken by nearly everyone, if the truth be known, and it is a legitimate enough recourse. There are, however, a couple of things to be said about it. First, the model chosen has only heuristic value. If it is a good model, it "opens up" the text and organizes all of Luther's subjects in a way that is cogent and interesting. The model is unimportant in itself and must be changed or even discarded if necessary. Most importantly it should never be allowed to take the place of the data. The model interprets Luther, not Luther the model.

Second, the model, in addition to working well over a large range of data, should have at least a *prima facie* relevance to Luther's own subjects and language and must be *demonstrably* relevant at the key points. You have to prove an hypothesis somewhere along the line. These two conditions can be termed the "reliability" and the "validity," respectively, of an hypothesis. Of the two, the question of validity is ultimately the most important. If an interpretative hypothesis is valid, it will in fact organize Luther as well and as extensively as he can be organized.

In this section I propose to develop such an hypothesis. The material from Luther's introduction to Ps. 51 we have been considering does give some guidelines. Let me summarize the results.

Luther occasionally can describe redeemed man as a "Christian-in-relation."[10] His introduction to the psalm is an excellent reflection of the purely relational character of Christian self-understanding. First, the fall of the creation into sin by no means broke its relationship to God, but rather changed it. The relation of dependence still obtains, but the understanding of the Creator and the creature becomes perverted. By mistaking itself as autonomous, as a *regnum,* the world—it is no longer properly called creation—thus also mistakes its Creator. It does this because instead of seeing God as He is, it sees and seeks itself in God. God, however, provides true knowledge of Himself independently of and therefore over against the false understanding of the world. In doing so God thereby also provides the correct understanding of the fallen world as a self-contradiction, and the correct understanding of the double relationship to both God and the world in which the Christian stands. Only in the revelation of God manifested in Christ and received in faith does the Christian discover himself both sinner and saved *coram deo,* and as both participating in and overcoming his fallenness *coram mundo.*

Luther's discussion, therefore, seems to play back and forth on three groups of subjects, each of whose meanings appears only in the relationships that obtain among the groups. We must thus now try to clarify the relationships themselves in order to gain appropriate and meaningful definitions for the subject groups.

The reality Luther has been combating is the *self*-understanding of the world. This self-understanding, no matter to what specific subjects it is applied, in fact is always characterized by an assumed viewpoint or relationship between man and his universe. Man is viewed as the autonomous possessor of self, world, and God. He is the measure of all, the center and meaning of all around him. This relationship—having self, world, and God around nearby for one's disposal—I shall call the *proximate* relation. It issues into a single, simple, or univocal "theological" assessment: *"I am righteous."*

This reality, Luther says, is rather to be interpreted as "fallen," the man-centered relationship is "idolatrous," and the univocal assessment should be that "man is a sinner." These judgments are possible only from the perspective of a second, contrasting reality. This reality is the understanding of Christian man. It too is characterized by an assumed relationship or viewpoint, but this relationship is *not* simple or univocal. It is rather dialectical or bivocal. Christian man knows on the one hand that he fully shares the "fallen, idolatrous, and sinful" viewpoint of the world. But he alone is able to make these correct judgments because he has, on the other hand, been given *another* viewpoint, one which is not *self*-derived. It derives rather from a reality which shares nothing with the world, but is in fact a judgment on the world. Luther must describe this reality, the understanding of Christian man in relation to self, world, and God, in dialectical,

29

or bivocal language, because the Christian stands in both viewpoints at once. The double relationship—understanding that one stands wholly within the world, yet at the same time judging that stance in terms of another reality or viewpoint distinct from the world—I shall call the *penultimate* relation. It issues into a dialectical theological assessment: *"I am both sinner and saved, unrighteous and righteous."*

Third, and most important, there is the viewpoint by virtue of which the proximate relation is shown for what it is and the penultimate relation is established in its dialectical perspective. This viewpoint is found in the Word of God. The reality it conveys is the self-revelation of God in Christ. For Luther there is simply no other, higher, or more ultimate bar from which to gain perspective and judgment than from the self-revelation of God in Christ. This relational perspective—God's own eye view, as it were—I shall call the *ultimate* relation.

The schema "proximate, penultimate, and ultimate relationship" is a modification of a model developed by Bonhoeffer in the third chapter of his *Ethics.* After long reflection and testing I have become convinced that with a significant alteration Bonhoeffer's construction provides a superb interpretative model for Luther. Not only does it clearly exhibit the relational nature of Luther's theology, but it also permits that theology to reveal its highly dynamic and eschatological character. I have come on no other model which so well achieves these results.

The modification is more exactly the formal addition of a third term, proximate, to Bonhoeffer's model. While the interpretation denoted by the term is implicit in Bonhoeffer, Luther's theology necessitated the shift in emphasis. The alteration was made necessary because, at least in the *Ethics,* Bonhoeffer's theology is more a "theology of the incarnation," while Luther's is more a "theology of the cross." Bonhoeffer therefore tends to make a more positive affirmation of the natural order than would be appropriate for Luther.

The three terms I have introduced are purely relational terms. Each finds its definition in the context of the others, and all three must be taken together in order to understand the meaning of each. While the terms have the substantive meanings I have given above, their primary functions are to express the relations which obtain among the subjects referred to, and more importantly, to emphasize the nature of the *judgment* which men make regarding those subjects. Thus "penultimate" and "proximate," for example, refer to the same subject, the world, but differentiate the two interpretations which men can place on it, and therefore on themselves and God.

Ultimate, Penultimate, and Proximate

Ultimate: the Self-revelation of God in Christ [11]

The relationship of the Word of God as the ultimate Word to the word of man is an eschatological relationship. The Word of God is "the last word" in two senses. First, the ultimate is final in a qualitative sense in respect to its contents. Luther is very critical of any attempt to gainsay the Word of God. In his introduction to Ps. 51, for example, he castigates those scholastics who want to add the "disposition of the heart" as a requirement beyond the Decalog. Nothing may be said beyond or in addition to the ultimate Word. And whenever that Word is spoken, it means the breaking off, the finish, of everything that has preceded it. Because it is a truly eschatological Word, the ultimate is qualitatively different from the penultimate word, and so is not the natural or necessary fulfillment of what preceded it. There is no method, no example, no extremity of thought or discipline whereby it can either reach the ultimate or insure its coming.

The Word of God is the ultimate Word in a second eschatological sense. It is final temporally. This means that it is always preceded by the penultimate. There is no future Word after the ultimate, but rather everything that follows is always that which has gone before the coming of the ultimate. You have to begin all over again all the time, says Luther. You cannot presume the ultimate and go on; rather you must "creep into your baptism" every day. The Christian is always a beginner. Moreover, in order that the ultimate remain unambiguously last, the penultimate must always be lived through in its entirety. Only the man of faith who lives in the penultimate can and must experience and reflect the full force of the Law, for example. One must be wholly slain by sin and the condemnation of the Law before the Gospel can be truly received as the ultimate Word. You must not and cannot short-circuit the fullness of life and death in order to receive the ultimate before its time. The penultimate, therefore, always remains in its completeness, just for the sake of the ultimate. And the ultimate, preserving itself as the last Word, therefore sustains and confirms the penultimate at the same time as it ends and invalidates the penultimate.

The ultimate Word, the self-revelation of God in Christ, is accordingly never mistaken for anything else. It is without question the Word of Christ, never the word of man. The ultimate Word is never defined in other than its own terms, and rather defines everything that precedes it. Against Zwingli as against the "doctors" Luther insisted that we

31

must understand and interpret our experience by the Word of God, never the other way around. And yet the Word of God, just because it is ultimate, is never "at hand," so to speak, ready at my disposal. It is not a quantum, an "already given," waiting merely to be applied. When a word which is falsely put forth as ultimate has these features, the relation between the ultimate and the penultimate has been misunderstood. This means that the ultimate had been made less than it is. The Word of God has become the word of man; the divine revelation a human doctrine.

The misunderstanding is based on the assumption that there is a univocal relationship between the ultimate and the penultimate. The coming of the Word of God might then mean only the destruction of the word of man, as Luther felt was the position of some "left-wing" reformers. A second position, too often exhibited among Lutherans, would affirm both the Word of God and the word of man, but hold them separate and essentially unrelated by means of a false application of the "two spheres" teaching, for example. A third option, one Luther felt was taken by Roman theology, would see no opposition at all. The Word of God simply confirms the word of man.

In these cases both the ultimate and the penultimate have been misunderstood and therefore the relationship between them perverted. Only in Christ and in faith does the proper relationship between God and man become manifest, as we saw above. The Christian knows he is both judged and saved. The incarnation is God's affirmation of the world; the crucifixion is His judgment upon it. And the resurrection provides the power whereby the Christian can be sustained in this double relationship, can be sustained in his penultimacy, in his "being-toward" the ultimate.

The ultimate, then, both confirms and invalidates the penultimate. We must now consider the reality which brings forth this double judgment.

Proximate and Penultimate: the World Interpreted by Fallen Man and by Redeemed Man.

We must consider these two terms together, because both refer to the same entity, the world, and both express a judgment on the world. In the case of the proximate the relationship to the ultimate is essentially denied, and the penultimate is considered at best illusory and useless. In the case of the penultimate the double relationship to the ultimate is affirmed, and the proximate is consequently accepted as real, though it is judged as a self-contradiction.

Throughout the introduction to Ps. 51 Luther referred to an attitude toward the revelation of God which maintained a univocal interpretation of the relationship between God and the world. This interpretation, Luther insisted, both impeded the Word of God and opposed the interpretation of faith. Dietrich Bonhoeffer, in the course of his exposition of the schema "ultimate and penultimate," also referred to such an attitude. He called it an "antitype," a "disorder" or "entanglement," and finally characterized it as "unnatural." It is this condition of opposition to the coming of the ultimate which I refer to as "proximate."

In this interpretation the world is seen as a collection of objects which bear no *intrinsic* relationship to God, man, or each other. This attitude is expressed in the philosophical approach we have seen Luther criticize—viewing things as "quiddities," things in themselves, rather than in terms of their relationship to God. In the practical order the collection is organized and related to man in terms of its usefulness. The world is *mine.* It consists wholly of things which are "handy," near at hand for my disposal, the value of which is assigned by me according to their degree of at-handedness or usefulness to me. As we have seen, even religious objects and observances can fall under this evaluation. The religious attitude becomes one department among the range of activities, and religious observances are justified in terms of their ability to effect certain purposes, to please God or mitigate His anger, for example. God Himself is no longer held ultimate, but becomes a religious object, an idol to be used like everything *else* in the world. In the world interpreted as proximate, *I* am the autonomous center, I assume the place of the ultimate to which all is directed and in which everything finds its being and its order. Luther has given the examples of lawyers, physicians, and parents as indicative of the "ownership" attitude. This attitude, he continues, seeks not God's glory but its own glory in God and in all creatures. Man's interpretation of himself as "the measure of all things," as the ultimate, thus produces an organization of the world which is consistent in its own terms and which implies its own autonomy and ultimacy. It thus exhibits the characteristics we have seen Luther refer to by means of his *regnum* perspective. From the point of view of Christ and faith, however, the world interpreted in this way is a false world whose self-understanding is a massive self-contradiction. It is false because in order to sustain itself the experience of the conscience must be avoided, the brute facticity of death rationalized away. It is a self-contradiction in the eyes of faith because it exemplifies creation denying its createdness, the totally contingent denying its dependence, the vehicle of divine self-revelation declaring its "value-only-for-itself."

While the interpretation of the world as proximate *denies* the relation to the ultimate, in the interpretation I have called "penultimate" the world is seen as everything inasmuch as it *affirms* that relation. The world is everything seen as "toward-the-ultimate," but only once the ultimate has revealed itself. There is, for example, no "history of salvation" until the revelation of the Savior in history. The "towardness" of the penultimate is not a judgment which man makes on himself and the world independently of the ultimate. As we have seen, it is only in Christ that this knowledge of man and of God becomes possible. The penultimate is then not a reality in which inheres a state or condition differentiating it from a perceived reality which is proximate. The Christian is "hidden," in Luther's words, and his holiness is not substantive, something in itself, but exists only in relation to Christ. The penultimate, therefore, is reality defined and interpreted exclusively from the point of view of the ultimate; reality *coram deo*. It refers to and reflects the judgment of the ultimate on everything preceding it, given upon man, and given to man in order that he might interpret himself and God correctly.

I have said that the penultimate is an interpretation which man has received from the ultimate. This interpretation is bivocal. It is characterized by "contrast"—the togetherness of the conjunctive and disjunctive dialectical forms we examined in the first section. The penultimate has this character because it receives itself from the ultimate, which as we have seen both confirms and invalidates all that precedes it. Redeemed man, who has appropriated the interpretation of the ultimate, can acknowledge the positive side of his relationship to the ultimate because he has received insight into himself as being "toward-the-ultimate,"—a phrase reflecting Luther's description of the Christian as *ingressus in ultimum* or *in Christum*. At the same time the Christian can acknowledge the negative side of his relationship to the ultimate, because he experiences himself as "being-for-himself"—a phrase reflecting Luther's description of the sinful man as *incurvatus in se*. The Christian, says Luther, knows himself both as saved and as sinner.

Here we see perhaps the most important feature distinguishing the penultimate from the proximate. While the proximate *denies* the interpretation of the world maintained by the penultimate, the penultimate *affirms* the interpretation of the world maintained by the proximate, although that interpretation is valuated differently. In Luther's terms fallen man views all things only *coram mundo*, thinking himself nothing but justified even though he is nothing but sin. Redeemed man views all things both *coram deo* and *coram mundo*, knowing himself both as sinner and as saved. The reason for this difference of interpretation, we have seen, is that the proximate interprets only itself, in its own terms, even when it speaks of God. The penultimate, however, interprets not only itself but also its relationship to the ultimate, and does so in terms of the ultimate.

Because of the *ingressus* character of the penultimate, it recognizes its function as that of preparing the way for the ultimate, but only once the ultimate has come to give the penultimate this understanding of itself. In Luther's terms the Christian is the man who constantly seeks the One who has already found him. It is necessary to define the relationship in this way because otherwise faith would become once again a work. The Pauline sequence of "indicative—imperative" would be reversed. The penultimate prepares the way, says Bonhoeffer, by acknowledging that it cannot prepare the way. This is a very important point to keep in mind if we are to avoid the error of interpreting Luther's dynamic understanding of the Christian life in terms of a simple growth in sanctification. It is vitally important not to view the penultimate as the locus of mutually exclusive forces, in which *ingressus* means the increase of holiness and the decrease of sin. Nor can the penultimate be viewed as the resolution of such exclusive forces. In both cases the dialectic in which the Christian lives is misunderstood as a rather static polar dualism, a "two-sphere" theory of reality with all its attendant problems. The dialectical tension in Christian life is precisely that tension between the experience of oneself as *incurvatus in se* and the faith that one is *ingressus in Christum*. With such a description we can adequately reflect the dialectical form with which Luther draws his picture of the Christian life without losing the highly dynamic character he gives to that presentation.

Because it incorporates the reality of sin into its self-understanding, the penultimate can distinguish its judgment from that of the ultimate. Because it sees all things from the point of view of the ultimate, the penultimate can similarly distinguish the proximate from the ultimate. But the penultimate never knows itself distinct from the proximate. Only God knows who are His own, and when the Christian comes to God, he does not distinguish himself from sinners. He confesses he is nothing but sin and leaves judgment to God. The unity between the penultimate and the proximate is further indicated by the fact that it is precisely the proximate in all its fallenness and disorder to which the ultimate has come and which is reconciled. The fallenness of the world is never a matter of indifference to the Christian, but just the opposite. The Christian finds his task that of declaring to the fallen world in which he himself wholly participates the true understanding of its relationship to God. The penultimate judgment declares to the world that God has broken its opposition, its pretensions of a *regnum*, and works to restore the intended relation of governance to the creation, that is, God's *mandates* to man for himself and the rest of creation.

Finally, the penultimate must constantly be self-critical. Luther condemns as *incurvatus* the highest spiritual goods, worship, love, and even faith, when they become the occasion for human pride. The Word of God cannot be mistaken for anything else, as we have seen. But the word of man, even of Christian man, can easily be mistaken as God's Word. Indeed the danger is greater than Christian man can fall into this error, since he may try to grasp at his salvation, make it his "own" rather than something given to him, and so deny his status as a sinner. The people of God, Luther says, live out of the hope Christ has given them, and constantly bring on themselves the judgment of the cross.

3

A Place to Stand

This essay began with a preliminary excursion into the rather forbidding jungle of Luther's language. We were able to form at least a crude map of Luther's verbal topography in terms of three dialectical perspectives. In the second section the task was to abstract from the initial empirical material in order to develop an interpretative model which would faithfully reflect the dynamic quality of Luther's theology and expose the interrelationships among his subjects in some systematic pattern. I tried to relate the model at every critical point to Luther's own more concrete language, both to keep us from getting entirely lost and to indicate the congeniality of the model to Luther's theological approach. In this section the task is to come back down to a more empirical reexamination of Luther's subjects and to integrate the results of the first two sections. In this way we should be able to develop an outline for the subjects we shall consider in this study, an outline which "hangs together" in an interesting and hopefully valid way. Almost more importantly, we should be able to discover a place to stand. Granting Luther's theology is holistic and entirely relational, there should be a perspective from which his subjects are best approached.

Let us return yet once more—it is a very rich passage!—to Luther's introduction to Ps. 51. It should be evident by now that what Luther considers true theology, discourse on subjects proper to the enterprise, is an activity of the penultimate. Theology is not the business of the ultimate, even though God's self-disclosure in Christ is the precondition for theological discourse. When God speaks, He does

36

not speak theology, but *revelation.* Theology is one form of the response the Christian makes to that revelation. But since Christian theology alone among human responses reflects the *conjunctive* side of the various forms of the dialectic of God and man, it is clear that it is not an activity of the proximate either. At the very beginning of his introduction to the psalm, Luther remarks that human reason, when it attempts to speak of God, speaks of something whose reality it does not and cannot experience. The Word of the Spirit is like a dream, Luther says, that is soon past and leaves no trace. A theology of reason without the Word is for Luther no theology at all, but something "mundane" or civil—in fact *anything* else. Theology properly so called, Luther never tires of insisting, is by contrast a formulation of experience. "A man becomes a theologian by living, by dying, and by being damned, not by understanding, reading, and speculating."[12] As we have seen, both parts comprising the true subject of theology are matters of the heart, of practice and feeling. But were the experiential character of theology all that distinguished it as an activity of the penultimate, it would be easy for the theologian to take that experience itself as the ultimate ground. The theologian would thereby fall back into a false theology, back into the proximate. True theology, says Luther, affirms its openness to and dependence on the ultimate Word. The theologian remains a pupil of the Word, and what he in part experiences is that his formulations cannot even remotely comprehend the reality of the ultimate. Luther has not only distinguished the penultimate as the locus of theological activity, but has also stated its relationship both to the ultimate and the proximate. Thereby he formulates the central theological statement: I am a sinner in myself, and in Christ not a sinner; I am righteous and justified through Christ who belongs to me a sinner. That, Luther continues, is the twofold theological knowledge of God and of man, and is the proper subject of theology.[13]

Since theology is an activity of the penultimate, of faith, this study must accordingly take the penultimate as its basic point of view. This means that the penultimate itself must be the central topic and that the world and God must be investigated from the perspective of the relationship of Christian faith to them. Among the three dialectical perspectives we developed in the first section, the dialectic "Christ and faith" emerges with particular importance. This dialectic is a contrast. Its explication requires a consideration of both the conjunctive and the disjunctive sides of the relationship.

The Day's Agenda

The reason for the difference of Christ and faith is the fact that faith participates in the fallenness that constitutes the proximate. At the same time faith differs from the proximate in its interpretation of that fallenness, of the relationships among God, man, and the world which sin has created. The difference of Christ and faith, of the ultimate and the penultimate, is the general theme of Part One. The title of the second essay, *Homo Incurvatus—Homo Ingressus,* indicates that what is at issue is the understanding of man in his relationship to God. The perspective *coram mundo—coram deo* is a singularly appropriate way of approach to this subject. This perspective reveals the situation of man as one who stands before Another. It is from this Other that man receives his identity, and it is to this Other that he submits his life for judgment. The perspective also reveals that there are competitive "others" before whom man stands. To faith, receiving one's identity from the world means becoming a sinner, *incurvatus in se.* When the Christian receives his identity from God, however, he understands himself as both sinner and saved, *ingressus in Christum. Ingressus* thus adequately defines the difference of the penultimate from both the ultimate and the proximate. The Christian has not yet become perfectly united to Christ (*pen*ultimate), and he is in the process of becoming united (pen*ultimate*) to Christ.

The third essay, *Lex et Fides,* in effect reverses the perspective, and considers the understanding of God in His relationship to man. Just as there are competing understandings of man, so there are competing understandings of God. The doublet that comes to mind immediately in this regard is "Law and Gospel." Some students hold this to be the basic dialectical expression of Luther's understanding of God's self-revelation. There are problems, however, if one refers the doubleness to the divine revelation. One way to formulate the general problem is to say that if "Law—Gospel" is the form of God's revelation, it is then God, and not the man of faith, who is doing theology. Some students, however, claim that "Law and Gospel" expresses not the ultimate form of revelation, but rather expresses Luther's anthropology. The approach I shall take partially shares this view. I shall argue that it is not "Law and Gospel" but Law and *faith* which defines the human response to the Gospel of God. Luther may finally compel me to abandon this thesis, but I feel much can be enlightened by maintaining it as long as I can.

While the difference of Christ and faith is the general theme of Part One, the identity of Christ and faith is the theme of Part Two. This indicates a shift in concentration from the relationship of the penultimate to the proximate to the relationship of the penultimate to the ultimate. Now the dialectic "Christ and faith," becomes the most appropriate perspective on the subjects. The fourth essay, *Fides et Promissio,* continues the analysis of faith introduced in the preceding essay, developing the "forensic" or "Word" side of faith relative to the issue of justification. The identity of Christ and faith will be grounded in the concept of promise. The fifth essay, *Initium Novae Creaturae,* continues the analysis of the dialectic of Christ and faith, but now on its "sanative" or "Spirit" side relative to the issue of sanctification. Thereby the consideration of man in regard to his *ego* and his *opus* becomes relevant as a new perspective on the anthropology developed in the second essay.

The grounds for both the difference and the identity of Christ and faith having been established, it then becomes possible to return to a consideration of the relationship of the ultimate and the penultimate to the proximate, the fallen world. For this purpose the dialectic *regnum dei—regnum mundi* becomes most germane. The sixth essay, *Ubiquitas Carnalis Christi,* will be an attempt to demonstrate that this teaching is not a problematic offshoot of Luther's doctrine of the Lord's Supper, but a result integral to Luther's eschatological approach. The idea will be investigated in terms of the relation of the ultimate to the proximate, that is, the world as God's gift to man. Thereby emerges the possibility for seeing the world in its intended nature, as creation rather than *regnum.*

The seventh essay, *Larvae Dei,* actually concerns the same topic, but is able, on the basis of the revelation of Christ in the Supper, to generalize the discussion of God's presence in the world. The *larvae* will be investigated in terms of the relation of the penultimate to the proximate, that is, the abiding *regnum*-character of the world as presenting God's task laid on the Christian.

The final essay, *Regnum Dei—Regnum Mundi,* will be much like this introductory essay in purpose. I will try once again, the results of the study now in mind, to consider Luther's theology as a whole and point up the eschatological quality which I think is its chief distinguishing feature.

PART ONE

God's Address

Part One is dominated by the perspective *coram deo—coram mundo.* If we translate *coram* as "before the presence of," the spatial metaphor connoted by this word will emerge. This connotation is the basis for the intended pun in the title of Part One. The first essay concerns where God is, that is, whether the relationship between God and man is theocentric or anthropocentric. The second essay concerns the nature of God's Word to man, and who man discovers himself to be in that revelation.

Essay II: *Homo Incurvatus - Homo Ingressus*

There is a right way and a wrong way to do theology, according to Luther. You can attempt to define man and God as they are in themselves and independent of each other. This approach is a *coram mundo* approach invented by that whore Reason at the instigation of the devil and has been swallowed by Luther's opponents, by Rome, and by the sinful world at large. It results in what Luther calls a "theology of glory," which ends up putting man in the place of God, thereby grossly perverting the true knowledge of both. There is on the other hand a truly theological, *coram deo* approach to theology. It defines man and God interdependently and in strict relation to each other. This is the approach Luther takes, and he shares it with Augustine (in his best moments), with Paul, with Christ, and presumably with God Himself. It results in what Luther calls a "theology of the cross" and a true theological knowledge which lets God be God and makes man be man.

As different as the two approaches are, they cannot go their separate ways either by remaining grandly oblivious to each other or by ecumenically defining separate areas of competence. The two viewpoints are competitive, not complementary. While "science" might think, erroneously, that it can legitimately relegate knowledge of God to the province of theology, faith can never relinquish knowledge of man to science. It is thus because both viewpoints claim an understanding of man that they are locked in a struggle. Man is the single subject of the anthropological discourse of both reason and faith. Not only does the common subject insure a real encounter of the two perspectives, but so does the mutually acknowledged unity of the subject. For "reason" accepts man's religious attitudes and practices as a legitimate subject for description and interpretation. And faith knows that it must take account of man in his sensuality, his bodiliness, rather than limit itself to what consequently would be a false interpretation of man's "spiritual side."

Man is the battlefield and every inch of the turf is in contention. The two approaches present radically contrasting interpretations of man, each bidding for his loyalty, each claiming to be the proper forum from which a man receives his identity and self-understanding. The self-understanding offered by the *coram mundo* approach is seductively attractive. As we saw in the preceding essay, man comes out with nature intact, with power sufficient to control himself and to make God his servant. And he has enough freedom of will and sharpness of mind to make choices in the best interests of his well-being. The *coram deo* approach is somewhat less flattering. For Luther it is precisely in man's understanding of God that his true condition becomes most clear. What emerges is man with nature totally corrupted by sin, his mind a school of lies, his will an engine of treachery. His freedom is an illusion, and in reality he is strangled in his own ego, trapped in himself, *incurvatus in se* in a tragically ironical sense.

At the same time, and for Luther the *simul* is the decisive matter, the fatal entrapment has been broken through. It is God Himself who broke the death-grip of sin by assuming and then overcoming human bondage in its most profound aspects. Only in the atonement is the true knowledge of God manifest, and accordingly the true knowledge of man. And only when a man has received this Gospel is he freed from bondage to his "incurvedness" and can also be *ingressus in Christum,* "becoming into Christ."

1

Flesh and Spirit

We must now begin to give substance to this summary. A consideration of the language Luther uses to describe man will provide us a rough draft of the contrasts between the two approaches to anthropology introduced above.

Luther, of course, recognizes the traditional definition of man as a "rational animal" whose intellectual ability distinguishes him from the lower animals. He also learned what was held to be the Augustinian psychology of a higher spiritual part and a lower sensual part, with the soul in between. Luther, especially early in his career, could use such a threefold distinction or evaluation when the occasion warranted it. At the same time, however, he denied the theological aptness of both the general definition and the psychology usually accompanying it. The traditional psychology, variable in detail though it might be, simply did not in Luther's opinion square with Paul.[1] Whether or not his sense of "flesh" and "spirit" exactly accords with Paul's meaning, Luther's theological psychology differed considerably from the more traditional interpretation shared by many of his contemporaries. To a student of the polemical writings of the 1520s it would seem as though a great deal of time, paper, and evangelical passion was wasted,

44

simply because the reformers could not or would not recognize the different meanings of "flesh" and "spirit" informing their positions.

When the Bible speaks of "flesh," says Luther with monotonous regularity, it includes the whole man. It is a generic term including all the components of human being and activity. "Flesh" can refer to the body, of course, but also to the will, the mind, even to the highest spiritual faculties, the most pious and idealistic of human yearnings. It is in fact to these latter that the term "flesh" can be applied with greatest accuracy and relevance. "Spirit" is similarly a word including the whole man. It is not to be restricted to the soul, even the "higher faculties" in general, but can and must characterize the body with all its activities and needs. The bodily sense of spirit plays a very important role in Luther's theology, especially in the issues of preaching, the sacraments, and Christian vocation.

Since the soul can be called "flesh" and the body "spirit," it is clear that the two terms do not indicate distinct parts of human physiology. That would be just the *coram mundo* approach of considering man in himself which Luther rejects. The terms rather distinguish man according to the dispositions moving him as a whole entity.[2] What Luther means is something like Martin Heidegger's understanding of man in terms of "care," or perhaps better, Paul Tillich's notion of "ultimate concern." The designations "flesh" and "spirit" properly refer to uses or functions, not to objects, Luther says.[3] The adjectival forms are in fact more accurate. The whole man is "carnal" or "spiritual," the whole man must be viewed either "according to the flesh" or "according to the spirit." The distinction thus refers to the opposite dispositions, attitudes, or purposes—the concerns giving man his *ultimate* identity, his *theological* identity. "Flesh" accordingly refers to anything outside grace and the Spirit of Christ, *any*thing apart from faith.[4] And that means *every*thing. For the whole world is flesh, i.e., opposed to God. "Spiritual" applies to anything done in the Word and in faith. It shows what comes from or is done by the Holy Spirit.[5]

Luther's anthropological language is wholly relational. Every definition of man developed independently of a definition of his relationship to God is irrelevant at best. And when such a definition is passed off as theological, it becomes instead a demonic attack on the Word of God. At this point it is most important to notice that Luther's relational understanding of man is automatically evaluative. By developing his meaning of flesh and spirit relative to man's ultimate concerns, he has focused on human motives, the judgments men make on themselves, the world, and God. It is this consideration of man *coram deo,* man in his *conscience,* which qualifies the discourse as theological. Luther's concentration on the evaluative or judgmental side of psychology exposes the radical opposition between the two approaches to the knowledge of man. What constitutes the "higher" and the "lower" aspects of man depends on the context or forum in which the discussion takes place, on who makes the judgment for what purposes. As Augustine had pointed out, the "hierarchy of goods" developed in the world by man and for his purposes was an antithesis to the order established by God for His purposes.[6] Although Luther's language and interests are different, he does share with Augustine the view that the *coram mundo* valuation of man amounts to a self-contradiction. Human judgment claims to reflect divine judgment. The world has its opinions of what sin and righteousness are, and drapes its theological wisdom with divine sanction. Yet in every case, Luther argues, the world's valuation of man and God's valuation of man are exactly opposite. What is foolishness, sin, and unrest *coram mundo* is wisdom, righteousness, and peace *coram deo,* and vice versa. This opposition of divine human valuation—sometimes the opposition seems to become an *a priori* principle—is most evident in Luther's earlier writings. It marks the "theology of the cross," God and His works hidden under the opposite appearance.

The very affirmation that God is hidden under contrary appearances, however, is an affirmation that can be made only by the Christian. As we saw in the preceding essay, it is only the penultimate judgment, only the judgment of faith, which is able to reflect both the divine and the worldly evaluations of man. It is thus only the Christian who can experience the contradictions between these viewpoints, embody them in himself, and formulate them in his confession of faith. Only the Christian is both "flesh" and "spirit" in Luther's sense of the terms. In a comment on Ps. 22:25 in his 1519 *Operationes in Psalmos,* Luther expresses this feeling of contradiction in a conclusion prickling with irony. The Gospel reduces man to nothing both before God and before men in order that

> by acknowledging our evil in this way we might merit the grace
> of the righteousness we bear before men on account of the Gospel
> of the cross. For we are found to be sinners before God because
> of ourselves and because of the world in which we live and move,
> but before the world we are found to be sinners because of God
> and His Gospel, in which we begin to live and move. . . . You see
> therefore the powers of the Gospel, justifying us before God and
> crucifying us before the world. There is thus a Word of salvation
> and a Word of the cross, a Word of wisdom and a Word of stupidity,
> and so on.[7]

The man of faith agrees with the world that he is a sinner. It is, however, only from the experience of the Gospel that such a confession becomes an honest one, and a man really merits the gratuitous (!) judgment of the world. The hook in this is that the grounds for the confession of sin are exactly reversed. God holds us sinners because we are "flesh"; the world holds us sinners because we are *beginning* (note well) to be "spirit." The world presumes to speak for God, but speaks against Him. Therein lies the self-contradiction of the *coram mundo* evaluation. There is no neutral ground between the two judgments. The contradiction within this worldly judgment, and between it and the judgment of God, is the major burden of Luther's *regnum* language. The realm of God and of freedom appears to the world as the realm of bondage and the devil. The Christian experiences God's grace and peace only along with the anger and tumult of the world, worldly peace only at the cost of divine wrath.

And yet this experience of contradiction is hidden from the senses. The Christian can affirm the penultimate judgment only because and insofar as he receives it from the Gospel, in faith. The ultimate is never present at hand as a datum. We *begin* to live and move in the Gospel, Luther says. In fact we are always, only, beginners. The experience is hidden from the senses, from the flesh, and thus from reason, Christian or otherwise. You just cannot "own" God and the Gospel in that way. Human reason invariably ends up contradicting God because its knowledge of Him is only partial or "left-handed," as Luther says. Reason praises God for His unjustified mercy but damns Him for His just wrath in spite of the fact that it sees God only in terms of Law or justice.[8] Reason is no closer to and no farther from God than any other human faculty. But it remains in itself, turns from the Creator to the creature, and corrupts both itself and the creation.[9] The problem is not that of an erroneous inference by reason from a supposed instinctive feeling of man for God. That too is simply not available. The *imago dei,* intended as a means whereby man might see God in himself,[10] is now so hidden that one can say nothing about it. In fact it is such an unknown quantity that human experience actually militates against its existence.[11] Without this guidance reason is thus left completely victim to itself, free to choke on its egocentricity, to self-destruct. It therefore ends up reversing the proper valuation of what is and is not to obtain *coram deo* or in the conscience. It attempts to gain freedom in the flesh, and via the Law becomes enslaved in conscience, when in reality the Law must be kept out of the conscience and in the flesh.[12] Moses and his Law cannot remove the terror of the bad conscience, which sees God and all creation thus opposed to it. Only faith and not Law can see the usefulness of this tyrannical onslaught.

Trapped in the I of a Storm

The preceding discussion has led right into the issue of the corrupted knowledge of God which is the result of, and which also most
clearly reveals, the entrapment of fallen man in his own ego. The
man of faith, embodying the penultimate judgment, alone interprets
reality in terms of contrast. Fallen man, embodying the proximate
judgment, interprets reality univocally, egocentrically. To the man of
faith this egocentricity reveals a massive contradiction in its subject,
a contradiction indicated both by the unbearable and inescapable scandal it sees when confronted by the Word of God, and also by its
own experienced self-contradiction. The contradiction in reference
both to God and itself is expressed as "bondage, entrapment," *incurvatus in se.*

Luther believes the vast mass of humanity lives as though there
were no God. The Gospel itself forces this recognition. In contrast
to the Biblical command to love God alone, and thus to hate oneself,
the law of nature is exposed as ultimate concern with self. To put
it most simply, "man cannot naturally want God to be God, but instead
wants to be God himself, and God not to be God."[13]

This state of affairs is the end result of sin and unbelief. Once
man has disbelieved God, he begins to be afraid of God. Thus he
flees from God, and his flight is always also a revolt. An analysis
of this flight from God[14] reveals how it should happen that the attempt
of the world to gain freedom by escaping life before God results in
the world's bondage to itself. We shall spend some time with Luther's
analysis, for in it we will find not only the intrinsic connection between
the *coram* and *regnum* language, but also the emergence of the relationship I have termed "proximate."

Luther's presentations of the growth of sin are varied in mood
and language, ranging from medieval academic exercises in his earlier
commentaries to the storm-lit autobiographical portrait in the 1526
Exposition of Jonah.

In his commentary on Rom. 1:21,[15] Luther develops a passage
on the "order and grades of perdition" to show how man ends up
separated from true knowledge of God and the victim of his own
persistent need for a god. The Fall has already taken place when the
first stage, ingratitude, becomes evident. For ingratitude is the consequence, Luther says, of self-complacency. Man has forgotten the
Giver and accepts the gifts as if he had not received them. So long
as he maintained an exclusive concentration on the Word of the Creator, man was unconscious of himself, knowing neither good nor evil.
He saw only God, not himself, and in this way remained perfectly

coram deo as a creature in free and natural service to his Lord. But once his attention became sidetracked, man became conscious of himself apart from God, and thus began that declaration of independence which is a self-contradiction. The "gift" is no longer a gift, but is one's "own." Some of the characteritics of the worldly *regnum* are already present. It claims autonomy, and its nucleus is the possessive ego. The egocentricity quickly manifests its self-destructive, *incurvatus* character. For now we are at the second stage, vanity.

"One feeds on one's own self and all that is created and enjoys that which lets itself be used, and so one becomes necessarily vain. . . . " To the one whose interests are now bound by his own ego, the sacredness of the creation is gone. Both he himself and the world are experienced as ready at hand, as disposable. The original relationship of governance is grossly perverted. To man directed by God's Word, the world could never be construed as being at man's disposal. It was rather at God's disposal, and put in the service of man by deputyship. "Being at one's own disposal" is a self-understanding of a world which has fallen.

We are now in a world of unreality, of vanity. Man has lost his bearings and wanders in darkness and ignorance. This is the third stage, "deluded blindness." He is in bondage, "blocked in upon himself," Luther says. Once he is caught in the delusion of the centrality of his ego, man in his *amor sui* becomes blind both to himself and to God. For now man, armed with a false self-definition, seeks to redefine God. This adventure is doomed from the start, for by defining himself apart from God, man has already committed the essential theological error. This is the fourth stage, "error toward God." Once the world has departed God's Word, it becomes victim to its own indomitable need for a god. "God" thus becomes the great cosmic screen on which man transposes his own fears and aspirations. "God" is now each man's creature, present at hand and at his disposal, like other things. He is a *deus inter alia.* This is the fifth stage, idolatry.

The unbelief at the origin of this disastrous flight from God is closely associated with man's relationship to the rest of creation. Not only does man lose God, but he loses the creation as well.

In his 1517 commentary on Heb. 3:13 Luther describes the rise of unbelief as follows.[16] Man finds joy in the creation. But then the Creator gets forgotten. This stage corresponds to the "ingratitude" Luther mentioned in the earlier *Romans* lectures. Having abandoned the Word of God which could have held him in the proper evaluation of creation, man becomes attached to material things as constituting the good in life. The fatal, natural attraction soon becomes complete.

Man loves the world and hardens his heart against God. The consequence is unbelief.

The sin does not lie in the creation. Only man exhibits this incurvedness. Only man sins and dies from it. Yet man's corruption flows over to corrupt the creation. The creation under man's hand becomes a world of things to be used and abused. Fallen man uses the world to blind himself to God and to deceive himself. The occasion for Luther's description of the rise of unbelief was the phrase in Heb. 3:13, "the deceitfulness of sin." To sinful eyes the good of the creation is deceitful. God could have been known from the creation. Luther maintained that if God's created ordinance were seen correctly it would be proper to argue for His existence on this basis.[17] The creation is properly the "veil" or covering through which man was to have seen God. This was in fact the only way man could have seen God, for apart from the covering God's love and majesty are simply too great for the human soul, heart, and body (!) to bear.[18] But sinful man makes the creation the ultimate good. He makes it into a god and thereby loses both creation and God. Luther is not exactly pitting love of creation against love of God. Only the sinful man's love of creation excludes love of God.[19] The creation now does not provide the true knowledge of God because man in his sin has lost true knowledge of creation. And he has lost the creation because he has lost true knowledge of himself.[20]

Luther draws the noose even more tightly. Back in the lectures on Romans once again, we find a passage on Rom. 8:7 in which Luther combines the themes of "the good" and "idolatry" to explicate man's incurvedness.[21] The perversity of human nature is so complete that even the *true* God and His works become "goods" for man's enjoyment, and so idols. Luther's hierarchy of goods makes an interesting comparison to the tradition. The ranging of these goods, from external goods through intellectual goods to spiritual gifts of grace, to God Himself, is more or less what was felt to be the divinely intended order. But while Augustine held that the *inversion* of this order in the worldly realm was a sign of its sin, Luther keeps the hierarchy right side up and argues that the sin lies in man's relating it to himself as "goods" to be enjoyed. Thus even that rare man who possesses a correct understanding of Scripture, exhibits the gracious gifts of the Spirit, and maintains the "proper" doctrine of God, does not escape the perversion of his nature. Even when man is right, he is wrong! For now God is kept in His glory as the highest good—for man. What is otherwise a legitimate form of revelation now becomes a human tool for keeping God pinned to the "highest good," for combating God's self-revelation in a "lower good." And when God would reveal Himself in what to man is not a good at all, but rather the opposite of good, the world's confusion and opposition is complete. The "theology of glory" is scandalized by the "theology of the cross." The "prudence of the flesh" is flatly contradicted by the "prudence of the Spirit."

One concluding observation on Luther's hierarchy of goods. The list is a list of *human* goods. It reflects man's understanding of himself. But at the upper levels we find God and His works mentioned. God is the highest human good. So that the doctrine of *God* is the highest expression of human *self*-understanding! Man's possessive egocentricity, in bondage to itself, knows no boundaries. The "theology of glory" is idolatry, self-glorification just where man thinks he is most glorifying God. Just as man lost the creation because he lost knowledge of himself, so he loses himself because he has lost God. And he has lost God just because he thinks he has God. But God simply will not allow Himself to be "had" in this way. The higher and more innocent the praise, the deeper and more guilty the sin.

Ludwig Feuerbach studied Luther's presentations of man the maker of idols.[22] He concluded that Luther himself supported the view that religion was ideology. How perfectly right Feuerbach was—and how perfectly wrong!

Sometimes scholarship becomes wondrously surrealistic.

Luther's descriptions of Jonah's oceanic experience with God reflect all the characteristics of the fall we have been examining. Throughout his commentary Luther compares Jonah to Adam, and proceeds to pour out all of his own experience into the description.[23]

Jonah the good Hebrew knows that God is "the God of Israel." But that confession has a hidden second clause: "—and of nobody else!" The Jews think they have got God, for He has revealed His law and observances to them. The Jews "keep" the Law, and so think they have the Giver of the Law and are themselves alone worthy of this ownership. That is why Jonah is scandalized when God bids him preach to the pagans.[24] The idol can remain an idol only if it remains your *own.* God's command poses a threat to Jonah's idol, and so rather than abandon the idol Jonah tries to flee from God.

The hurricane God brews up for the occasion causes the shipmates to call on their own tiki gods for assistance. But Jonah's blindness is more complete. For he is dead asleep, blissfully and innocently unaware of what is happening to him.[25] Once he is awakened his immediate response is one of fear of the idol's wrath. His own knowledge of God is as false as that of his shipmates. But Jonah's perversion is even more profound, for he has the gall to boast that he alone fears the true God![26]

51

The self-destruction of sinful man's understanding of himself and God is soon complete. There is finally no choice left for Jonah but suicide. He must destroy himself rather than give up his idol. "Law" was his highest self-understanding, and he betrayed himself. The Law becomes a tyrant when you make it God. It kills those who would live by it.

The Law is good, Luther says, but not for man, since he misuses it both in reference to himself and in reference to God. As we shall see, Luther understands human nature in terms of Law. Yet he argues that man hates the Law, regardless of appearances to the contrary. And this is the self-contradiction which binds and finally kills man. The Law experienced in its binding, damning character appears to sinful man to be a tyrant. As do all Luther's "tyrants," so the tyrant Law exposes the self-contradiction in which man is trapped. Death, hell, sin, the devil, are all scandals, disasters, contradictions, because they comprise the existence and the future of sinful man, whose intended existence and future was to have been life, heaven, righteousness, and God.[27]

Of course, there is no way out of this scandalous self-entrapment for man. Jonah tried to flee from himself, from God, but God hounds him to the ends of the earth. Yet the divine interest is for Jonah's own good. Only the action of God creates the possibility for sinful man to escape the deadly *incurvatus* of his own egocentricity and become also *ingressus*. In fact, however, Jonah never did repent, not finally. The Ninevites repent, to Jonah's surprise; God spares the city, to Jonah's outrage. He will not let his idol go.

To Luther the only effective antidote to man's terminal condition of sinful bondage to the Law is God's revelation in Christ. In fact it is only in Christ that the man of faith can even become aware of the self-contradiction. We are driven to Christ not only for escape from this self-strangulation, as Luther describes it, but also in order to understand what *"incurvatus"* and *"ingressus"* mean in their deepest senses. We must, therefore, now turn to Luther's presentation of Christ's atoning work in order to gain the true sense of the bondage which constitutes the fallen world. In doing so we will also gain a better position for understanding the issue with which this essay began, the dialectic of flesh and spirit.

3

Breaking In, Breaking Out

In section 1 the competitive *fora* before which man stands for his identity were introduced in a preliminary fashion. In section 2 we followed Luther's presentation of the bondage or entrapment into which man is led once he has committed himself to the "wisdom of the flesh." The form of definiteness achieved by this attempt to grasp at freedom from God is "bondage." It would be quite proper to say that Luther defines man not as a "rational animal," but as one "in bondage to sin." "Bondage" in two senses at least. First, man has no alternative to rebellion and the consequent self-destruction. He is bound to do it. Second, he is forced in this direction by the power of sin. The power of sin is, of course, located in his own corrupt individual nature. Yet Luther also feels that sin is a power transcending individual man, transcending even the race. While it would be possible, indeed traditional, to express the transcendence of sin in terms of the doctrine of original sin, Luther's special approach to this aspect of the power of sin is rather in terms of the "tyrants."

Luther does incorporate aspects of both the so-called Anselmian and the Abelardian theories of the atonement in his description. Yet the most characteristic feature of his presentation is the rather cosmic power struggle of Christ with the tyrants—a struggle taking place "outside" man. This kind of interpretation, memorably formulated in the 1535 *Galatians* commentary, is called the "classic" theory by Gustav Aulen, its chief advocate.[28] It exhibits the power of Christ breaking the transcendent power of sin, the tyrants, and thereby exhibits Christ empowering man to struggle with the sin in his flesh. Luther's presentation of the atonement thus picks up the "power" side of his discussion of human bondage. Christ both reveals sin in all its transcendent power and breaks through that *regnum* from the outside. And therein the other aspect of bondage is overcome. For now man has an alternative. Christ breaks man out of himself, creating in the man of faith the life which, while remaining *incurvatus in se,* is now also *ingressus in Christum.*

The atonement thus provides the true knowledge of man in its radical dimensions. But it does so only because it provides the true knowledge of God, also in radical dimension. God remains free above His Word, of course. He is never simply present at hand, even in Christ.[29] Yet Luther warns of the danger of seeking God apart from His covering in Christ. For man God is to be found only in Christ. The cross is the paradigm, the norm, for the true encounter with God, and whatever is thought of God apart from Christ is speculation and idolatry. The close interrelationship of the knowledge of man and of God is a premise which Luther exhibits most clearly in his treatment of the divinity of Christ in the atonement. It is Christ's work which proves that at the cross we encounter the true God rather than a fiction. The man Christ has, according to Paul, given us salvation, overcome the tyrants, in fact has entered the depths of the human condition more deeply than is humanly possible. Only God could become *that* human. Therefore Christ is divine! This sort of argument for the divinity of Christ is very interesting in itself. But it is also an excellent way of indicating the depth or the transcendence of the bondage to which sin leads. Sin has become so profoundly transcendent that a man in sin cannot even experience what it is to be man in sin. Jonah sleeps in fake innocence while the storm rages. So Christ's suffering both exposes and overcomes the self-contradiction which is man. Christ's ability to do this reveals His divinity. It is in the supra-human depths of human bondage and suffering that the true God is manifested. What is manifested there is God the Savior, not God the judge and tyrant.[30] If Christ is ever separated from the sinful bondage of the human condition, the atonement itself is in a sense lost. This is because Luther insists that the *pro nobis* aspect of discourse on the atonement is a constituent of the event itself. When this is denied or forgotten, the sacrifice on the cross loses its "for us" character, its existential reference. It then becomes merely an exemplary event, the norm for an *imitatio,* and that means a temptation to works-righteousness. The atonement becomes an instrument of the Law. And because the ideal thus exemplified is so radical, so impossible to fulfill, and yet seemingly the condition to salvation, Christ is again wrongly experienced by us as a judge and tyrant. To sinful, disbelieving men he becomes—Luther is a genius with words—a "white devil," the tempter in divine raiment.[31]

So Christ must be kept close to His saving work. Just as a proper theological definition of man would be "he who is in bondage to sin," so the proper definition of Christ is "He who gave Himself for my sins." For Luther Christology *is* soteriology.

If Christ's "humanity for us"[32] is the locus for our knowledge of God, so is it also the locus for our knowledge of man. Christ's passion provides Luther the opportunity to develop a language as radical and profound as the human sin he seeks to reflect. This language is the language of the "tyrants," and of Christ's struggle with them. Somewhat strange to the ear at first, and suspiciously dualistic, this form of talk has been criticized or simply dismissed by many students. It appears to show Luther at his Teutonic worst, unconsciously appealing to and exploiting medieval Germanic superstition and mythology. It seems theologically unjustified, and in fact a hindrance to understanding. But Luther had a fair intellect, and a rather well-trained one at that. He was a superb dramatic artist, to be sure, but is it not a fair assumption to presume that Luther was conscious of what he was doing, especially in regard to what by his own conviction was among the most central of Christian teachings? With only this much generosity of attitude, we can approach the "tyrant" language more productively.

In the famous opening lines to his *scholia* on *Romans,* Luther said that the sum and substance of the epistle was to pull down, to pluck up, and to destroy all wisdom and righteousness of the flesh, "and to implant, establish, and make large the reality of sin." The "tyrants" make large the reality of sin. Perhaps such mythical and dramatic language was the only way, or the best way, to portray the power of human sin in all its transcendence.[33] Such a presentation may have been alien to our forefathers, but Albert Camus' *The Plague* is only one sign that Luther's sense of the demonic, transcendent, personal, and self-conscious character of evil is not lost on our own generation.

It is thus that Christ's struggle on the cross with the tyrants reveals the radical disjunction between the judgments of God and the world, the radical self-contradiction of the latter, and the possibility for life in faith which Christ's victory assures. Nowhere is the opposition of judgments more radically revealed than in Christ's humiliation. Christ on the cross is the ultimate of righteousness and the ultimate sinner, at once the ultimate lie and the ultimate truth, the ultimate glory and the ultimate despair, ultimate blessedness, ultimate damnation.[34] It is in Luther's ecstatic and paradoxical language that the contradiction of the world is revealed. This language is most classically represented in his 1535 comments on Gal. 2:19 and 3:13.

> Therefore Paul would like to draw us away completely from looking at the Law, sin, death, and other evil things, and to transfer us to Christ, in order that there we might see this very duel: the Law battling against the Law, in order to become liberty to me; sin battling against sin, in order to become righteousness to me; death battling against death, in order that I might have life. For Christ is my devil against the devil, that I might be a son of God; He destroys hell, that I might have the kingdom of heaven.[35]

What is revealed in this language—and it goes on page after page with the same intensity in the *Galatians* commentary—is the self-contradiction of the fallen world in its self-destructive character. Incurvedness feeds on itself. Because the forms of definiteness which characterize fallen man have a transcendent, supra-personal character, the tyrants cannot be overcome by man. Their quality as "tyrants" simply indicates the profundity of human entrapment. Sin was a creature of man that has become a monster destroying its creator. The tyrants kill man before man can kill them. Only God has the power to assume both sides of the struggle of man against himself. Only God can sustain the full power of the tyrants, and by sustaining their heaviest onslaught destroy them on their own terms and so reveal their self-destructive essence. Only in Christ is there occasion for the Law to bind itself, death to kill itself, and so on. And thus only in Christ is the transcendent power of sin both revealed and overcome.

As important as it is to emphasize the "cosmic," or if you will the "objective" character of the tyrants and Christ's struggle with them, it is no less important to emphasize that "tyrant" is "*human sin*" writ large. The struggle of Christ on the cross is with *my* flesh, in *my* flesh, and the victory is for *me*.[36] Not only does the atonement reveal Christ the Savior but also man the sinner, for God does not save anyone except *real* sinners. "Therefore sin boldly . . ."! "But believe more strongly still," for the atonement also indicates the principle under which the Christian lives and in terms of which he experiences himself.

> For all that comes from God must be crucified in the world (and so long as it is not led to the cross, i.e., the readiness to endure shame, it cannot be recognized as coming from God). Even his only-begotten Son was not exempted from this but was placed before us as an example for this.[37]

While Luther would not have formulated this conclusion in a way so apparently close to the idea of an *imitatio*—piety in his later writing as he does in the *Romans* commentary, the principle is a sound expression of the "theology of the cross." The experience of contrast is not a human achievement. It is the gift of God, and both makes possible and characterizes the penultimate judgment, the life of faith. The Christian alone can recognize in himself the struggle between God and the world manifested perfectly and finally by Christ on the cross. It is only in the life of faith that this struggle, the struggle between flesh and spirit, can be clearly understood. We are thus now in a better position to evaluate the theme with which we began the essay. For where there is faith there is the struggle between that which is "from God," the Spirit, and that which is "in the world," the flesh.

In the introductory essay I noted that to an extent Luther's dialectical pairs are interchangeable, and that even the members of a given pair varied. Thus sometimes Luther can discuss man in terms of the dialectic "nature—spirit," associating "spirit" very closely with "grace." Occasionally the dialectic "wrath—grace" can be used anthropologically.[38] Especially in his earlier writing the dialectic "inward —outward" can be used equivalently to "flesh—spirit."[39] Yet it is the dialectic of flesh and spirit that is by far Luther's most important formulation for describing the human condition. Luther says that when he, following Paul, uses the term "flesh," it must refer to the Old Adam, the whole man in sin, and not to some "part" of him.[40] The most important thing to remember in this connection is that *neither* the conjunctive *nor* the disjunctive senses of the dialectic "flesh—spirit" can properly apply to the man sunk in sin. The carnal man always consents to his flesh, becomes one with it, *"idem cum carne,"* Luther says.[41] And that means he is wholly included in the self-destructive nature of sin.

> The flesh, however, accomplishes what it wants to do in so far as it fulfills its desires with joy and without any struggle and hesitation. This is the way of life, nay, rather, it is the sign of death: it shows that the world is lost; it is so easy to do evil.[42]

The Christian by contrast does not exemplify the deadly unification with the flesh. He is not "well-adjusted." The Christian is wholly spiritual, and this means it is the Christian alone who can be described dialectically. Only in the wholly spiritual man is there a struggle between the flesh and the spirit! Only in the Spirit is a man almost literally beside himself, two men struggling with each other.[43] We can make sense of this only when we do not interpret the struggle as that between the flesh of man and the spirit of man. This would be to fall back into the anthropology Luther has rejected, in which the soul—here the Christian—is seen as the locus of a struggle between his "higher" and "lower" powers. The consequence would be a false conception of Christian growth in sanctification. It would be Law, works-righteousness, all over again. Rather the conflict taking place in the wholly spiritual man is that between the flesh of man, the whole man, and the Spirit of *God.* It is the Spirit of God who by His presence stirs up the conflict, and who is master over the flesh of man.[44] It is the presence of the Spirit and not some inherent quality of the Christian that distinguishes him from fallen man. And now we have one application of the disjunctive sense of the dialectic. A man is mastered *either* by the devil *or* by God.[45] He is either flesh or spirit. In the first case fallen man is wholly at one with himself. He embodies the single, proximate judgment: he is flesh. But in the second case redeemed man is not one man, but two. He embodies the double, penultimate judgment: he is both flesh and spirit. This is true because a man does not by any means cease to be a sinner, a man of flesh, just because he is a Christian, a man of the Spirit. So a man can be *either* one man (flesh) *or* two men (flesh and spirit). The Christian is two men. He embodies both the conjunctive and the disjunctive senses of the dialectic. Since he is wholly flesh, he embodies the struggle of the world against God. Since he is wholly spirit, he embodies the encounter of God with the world.

> There are two whole men, and there is only one whole man. Thus it comes about that a man fights against himself and is opposed to himself. He is willing, and he is unwilling. And this is the glory of the grace of God; it makes us enemies of ourselves.[46]

The Christian is "one man" because it is just within him, and not between him and someone else, that the struggle of the flesh against the spirit takes place. The Christian is "two men" because in him the encounter of God and the world allows no compromise. The "one man" is the man as seen through faith, inasmuch as he shares the fallenness of the world. The "two men" is man as seen through faith, since the Spirit of God works within the fallenness.

The designation "flesh," therefore, refers to man wholly sunk in sin, the man of whom it is true to say only that he is *incurvatus in se.* "Spirit" refers to man wholly sinner and wholly justified, to man who is both flesh and spirit, the man of whom it is true to say that he is both *incurvatus in se* and also *ingressus in Christum. Ingressus* is a term connoting both the "toward" and the "not yet" character of the faith relationship. The Christian is "toward" Christ, and it is his "towardness" which distinguishes him from fallen man. The Christian is "not yet" Christ, and it is this which distinguishes him from God. Luther's *partim* language can be interpreted in the same way. To the extent *(partim)* man remains flesh, he is not one with Christ; to the extent he is spirit, he is not one with sin.[47] The reality of faith is a penultimate reality.

In this essay I have concentrated the analysis on the dynamics of the "flesh" or *incurvatus* side of Luther's anthropology. The dynamics of the "spirit" or *ingressus* side must await fuller treatment later. The presentation of the work of Christ indicated the self-destructive character of the contradiction reflected in that judgment I have called proximate, and that Luther terms *incurvatus.* It also indicated that the penultimate reality or judgment is made possible and is characterized by something outside itself, namely, the ultimate. *Homo ingressus* is two men, flesh and spirit, but the spirit is not his, but God's.

The second section of the essay introduced a discussion of man's perverted knowledge of God in order to bring into greater relief human incurvedness. Now I must return to this subject in greater detail, but with a shift of perspective from man's relationship to God to God's relationship to man. Thereby the true character of God's Word, and both a new perspective on human incurvedness and also a fuller understanding of Christian becoming, will be obtained.

Essay III: *Lex et Fides*

Let the Writer Beware

Most students of Luther do not begin to appreciate the holistic and systematic character of his theology until they venture into print with an interpretation which, one learns soon enough from the critics, has come to grief. A small lapse of interpretive sensitivity at one point, and Luther's *theologia relationis* snowballs the misjudgment into a magnificent distortion of the whole. You begin well, easily, naturally, and end with a labored interpretation full of pseudo-problems and smelling of artificiality. Something has gone wrong, but you don't know where. And Luther has escaped again.

Make a good judgment at a critical point, of course, and you are home free. If you are a German, you can create a school of interpretation after you that will last forty years.

One such consequential judgment was made in the preceding essay. On the assumption (I don't wish to argue it now) that Luther's understanding of Christ's atonement is central to his theology, I decided that his presentation of the "tyrants" must be taken seriously. I introduced the subject as an expression of Luther's anthropology, arguing that for all its "objective" or transendental appearance the tyrant-language expressed the "depth-dimension" of human sin. This decision was not made to make Luther's ideas more acceptable or, forgive the word, relevant, but rather because of the presence among the tyrants of one tyrant who in a sense was the essence of them all. This is the tyrant *Law.*

If one refers "Law" to divine revelation, or revelation alone, rather than primarily to the human condition, Luther's presentation leads into a very difficult interpretive position. When we think of "Law," the dialectical counterpole immediately coming to mind is "Gospel." So that Law and Gospel are then interpreted as God's revelation(s?) to us. The hesitation indicates the problem. We make revelation one revelation because God is one. This is correct instinct, but now Luther troubles us. For his presentation of Law and Gospel forces us to the view that Gospel suceeds Law, as the perfect succeeds the imperfect, for example. We begin to get uneasy. Is Law an inferior, non-ultimate form of revelation? Does God not expect the Sermon on the Mount to be taken at face value? Luther pushes us further. His animus against the Law led many would-be friends to conclude that Luther fell into theological *dualism.* He is called a Manichee, a not-so-crypto-Marcionite. And it is just the tyrant language that cinches the impression. We have here at best revelation opposed to itself: Law and Gospel in combat. A short step to the view that the God of Law battles with the God of Gospel. An even shorter step to the view that there are two gods. All of Luther's dialectics fall in to support this view: God's "two wills," the "alien" and "proper" work; God *in se,* God *ad extra;* the "theology of glory" and the "theology of the cross." And so on.

We turn attention from knowledge of God to knowledge of man. The analog to "Law—Gospel" is "works—faith." Again a host of problems arise. By putting these terms in polarity we make them appear to belong in the same category: responses to God's revelation. It is now very easy to turn faith into a work. For when one says "faith or works" the meaning is "by means of faith or works." What is meant is one's attitude of response, what faith or works are intended to be: responses to requirements. Faith is then a work of a different kind, perhaps. More difficult, but still a work. And that means Law.

In order to keep faith from becoming a work, we set it in strict opposition to work: "either by works or by faith." This opposition reflects the opposition of Law and Gospel. And now all the familiar problems of Christian living emerge: the relation of justification and sanctification, freedom and discipline, and so on. Reflexively, the dichotomies of Christian experience color the nature of revelation itself. For now antinomian and legalist contend for Scripture. If there is a word of forgiveness, of healing grace, of freedom, there is Gospel; if there is a word of judgment, of bondage, of requirement, there is Law. Revelation is again the idol, the ultimate self-justification of the proximate, which in its self-contradiction produces contrary gods and forms parties of scholars in their respective defenses.

Let us begin all over again. Something has gone wrong. For Luther opposed himself to the antinomians as well as to the legalists, and does so on the basis of the single Word of God. We seem to have lost the fact that for Luther "works—faith" and "Law—Gospel" are *contrasts.* They admit a *conjunctive* as well as disjunctive sense. Works are very much a part of the Christian life of faith. Because the Christian is a sinner, the temptation to works is an opposition to the work of Christ. Because the Christian is justified, works are the realization of Christ's presence in him. Similarly, the Christian does not experience the Law in its depth, in its true meaning, until he has received the Gospel, just as the Gospel itself achieves its meaning and efficacy only in the context of the preaching of the Law. We must therefore reconsider the referents to and the interrelations among "Law," "Gospel," "works," and "faith." The decision taken in the preceding essay to interpret the tyrants as descriptions of fallen man means that "Law" is to be interpreted this way. Now the dialectic "Law—faith" can emerge as a proper anthropological contrast. Is "works—Gospel" a proper contrast? It might be, for if works are understood by faith as an expression of Law, what we do in fulfillment of a demand, then Gospel can be understood as what we receive in fulfillment of a promise. "Demand and promise" might therefore be a much better way to construe Luther's understanding of revelation than "Law and Gospel," while "Law and faith" might be a better way to understand the human response to the Gospel than "works and faith."

Such an interpretation of Luther, besides other advantages, would expose both the dynamic and the relational character of his theology in a particularly forceful way. The key to such a possibility of interpretation rests on what Luther means by "Law," or more exactly, what he means and does not mean by the dialectic "Law—Gospel."

1

Out of One, Two

According to Luther everything revealed about God is revealed only through the Word of God. Whatever God may be for Himself, for us the only God available is the God who is identifiable with the Word.

From this identification of the Word with God one might be led to investigate whether Luther applied the attributes of the divine nature to the Word. And we could find any number of passages such as the following to suggest the omnipresnce of the Word.

> Therefore, since the Word [sermo] of God is over and above all things, beyond all things and within all things, before all things and behind all things and therefore everywhere, it is impossible to escape from it anywhere.[1]

It would be easy to develop Luther's theology of the Word in this direction. And it would be dead wrong. For in identifying the Word with God, Luther intends, not to generalize or abstract the Word into a universal divine form, but to incarnate or concretize God into the particular physical reality of the written and spoken Word. We could better express the sense of Luther's identification by reversing the way we began and say: God is identified with the Word. For God can only have the form of the Word as His form, and what we do with the Word we do with God. Again, it would be wrong-headed to say that we come to God through the Word. Rather God has come to us in the Word, the Word to which He has bound Himself,[2] and alone through which His self-revelation is manifest and made efficacious. The Word to which God has bound Himself is found in the Scriptures. Apart from that Word the highest piety is idolatry, opinion in the guise of truth. Unless we keep to the Word of Scriptures like a hare to its hole, as Luther put it so quaintly in a sermon of 1522, all is lost. Presence everywhere is presence nowhere. If we wander about "under our own recognizance," as the saying goes, we will be hounded everywhere and end up not knowing where either God or we ourselves are.[3]

One of the most consequential discoveries made by the young exegete was that the speaking or discourse of God in the Scriptures has the character of a Word of *promise.* This discovery, the nature and applications of which we will consider in the next essay, gave Luther the basic dialectic for his understanding of revelation: the Word of God as composed of promises and threats or commands. Occasionally Luther will say the Old Testament contains threats or Law, and the New Testament promises or Gospel.[4] But usually he sees the dialectic of promise—Law applicable throughout the Scriptures. The important thing is to distinguish properly the words of promise and the words of Law in their interrelated, mutually dependent functions, whether they occur in the Old or the New Testaments.[5]

As vital as it is to distinguish correctly God's words of promise and of Law, it is impossible to do so unless one first knows the point of God's speaking in these modes. The whole Scriptural revelation, Luther says, begins and ends with, and has as its only purpose and reality, the revelation of Christ and His atoning work for us. Conversely Christ can be found nowhere else but in God's words of promise and Law. God achieves concreteness in His words finally and perfectly only in the concreteness of Christ. Christ alone is the enfleshed Word of God that is within our reach. Christ is the Word that is "abbreviated," "cut short," or "consummated" for us, Luther says in the *Romans* commentary.[6] Every word before and after Christ is penultimate, and every word which does not find its concreteness in Christ is not a Word of God but a vacuous word of man. Thus while the entire Scripture is God's words of promise and Law, these words achieve their meaning only in Christ.

It is at this point that we gain the first of the terms we are considering in this essay. For it is the preaching of Christ and His resurrection which is the content and definition of the Gospel, and it is ultimately the Gospel which is therefore the Word of God.[7] The Word of the Gospel is the Word of the cross, however, and so what is revealed in the Gospel is not simply the good work of God but also the evil works of men. The Gospel, Luther consistently argues, is the preaching of justification, the good Word bestowing grace, peace and forgiveness, the Word of salvation. It is thus in the proclamation of the Gospel that there is exposed the fallen human condition of total opposition to God from which Christ has saved us. The Gospel proclaims the righteousness, grace, and salvation of God in the work of Christ, and therein reveals the damnation of men apart from the work of Christ. This double revelation alone is the proper knowledge of God.[8]

Our task in the first section of this essay is to discover the locus of a mutually exclusive opposition with respect to God's revelation. God's words of promise and of Law function jointly to lead men to Christ. And the opposition exposed by the Gospel is not an opposition *in* the Gospel, but *between* God and man. In fact this opposition is not a true opposition at all. The Gospel does not expose God's righteousness *and also* human sin, but rather proclaims God's righteousness *overcoming* human sin. Knowledge of God and knowledge of man must be defined in terms of each other, as we have seen in earlier essays. Were God's righteousness and human sin separated, the Gospel would no longer be God's good Word, but a word of Law and damnation.

Yet we are not wrong in seeking the opposition in the context of the Gospel, if for no other reason than that the human opposition to God which Christ has overcome is fully manifest there. Luther has, however, given further indications of the path we must follow. He has consistently defined the Gospel not as a given body of doctrine but as an *act*. The Gospel is the *preaching* of forgiveness of sins in Christ. It is something, therefore, in which men participate. The preaching of the Word involves the hearing of the Word. The Gospel, Luther insists, consists in its activity, in its effects, in its use. Thus we cannot even understand what the Gospel is unless we know what it does in men, and what men do with it. Now Luther says there are two uses or responses men make to God's Word, and it is just the Gospel which shows them to be mutually exclusive uses. It is in man's responses to the revelation of God that we will find the opposition we are seeking.

If the Gospel is known in its effects, then *faith* is the Gospel made effective. The preached Word of God can only be received by faith, the faith created by the Holy Spirit in and through the preaching of the Word. It is faith alone which properly "grasps" or uses the Word of God; faith alone which sees the benefit of the tyrants, the hidden good of the Gospel.[9] Faith is the only true use of the Word because faith alone is the true form of Christ. And thus only through the preaching of Christ does faith arise and become the true knowledge of God.

The Word in which faith arises is a spoken Word, and thus faith arises *ex auditu,* from the hearing of the Word.[10] What faith hears in the preaching is the Word of promise. The connection of faith and promise was one of Luther's most important theological discoveries, and from the time of the breakthrough on this point in his commentary on Rom. 3:2 ff., he never ceased to insist on the strict togetherness of faith and promise. Not only do faith and promise require each other, but since Christ is the fulfillment of the promise, faith is the fulfillment of the promise.[11] And since faith alone has Christ, *faith alone has the Gospel.* And this means, Luther never tires of repeating, that *faith alone properly distinguishes Law and Gospel.*[12]

How faith distinguishes Law and Gospel is a theme of the next section. At this point we must introduce the other "use" men make of the Word. In the revelation of Christ there becomes manifested another use or response to the Word of God besides that of faith. This use does not take Christ as the explication of the Word, but judges the Word by human nature. The Word thus appears in opposition to human nature, which experiences the Word as a cruel, incomprehensible tyrant bringing the world's evil to light and forcing the world into rebellion.[13] Since it does not and cannot see God's promise fulfilled in Christ and in faith, human nature sees Christ only as another lawgiver. It sees the entire Word of God as nothing but Law, and so is driven to despair. This use of the Word is opposite that of faith, and it can be termed the use or response of Law. Because this response to the Word is not a response to Christ, Law does not have the Gospel. This means the response of Law *cannot properly distinguish Law and Gospel,* but confuses them, and thus has only Law.[14]

We shall examine this theme more carefully in the next section. But now we are in a position to assess the opposition Luther always develops when he is speaking about Revelation. There is indeed a mutually exclusive opposition, but it is to be located in the *responses* men make to the Word of God, responses which the preaching of the Word creates in its hearers. Now this opposition is not between "works" and "faith," and it is not between "Law" and "Gospel." These dialectical themes only admit of *contrasts;* the terms have an interdependent relationship in Luther's descriptions. This is true even

64

in Luther's *Galatians* commentary, where the distinction between Law and Gospel is most sharply drawn. For if we look carefully we find that Luther does not quite make Law and Gospel into an opposition. Luther sometimes presents a mutual opposition in the context of a discussion of promise and Law.[15] But the opposition is between *justification* by faith in the promise or by works of Law. The same obtains in his contrast of grace and Law: the mutual exclusion is not in terms of grace or Law, but rather in terms of which is to reign in the *conscience*. It is the two *doctrines* which are opposed.[16] The clear division of Law and Gospel, Luther says, is the essence of good doctrine.[17] And where the distinction of Law and Gospel seems most explicitly stated, Luther is invariably talking not about Law and Gospel, but about the *justification* of the Law or the Gospel.[18] The Law becomes opposed to the Gospel only when it is misused.

> In its *proper* use the Law ought to support the promises and grace. If it conflicts with these, it is no longer the holy *Law* of God; then it is a false and diabolical *doctrine* that only produces despair, and therefore must be repudiated and excommunicated[19] (emphasis mine).

The opposition is not rooted in the Word of God. It is rooted in man's varied appropriation of the Word. We have seen Luther posit two "uses" of the Word of God: the use of faith and the perverted use which I have characterized as "Law." Now the opposition is not exactly between faith and Law, but between the two *uses*. There is a mutual opposition, that is, between the *righteousness* of the Law and the *righteousness* of faith.

The Word of God is the ultimate Word which, when it comes, exposes all else as penultimate. We have seen how the proclamation of Christ functions as a sort of catalyst producing two kinds of responses or uses. Which response men make depends on God's election, and Luther will not finally debate *that* matter with you, so you might as well accept it. The proper or true response to the Gospel is the response of faith. It is faith which has the identifying characteristic of the penultimate. Faith embodies the correct dialectic between sin and righteousness. Only faith knows how to properly distinguish and apply Law and Gospel. The improper or false response has the character of the proximate. Law is a univocal understanding which is self-destructive. It confuses sin and righteousness, and thereby confuses Law and Gospel. It turns God's Word into its own word, into simply Law. The mutual opposition is between these two modes of response to the Word of God, and this opposition is manifest in the two theological assessments made of the commands and promises in God's Word. Law and Gospel go together and require each other. The righteousness or justification of the Law (works) and of the Gospel (faith), however, their status as doctrines and their place in man's life *coram deo*—these positions are mutually exclusive.

2

The meaning and use of Law is the guiding issue of this section. There are two ways of approach to the issue. We could first establish the meaning Luther gave to the word "Law," and then attempt to make sense out of his rich and apparently confusing presentation of the function or use of the Law. The reverse procedure, however, would be at least as appropriate. For a strong case can be made for the thesis that in Luther's theology the meaning of the Law is established by its use. More often than not Luther takes the latter approach. I shall take the former, but only because things can proceed a little more simply that way. Misjudgment can be precluded if we bear in mind that for Luther the full recognition of the true referent of the Law is in fact the only valid theological use of the Law.

And now an important *caveat* emerges. The discussion in this section has essentially nothing to do with Luther's well-known distinction between the "civic" and "theological" uses of the Law. *That* distinction will be important for us later. In this section we are interested solely in the "theological use" of the Law. It is this use alone which effects, in accordance with divine election, the two different states of affairs which were introduced in the preceding section, and which now must be fleshed out in greater detail.

The Law Is *Schon Da*

When men hear the word "Law," Luther says, they respond in one of two ways, both as wrong as they are natural. Some "disciples of the Law" conclude from the fact that the Law is preached that they ought to and can in fact keep it and so find life. Others, less sanguine about their capacities, acknowledge the "ought" but are driven to despair because of their incapacity.[20] Differences of estimation aside, the two responses share the assumption that the relation to God is a legal relation. All men, Luther concluded, by nature think that they are justified by the Law, even though some would like to be free of this arrangement.[21]

This natural, one could say instinctive estimation of the human relation to God in terms of Law is contravened, however, by another phenomenon. If man's natural corruption leads him to think instinctively in terms of Law, his corruption by sin[22] leads him to defect from and to deny this relationship. The true definition of the Law is actually the opposite of what men think, Luther insists. It is in fact a denial of all our experience to say that we love the Law. We rather hate it, love sins, hate the fact that the Law forbids sinning.[23] The opposition of the Law and man's will is a dogma with Luther from the beginning. If the Law is good, the will's desire is opposite. If man appears to love the Law, he really hates it and keeps up appearances merely for his own interests.[24]

Two short paragraphs and we are already in the rip of a contradiction: man in his fallen nature instinctively responds to God in terms of Law, yet in his sinful will hates and opposes the Law! We seem to have three elements here: sin, nature, and Law. If we investigate the relationship Luther sees among these elements, we may begin to gain an understanding of the meaning and function of Law.

Luther was able to clarify his understanding of the relation between Law and human nature only with some difficulty. He ran into trouble right at the beginning with his 1515 commentary on Rom. 2:12-14.[25] The Gentiles can be said to "perish without the Law" (2:12) only if "law" refers, not to the written Law of the Jews, but to the "spiritual" law which is "natural" in all men. Alternately the Gentiles can be saved if they have fulfilled "the things of the Law." But Luther is not exactly sure of the rationale on this matter, and so he backtracks to v. 11 for help and comes up with a goodly advance in his understanding of Law. The spiritual or natural law

> . . .is a law which is inborn and indigenous *[nata et concreata]* to them, not given; a law which was there before they came into being *[inuenta]* and is therefore no mere tradition; a law which is alive and not merely written down (LCC 15,48).

But Luther is still having trouble with the phrase "perish without the Law." His text is full of marginal insertions, and as usual at this point in his career, Luther runs to Augustine for aid. The phrase suggests an opposition between "nature" and "Law" which Augustine reinforces, but which thereby moves the discussion in a direction opposite that taken in the passage quoted above. The Augustinian direction gets Luther through v. 13, but v. 14, "the Gentiles . . . do by nature the things of the Law," again suggests the proximity of Law and nature. Luther goes to Augustine once more, develops a couple of complicated and unsatisfactory solutions, admits great puzzlement at Paul's usage, and concludes rather irrelevantly that all men are sinners and need grace.

But now Paul delivers the final blow. Rom. 2:15, "the work of the Law is written in their hearts," demolishes Luther's attempt to keep to the Augustinian separation of Law and human nature. Luther decides to let Paul interpret Paul, and appeals to Rom. 5:5—but with a startling application. He equates "the Law is written in their hearts" with 5:5: "love is shed abroad in *their* [sic] hearts through the Holy Spirit." A change of pronoun and the description of Christian life is applied to the Gentiles![26] And now another advance in Luther's understanding of the natural, spiritual Law occurs. For he continues,

> This love is the law of Christ and the fulfillment of the law of Moses or, rather, it is a law without law, without measure, without end, without limit, but extended above and beyond everything the law prescribes or can prescribe (LCC 15, 52).

Luther has tentatively committed himself in the direction of a close relationship between human nature and at least the "unwritten" or spiritual Law. By 1519 he was prepared to interpret even the written Law in this way. In his commentary on Gal. 2:19, for example, Luther develops a definition of "the Law of the letter" in terms of "flesh," and does so in a way suggesting the "tyrant" language.

> The Law of the letter is everything written with letters . . . . This is the Law of works, the old Law, the Law of Moses, the Law of the flesh, the Law of Sin, the Law of Wrath, the Law of death. It condemns everything, makes all men guilty, increases lusts, and slays; and the more spiritual it is, the more it does so . . . .[27]

By the time of the 1535 *Galatians* lectures Luther is using the words "flesh" and "Law" almost interchangeably to refer to the same thing. Nature is inclined to observe the Law, and natural reason cannot but think according to the Law. So long as man is alive and in the flesh, Luther says, he is under Law.[28]

It is with the *Antinomian Disputations* of the late 1530s, however, that Luther seems to have completed his development. Law, sin, and death are inseparable. While man is alive the Law reigns.[29] No longer does the distinction between the spiritual and the written Law complicate the association of Law with human nature. It may be true that some men are unconscious of the Law. There may be no explicit or written Law. Some may not feel the damning power of the Law, or do so only vaguely. But the Law is nevertheless common to all men.[30] The Law, says Luther in a passage suggestive of his first definition in the *Romans* commentary, is already there: *"iam adest, ist schon da. Lex prius adest in facto."*[31]

So far we have been following, somewhat elliptically, one line in Luther's developing understanding of the referent of "Law." The Law is spiritual, alive, indigenous to man's being *(Romans)*. It names all the ills of human experience (1519 *Galatians*) and reigns over men so long as there is life and flesh (1535 *Galatians*). Whether its terror is experienced or not, the Law is common to all mankind: it is already there *(Antinomian Disputations)*.

It is just at this point that we must pick up another and in fact more important angle on the Law. At the beginning of the section we found a contradiction: man is by nature inclined to the Law, yet he is completely opposed to the Law. It is in the revelation and exploitation of this self-contradiction that the preached Law finds its chief function. It reveals man to himself. It convicts him of sin.

Throughout his career Luther maintained that the Law functioned as a mirror in which man could see his true sinful self. So close is the relation between Law and sin that the words seem interchangeable. This is because the sum and substance of the Law, its "subject matter," is the sinner.[32] There is nothing strange about the Law. Whether written down by Moses or preached by Christ, the Law simply shows man who he is: a creature of Law who betrays the Law and who in his impotence and hatred is therefore convicted of sin and justly sentenced to death. The Law is not strange or heteronomous. The wrath and damnation of the Law do not come from afar. The Law shows man damned on his own terms. As Luther put it so characteristically in a 1537 sermon on John:

> In sum: the law shows me what I am, reveals my sins and grabs me by the throat—and it does so justly.[33]

It is in fact only when we view the Law as a mirror of the sinful human condition that we can understand an otherwise "hard saying" of Luther's. This is his conviction that the Law when proclaimed *increases* sin, hatred, and disobedience. It takes the work of the Holy Spirit to crystalize man's knowledge of himself by means of the preaching of the Law. Otherwise—and Luther is at his descriptive best on this point—man wanders about in a great "cloud of unknowing." Blissful, at peace, wondrously unself-conscious. And, of course, all the more hopelessly bound to death and hell. But when the Law is proclaimed, when man is shown unmistakably who he is, the shock of recognition is almost too much to bear. There are simply no words, no language—no, not even Luther's German—adequate to describe the virulence and foulness of the sin disclosed in the light of the Law. It is in this way that the Law proclaimed reinforces what is in fact *"schon da"*: the Law betrayed.

So far we have been examining one kind of human response to the Word of God. The Word of God appears simply as a Word of Law to man, no matter whether that Word concerns Moses or Christ. The Word of Law is the outward sign revealing not a heteronomous set of rules to be observed but rather the sinful human nature in which man is trapped by his own self-contradiction. The revelation of the Law is the revelation of man fatally curved in upon himself, against himself, man locked in self-destructive bondage to his fallen nature and sinful will. This reality I have termed "proximate." We can call it "Law." The Law is the content and expression of man's being. Many students of Luther have suggested this identity,[34] but no one has done so better than Gerhard Ebeling.

> . . . Law is for Luther an existentialist *[existential]* category which sums up the theological interpretation of man's being as it in fact is. Law is therefore not an idea or an aggregate of principles, but the reality of fallen man.[35]

The Law Is Good, But

Were the preaching of the Law simply to effect human self-recognition, driving man to hatred and despair, the Law would not be doing its proper task. The Word of the Law would not in fact be the Word of God at all, but rather the word of man, of the devil, of the tyrant Law. My description of the function of the Law as revealing the human condition, if left at that point, would be a description of the *misuse* of the Word of God. The preaching of the Law is not intended to drive man to despair, condemned in his own eyes. As Luther says so frequently, often right in the midst of otherwise unrelieved descriptions of the killing power of the Law, the Law does its proper work only when it sets me *before God.*[36] This alone is the *theological* use of the Law. Only when the Law brings us before God at the same time as it brings us before ourselves can we learn that we are *sinners.* Sinners, moreover, who are saved, for men are revealed for what they are only as God in the Gospel reveals who he is: the Christ who has borne the judgment of the Law on sin and accomplished our salvation.

Whether the proclamation of the Word leads us to despair or to Christ is a question of divine election. But in those whom God has chosen, the Holy Spirit works the true task of the Law, which is to lead us to the Gospel. It is thus only the man of faith who properly responds to God's Word, and who alone is able to distinguish the Law and the Gospel correctly.

Law and Gospel, properly distinguished and applied, is the sum and substance of Christian doctrine and the whole business of Christian theologians. The key to the correct understanding of the relationship of Law and Gospel is Christ and His work. Remove Christ from God's Word, Luther says, and you can't understand the distinction.

Luther provided his young theological students an almost endless

70

variety of analogies for the proper relationship of Law and Gospel. They ranged from the traditional contrast of nature and grace to the more problematic contrast between the "right-" and "left-handed" knowledge of God. By far the most frequently occurring analogies, however, describe the contrasting functions of Law and Gospel, or the human locus to which the functions apply.

The function of the Law, for example, is to proclaim the commandments, and in so doing to humiliate man, make him guilty and sick, to condemn and kill him. The function of the Gospel, by contrast, is to proclaim the fulfillment of the commandments by Christ, to console man, forgive and cure him, justify him, and make him alive. These kinds of images imply that the Law and Gospel not only contrast with each other, but also require each other in order to function properly. Now Luther for quite understandable reasons does not like to emphasize the dependence of the Gospel on the Law. But he does clearly affirm that dependence on occasion.[37] Much more frequently, of course, he describes the function of the Law as leading to the Gospel. The Law by breaking our self-esteem drives us to Christ. It produces a need for the Gospel and makes the Gospel lovely and desirable. The Law, therefore, is not against the Gospel, but by convicting us of sin prepares us for receiving the Gospel and its benefits.

Luther's descriptions of the interrelated, mutually dependent functions of God's Word are matched by an equally rich presentation of the proper *loci* for the application of these functions. Only the Christian, the man who lives in the penultimate, experiences the dialectical tension between his participation in sin and his justification by Christ. Thus only the Christian can rightly appropriate the two functions of God's Word. He may do so because he experiences himself living both in the flesh and in the spirit, as we saw in the preceding essay. As did the Paul of Rom. 7, the Christian experiences two laws: the law of his flesh and the law of his mind. Luther knows that only love is the true fulfillment of the Law, and that this fulfillment takes place under the agency of the Holy Spirit in the mind or heart of the man of faith.[38] Thus one can say there is no Law for the Christian conscience, in the sense of a law which convicts by its demands.

> . . . In so far as he is righteous he has all the virtues which the law demands. He is already above the law because he owes nothing to the law: he keeps the law and his life is the very law itself, living and fulfilled.[39]

The Law, Luther never tires of repeating, must be kept completely out of the conscience.[40] Out of the conscience, the mind, the spirit, and in the flesh where the work of the Law is still necessary. Not only is the Christian still in the flesh, and so requires the binding, disciplining function of the Law, but it is also "in the flesh" that the works of love are to be manifested.[41]

This understanding of the proper uses and objects of God's Word is not a refinement or minor correction of that understanding which I termed "Law." It is rather an exact and complete opposition to it. The Law, that wholly sinful human response to God's Word, confuses and misapplies Law and Gospel, and ends up identifying God's Word with the only reality fallen man experiences: Law. The Christian, the man of faith, lives in the penultimate. Only faith experiences the tension between human fallenness and the restitution of Christ. Only faith is therefore capable of properly distinguishing and applying the Law and the Gospel. And this means that only faith has God's Word as it really is: Gospel. Faith alone does not pervert and transform God's good news into Law. Faith alone is therefore the only proper use of the Word of God, and the only proper theological sense of the Gospel.[42]

Earlier I developed the thesis that for Luther "Law" indicated the mode of response to God's Word characteristic of the reality of fallen man. It now seems to me most appropriate to suggest that "faith" can be understood in a comparable fashion. Faith is then the existential mode of response to God's Word characteristic of *redeemed* man.[43] "Law" and "faith" emerge as the two mutually exclusive modes of human response to divine Revelation. Does Luther afford sufficient basis for such an interpretation? We have already seen him describe the misinterpretation of God's Word as a misuse characteristic of fallen man, who can be characterized as Law. We have also seen him describe faith as the only proper use of God's Word, and have at least the beginnings of support for the view that "faith" like "Law" describes an existential human reality. A fuller presentation of this matter awaits Part Two. But the most important initial confirmation of my hypothesis comes when we find Luther making explicit comparisons between faith and Law in terms of human response to the Word of God.

We find such comparisons scattered throughout Luther's writing. He will occasionally contrast faith with flesh—"flesh," recall, closely associated with "Law." Sometimes the relation of promise and Law, of person and work, spirit and letter, Gospel and commands, will be used to clarify the relation of faith and Law. As we should expect, however, Luther's richest and most intense discourse on the opposition of faith and Law occurs just where the issue of the doctrine of justification—and this means the issue of the proper distinction and application of Law and Gospel—most occupies his pen: the *Galatians* commentaries.

72

Even in the generally disappointing commentary of 1519, Luther achieved the explicit modal opposition between faith and Law in regard to justification. The comparison comes up first at 1:24. The Christians in Judea, Luther says, observed a "mixture" of faith and Law which Paul opposed. They made salvation rest on the Law, and almost blotted out faith. We make Law a tyrant over faith; Paul makes faith master over Law.[44]

The comparison of these two contrary ways of salvation is fleshed out in greater detail at 2:16-20.[45] Here we have all the familiar associations brought in for assistance: the contrast of faith and flesh, of promise and Law, for example. There are two mutually opposed ways of justification: Law or faith. The former is doomed to self-destruction. The latter means the "end" of the Law, both in the sense that the Law no longer condemns man, and in the sense that faith is the fulfillment of the Law.

The systematic use of the modal distinction between faith and Law in terms of justification is most in evidence in the 1535 *Galatians* commentary. Throughout the text we find extensive passages on the confusion that occurs when one approaches the Gospel according to Law, or reason, or the flesh, rather than according to faith, or promise, or the Spirit.[46] So basic and useful is the distinction between faith and Law that Luther, at the beginning of the commentary, sketches the whole argument in these terms.[47]

The issue, Luther begins his précis, is the proper understanding and application of the doctrine of Christian righteousness, in contrast to all other kinds of righteousness, chiefly the righteousness of the Law. While both the righteousness of faith and that of Law are gifts of God, they must be cleanly separated. *Coram deo,* only the doctrine of faith must be considered. Only after this doctrine is established may we talk about the righteousness of the Law.

The passive character of Christian righteousness is difficult for man to understand and accept. Invariably men bring an active righteousness into their consciences, the effect of which is simply to increase human misery. The antidote is the righteousness of faith. The Christian knows how to distinguish. The passive righteousness of faith belongs in his conscience, *coram deo,* while the active righteousness of Law belongs in his flesh, *coram mundo.* The doctrine of Law is appropriate to the old man, to the flesh, to works, and the doctrine of faith is appropriate to the new man, to the Spirit, to grace.

As clearly as the two doctrines are to be distinguished, they belong strictly together for the Christian, since the Christian always lives in both realms, is both saint and sinner. It is only the man of faith

73

who knows that he stands both under Law and under faith. Everyone else will invariably confuse these mutually exclusive doctrines of righteousness. The result is that the doctrine of Law will prevail throughout. Whether it comes from Jerusalem, Rome, or Zurich, it is still a doctrine of works, and that means Law.[48] If we don't distinguish between the passive righteousness of faith and the active or works-righteousness of Law, we are under Law and Christ is lost as Savior. If we are under faith, we can observe and apply the distinction. And thereby we will enjoy peace of conscience on the one hand, and spontaneously fulfill the commandments with works of love on the other. These, Luther concludes his précis, are together the signs of a Christian life.

3

In the preceding essay we investigated Luther's understanding of the relation between man and God in terms of the contrast "flesh—spirit." As we saw, fallen man could be described as "flesh" and redeemed man as "spirit." In the first case "flesh" named the whole reality of fallen man in opposition to the Spirit of God. "Either flesh or spirit" was then the appropriate way to distinguish fallen man from redeemed man. In the second case, however, "spirit" named the whole reality of redeemed man who was both in opposition to God and in agreement with God. "Both flesh and spirit" was therefore the appropriate description of redeemed man.

In this essay we have been examining the same subject, but from a different perspective and in terms of a different language. Fallen man's response to God was named "Law," that of redeemed man "faith." In the first case "Law" described fallen man's response to the Word or Gospel of God in complete opposition to the response of redeemed man. Thus "either Law or faith" was the appropriate way of distinguishing the two uses of God's Word. In the second case, "faith" described redeemed man's response, a response which recognized both the commands and the promises in the Word of God and applied them correctly: the commands to the *flesh,* the promises to the *spirit.* Luther's identification of "flesh" with "Law" and "spirit" with "faith" then made it possible to describe redeemed man's response to God as "both Law and faith."

There is, therefore, *an exactly parallel relationship between Luther's use of the "flesh—spirit" contrast and the "Law—faith" contrast.* The two terms on each side of the hyphen are materially identified, and the linguistic shift from one contrast to the other indicates not a change of subject but rather a change of perspective on the subject. The two sets complement and explicate each other.

In both essays it was the issue of the relation between justification and sanctification that called forth Luther's contrasts. We are now in a position to sketch a formal presentation of this issue. Once again the language changes. But we shall see that the view that man is wholly sinner and wholly righteous, and at the same time partly sinner and partly righteous, is again a formulation exactly parallel to Luther's understanding of flesh and spirit, Law and faith. Luther is systematic!

Simul

I shall be bold, or merely young and arrogant, and say that Luther's doctrine of justification and sanctification is not all that difficult to understand. Don't be put off by all the literature on the subject. Most of it is about equally divided among investigations of how and when he developed the teaching, attempts to assess its faithfulness to Scripture and tradition, and attempts either to affirm or deny the doctrine on other grounds.

We can be easily confused, however, if we begin the explication in terms of that most famous battle cry, *simul iustus et peccator*—"at the same time justified and sinner." That formulation is not a constitutive statement, but rather a summarizing one. It does not, moreover, tell us anything about the referents or meanings of "justified" and "sinner," hence nothing about their relationships to either justification or sanctification. What has unfortunately dropped out of the famous phrase is an extremely important qualifying contrast of Luther's. This is the contrast *totus—partim.* From one perspective Luther can say the Christian is at the same time *(simul)* wholly *(totus)* sinner and wholly just. From another perspective he can say the Christian is at the same time *(simul)* partly *(partim)* sinner and partly just. Only by *combining* the two perspectives do we arrive at the complete formulation of his teaching: the Christian is at the same time *(simul)* wholly and partly sinner and justified. Three senses of *simul.*

The first sense of *simul* concerns man in the spirit, in the conscience, in faith. How does he stand before God and before himself? What is the theological assessment of his relationship to God? We may call this perspective the issue of justification, but we should remember that the distinction of justification from sanctification, as important as it is, is still an abstraction.

When it is a matter of man's status before God, only the adverb *totus* applies. This is true simply because God's righteousness—his commands and his grace in Christ—is *absolute.* There just can be no possible qualitative or quantitative gradation in this regard. All works are equal. To have "almost" fulfilled the Law is identical to total failure, and it is only by God's imputation that our faith can be "perfect."[49] Only the righteousness of faith is appropriate here. The righteousness of the flesh, of works, of Law, is by its very nature concerned with qualitative and quantative distinctions. On the matter of justification, therefore, the introduction of the righteousness of the Law is a deadly mistake. The two righteousnesses are mutually exclusive. There is no middle ground. We are either righteous before God or we are damned. We are either free or enslaved. No qualifications. If we trust in our own works, our righteousness is a devilish righteousness. It is the tyrant Law, the idol we have made of ourselves.[50] This is why Luther never tires of insisting that the central issue posed to man by the Gospel is whether he will seek to be justified by Law, and be damned, *or* accept justification by faith, and be saved. One option excludes the other.[51]

Man is wholly a sinner in the eyes of the righteous God. Man must accept the judgment on himself unconditionally if his trust in the justification of the Law is to be rooted out. He must believe God. When the gift of faith is given to him, he is wholly justified. This is what Luther means by *totus iustus, totus peccator.* Already in the *Romans* commentary the teaching is clear. In his first attempt to understand Rom. 3:4, Luther tried to make man's confession the basis for the "justification of God's words." But once he was able to utilize the concept of *promise,* the works-righteousness latent in the earlier formulation vanished.[52] We do not and cannot ourselves acknowledge that we are sinners. It is only the man of faith who—against his experience—can confess that he is *totus peccator,* and so accept before himself, intrinsically, what he is before God.[53] *By faith alone we must believe we are sinners.* This faith is of course not our doing, but the act of God.[54] It is on this basis that God extrinsically declares the man of faith *totus iustus.*

With this formulation Luther can somewhat later in his commentary arrive at the full meaning of the first sense of *simul.* The saints are intrinsically always sinners, and therefore they are extrinsically always justified. To God the saints are at the same time righteous and unrighteous; they are knowingly righteous and knowingly unrighteous, sinners in fact but righteous in hope. Sin remains and simultaneously does not remain in Christians. And God takes the ungodly at the same time for unrighteous and righteous. He both does and does not take their sin away.[55]

Whichever way you put it, the relationship holds. The saints are wholly justified, yet they are wholly sinners. The ungodly are unrighteous; yet they are righteous. *Simul totus iustus et totus peccator.*

The second sense of *simul* usually emerges right in the context of Luther's discussion of justification. Christian man by faith recognizes he is wholly a sinner. God by imputation recognizes him as wholly justified. Yet man is still unrighteous; he still sins. As Luther will put it with a subtle shift of phrasing, the Christian "is a just man who at the same time sins."[56] He is no longer under the tyrant sin, but he sins nevertheless. Because he is still a man of flesh, the sins of the flesh are only in the process of being removed. They are there in fact, Luther says in the *Romans* commentary, and taken away in hope.[57] While fallen man is *incurvatus in se,* redeemed man is also *ingressus in Christum.* It is thus from the perspective of *sanctification* that Luther says the Christian is at once partly righteous, partly sinner, partly bound by Law (in his flesh), partly free of it (in his mind).[58] Because he is still in the flesh, the works of the just man are good, yes, but riddled with sin. It is precisely the wholly justified man who knows his works are partly corrupted by sin and so cannot and must not be brought before God in regard to justification. Empirical piety is always ambiguous. Only the spiritual man knows how to distinguish.[59] In fact the spiritual man instinctively keeps his works directed to their proper end: the world. His works flow from his faith freely and naturally. They are the incarnation of Christ in him. They demonstrate God's righteousness in the world and for the world.[60]

Everything just said about the *partim* quality of works is said only of the works of a man who is wholly justified. The continuing struggle against the sins in the flesh, and the continuing growth in works of love, is the process of sanctification which is a consequence of justification. The two perspectives must be cleanly distinguished, yet they are inseparably bound together. This is the third, summarizing sense of *simul.* Early in his career Luther expressed the togetherness by means of distinctions such as "intrinsic-extrinsic" and "interior-exterior." Soon enough, however, the language became more identifiably Luther's, God works not only *in verbo,* but also *in re.* Righteousness is twofold: the "alien" righteousness of Christ—the forgiveness of sins and free imputation of righteousness with which God covers the sinner because of the work of Christ, and the consequent growth of "proper" or active righteousness.[61] The latter includes the works of love to one's neighbor, and the discipline of the body which is the daily work of the indwelling Christ and the Holy Spirit. One can say, correspondingly, that justification is twofold: between man and God, and between man and man. *Coram deo* faith is the proper relation; *coram hominibus* works of love.[62] The Christian, Luther says, is always a sinner, always repentant. He is righteous and is being made righteous; partly sinner and partly righteous, i.e., he is nothing but repentant.[63] *Simul totus et partim iustus et peccator.*

Getting It Together

In this section I have only provided a sketch of Luther's understanding of justification and sanctification. These issues will occupy us in greater detail in Part Two. But notice that his teaching takes a form which is by now very familiar to us. There is the "either-or" side of the contrast: justification is either wholly by the righteousness of the Law and not of faith, or it is wholly by the righteousness of faith and not of Law. Then, granting that justification is by faith, it is now possible to speak of the process of sanctification in terms of the "both-and" side of the contrast. The Christian and only the Christian is partly righteous and partly sinner. The Christian alone is both under the Law and free of the Law.

The structure of Luther's teaching on this matter is exactly parallel to that concerning the relationship of Law and faith, of the commands and promises of God's Word, of flesh and spirit, of man *incurvatus* and man *ingressus*. And it is exactly parallel to the *coram mundo-coram deo* dialectic he established for theological discourse.

In Part One our task in general has been methodological in character. The major problem has been to develop a pattern of interpretation which on the one hand makes sense out of Luther, and on the other exposes the highly dynamic quality of his theology. Hopefully, of course, the interpretation is also expected to be faithful to its subject! The pattern which I have developed is the result of what amounts to a no-holds-barred wrestling match with Luther. He will thrash you to within an inch of your life, but if you can stay on your feet there are blessings to be had in the morning.

The dialectical pattern which has emerged I have baptized as the relationship "proximate-penultimate-ultimate." Or in more reasonable language, the relationship "fallen man-redeemed man-Word of God." Of the first element in that relationship, only a univocal reality obtains. Man is fallen, or flesh, or Law, or sinner. Because the Word of God has entered that fallenness, however, another reality emerges. And concerning this reality the language is bivocal: Christian man is sinner and saved, flesh and spirit, faith and Law. Now these dialectical forms are contrasts. They admit both disjunctive and conjunctive senses, depending on Luther's perspective. Thus the following set of propositions, which sum up our results so far, are only apparently paradoxical. In each case the first member reflects a *disjunctive* sense. It is based on the relation "fallen man-man of faith," and expresses the mutually exclusive ways they relate to the Word of God. The second member of the proposition reflects the *conjunctive* sense. It is based on the relation "man of faith-Word of God," and expresses the double relationship in which the man of faith stands to the world, the recognition of which double relationship becomes possible and necessary only when man has given himself over wholly to the divine judgment.

From Essay I:

1. The theological eye sees God, man, and the world *coram deo* and not *coram mundo.* Since it is only from this perspective that both God and the world can be seen as they really are, the theological eye *therefore* sees God, man, and the world both *coram deo* and *coram mundo.*

From Essay II:

2. The Christian is not trapped, *incurvatus in se,* but is rather free, *ingressus in Christum;* the Christian *therefore* perceives himself as he really is, as both *incurvatus* and *ingressus,* both bound and free.

3. The Spirit of God has conquered the flesh of man, and the Christian thus lives in the Spirit and not in the flesh; the Christian *therefore* is perceived as he really is, as both in the flesh and in the Spirit, both carnal and spiritual.

From Essay III:

4. The Christian responds to the Word of God not in the way of Law, but rather in the way of faith; *therefore* the Christian knows that his response is always both in terms of Law and in terms of faith.

5. The Gospel has overcome and broken the power of the Law, and the man of faith is thus no longer under Law but under Gospel; *therefore* the man of faith sees God's Word meeting him as it really is, as both Law and Gospel.

6. Before God the Christian is wholly just and wholly sinner, by his faith alone and not by his works; *therefore* the life of the Christian before God is composed both of faith and of works, and he is partly righteous and partly sinner.

PART TWO

God's Futurity

The general theme of the preceding essays was the disjunctive side of the divine—human relationship, and the discussion was essentially methodological: *how* God and man are known. In this part the perspective is shifted to the conjunctive side of the relationship, and the discussion is basically epistemological: *where* or on what grounds the knowledge of God and man is certified. There are both extrinsic, formal, and intrinsic, material grounds. The former are discussed in the first essay, *"Promissio et Fides."* Herein I continue the analysis of faith begun in the preceding essay, with what will be a growing emphasis on Luther's portrayal of Christian becoming. The second essay, *Initium Creaturae Novae,* examines the intrinsic grounds for the knowledge of God and man. In this essay I continue the emphasis on the process of faith becoming, and develop a more dynamic interpretation of the anthropology introduced in essay two.

The two essays thus comprehend what I am suggesting by "God's futurity"—which is of course also man's futurity. God's self-disclosure, His promise, is the lure creating faith and directing it toward its future. And God's activity within faith, His re-creation of man, provides the motion toward and the firstfruits of that future.

Essay IV: *Promissio et Fides*

Almost Virgin Land

In the preceding essay I developed the thesis that it is only the Christian who is capable of seeing himself both in terms of Law and in terms of faith. This self-understanding is not available to natural man, according to Luther. He cannot assemble it from his sense experience and cannot certify it by demonstrating the adequacy and fidelity of his reason. Yet one aspect of that self-understanding—man as *lex*—does have to do with a human reality. It is true that God's Word reveals Law, but that which is revealed is not, so to speak, "of God," but is in a radical sense "of man." Law and works are man's reality, not God's. If God's Word is required, according to Luther, for man to know himself animated by Law and occupied by works, it is not because Law and works are alien to him, but because sin has so massively vitiated his self-knowledge. It remains true of man, whether he knows it or not, that Law and works are *his.*

Because of this fact, my construction of Luther's theological anthropology in terms of Law and faith might lead to a misunderstanding. If Law and faith are descriptions of Christian life, and if Law belongs to man, would not faith also belong to man? To continue the parallel, should we not say that faith was always theoretically within human capacity, and that the revelation of Christ and His work in the Scriptures was a revelation to man of that highest ideal of which he was capable, but from which he had been blocked because of sin? Much "evangelical" theology has been done along these lines. Yet one can scarcely imagine a viewpoint more alien to Luther.

As we enter Part Two of this study, our first major task is to explicate one of Luther's more profound convictions: that faith and the Christian life of love are in the most radically conceivable sense *gifts.* They are in no sense man's possession, actually or potentially. They are gifts of God, of Christ, unmerited, unprepared for, unpossessed, and unavailable as evidence of human righteousness before God. Heb. 11:1, "Now faith is the substance of things hoped for, the evidence of things not seen," can hardly be overestimated with

83

regard to Luther's understanding of the source of Christian self-under-standing. The Christian almost literally receives himself from God, according to Luther. The epistemological grounds for faith and the Christian life of love lie wholly outside human capacity and experience. This thesis must now be emphasized, and emphasized without qualifi-cation, if we are to understand Luther at all. Otherwise we will end up with the situation I alluded to in the introduction to the preceding essay: we shall have turned faith into a work.

This emphasis, however, does not at all mean we have to introduce new materials to supplement or counterbalance the results of the study to this point. In the preceding essay we worked with basically four interrelated elements: God's revelation of demands and promises, and man's response of Law and faith. "Demand" and "Law" were the major foci of attention there. In this essay, "promise" and "faith" provide the guiding interest. In the first section I shall attempt to sketch Luther's developing understanding of revelation as promise, especially as it affects his understanding of faith. In the second section I shall concentrate on faith as a gift of God, faith as "hanging upon" the promissory Word from the outside. In the third section I shall combine these themes to produce a sketch of Luther's understanding of the Christian as *viator*, "wayfarer," as one who lives out of his future, his becoming a response of hope to the promises of God.

It is a truism regretted by many and welcomed by some that the history of scholarship, even the best and most impartial scholarship, reflects the changing sensitivities and interests of the scholar at least as much as it reflects the accumulation of so-called assured results of scientific research. In the field of historical theology it seems that Luther more than any other figure provides occasion for the best demonstration of the sociology of knowledge.

The subject of this essay is one such evidence. One looks almost in vain among the older works on Luther for even a cursory reference to the meaning and function of promise in Luther's theology. It comes up as an incidental element in presentations of Luther's exegesis of the Old Testament, and as an identifying feature of a passing phase of his approach to the sacraments, and that is all. But whether because of recent discussions of "futuristic" or otherwise eschatological theol-ogy, or because of continued interest in the young Luther, there has emerged within the past decade a growing hunch that the concept of *promissio* is among the most systematically important and fruitful of Luther's discoveries. Maybe it's just our out-of-joint times. In any case there is now a small but serious research afoot on the subject.[1] In recent works *promissio* has surfaced as the guiding approach to Luther's first exposition of the Psalms.[2] But while it has become evident that the concept of promise grows in importance and application throughout the course of Luther's theological development, there are only the merest beginnings of detailed study of the concept outside the *Dictata*.[3] A general overview of the issue is therefore necessary, though unsatisfying. In any case it is the most I can do in this essay.

<h1 style="text-align:center">1</h1>

The Once and Future Christ

During the late summer of 1515 Luther was finishing his *Dictata* on the Psalter and beginning work on the *Romans* lectures. Toward the end of his work on the Psalms Luther became increasingly aware of the value of "promise" for his exegesis. Ps. 118 (119) was a particular stimulus since the word *eloquium,* which he held to be equivalent to *promissio,* appeared so frequently.[4] The same psalm was also very influential in consolidating a profound shift in Luther's theological anthropology. For in the course of these lectures Luther developed a rather astonishing theological definition of *substantia* as "that upon which one stakes his life." And for the Christian, his *substantia* is faith, the faith and hope which hang from the promise of God and not from anything man can call his own.[5]

The lessons he learned from the psalter on the importance of the equation of *eloquium* and *promissio,* and the appropriateness of faith in the promise as the *substantia* of Christian life, served Luther well in his *Romans* lectures. All but a few references to promise come in the first four chapters, completed in the late fall of 1515. Thus it is during the summer and fall of that year when Luther was most preoccupied with *promissio* and the rather massive consequences it entailed for his theology.

As Luther begins his *scholia* to the first chapter of Romans, we notice traces of his work in the *Dictata* on the kinds of promise and the extraneousness of our righteousness.[6] There is no further mention of promise until the third chapter. At the beginning of this chapter vs. 2 and 3 give Luther the occasion to use the connection of *eloquium* and *promissio* to argue that God has bound Himself to His promises and that faith is the fulfillment of the promise.[7] But Paul's quotation of Ps. 51:4, "that you might be justified in your words," presents Luther with grave difficulties.[8] His first solution to the issue of how God is justified is that God's righteoueness is set off by our confession of sin. No mention of promise. But at 3:7 Luther abandons this approach to the question and starts all over with a summary. All of a sudden he recalls 3:2 and the equation of *eloquium* and *promissio* (LCC 15, 74). And now his second solution is easier. For by utilizing the concept of promise, Luther is able to conclude that God is justified in His words *[sermonibus!]* when we believe the Gospel about the fulfillment of God's promises. The "tropological" sense is that sin can be said to enhance the truth of God

> . . . by its being what it is, i.e., the trust by which we believe God that we are sinful, though we ourselves do not think or imagine that we are—this very faith establishes us as sinners and gives God the glory (LCC 15, 78).

A breakthrough has been remembered! And now the text up to 3:12 is peppered with corollaries abounding with ideas on the nonevidential character of faith, the intrinsic connection between faith and the promise, our alien righteousness, and the Christian faith which lives out of its future, constantly seeking itself in hope.

The fruits of this development reappear in the comment on 4:7, where Luther utilizes "hope" to arrive at a formulation of the *simul* character of the Christian's experience of himself, which Luther sums up in the couplet *peccatores in re, iusti autem in spe* (LCC 15, 125). In the corollary *promissio* breaks through again to explicate the relationship wherein the sinful Christian is nevertheless justified by living out of his faith and hope in the promising Word (LCC 15, 127 f.). As the text continues and Paul calls Luther's attention to other matters, *promissio* does not appear in the *scholia.* But the glosses to 4:13-21 continue the development, Luther noting the mutual dependence of promise and faith, the opposition of promise and Law, the nonevidential character of faith, and its substance in the promise.

In his commentary on Rom. 8:19 Luther picks up the matter of the "essence" of created being, saying that this is what Paul is speaking of in "a new and strange" theological way by speaking of the *expectation* of the creature.[9] The understanding of creation in terms of its future rather than its present substance is a generalization from what Luther concluded about faith's "substance" in the *Dictata.* In the somewhat disappointing 1519 lectures on *Galatians* this line of development is again mentioned. Luther, following Melanchthon's expert opinion, interprets "hypostasis" or "substance" as "existence" or "self-subsisting essence." But he says it can also mean on the one hand a promise, agreement or expectation, a faith directed to God and believing His promises. On the other hand it can mean truthfulness, faithfulness, honesty, a faith directed to man, in which we keep our promises.[10]

The remainder of the *Galatians* commentary is almost barren of reference to promise, except for a few occasions in chapter three.

If we are somewhat diasppointed at the lack of development of

86

the "faith-hope-promise-substance" complex in the 1519 *Galatians* commentary, we are amply compensated by Luther's second attempt on the Psalms, his *Operationes in Psalmos* of the same period. This work buries us deeply within the *abscondito sub contrario* patterns so characteristic of Luther's "theology of the cross."

At Ps. 5:11 Luther explodes into an intense 20-page excursus on "hope" which culminates with the statement, *"CRUX sola est nostra theologia"* (W 5, 176.32 f.).[11] In this excursus Luther renews what he had done before and begins to develop applications of the promise-faith-hope complex which he will emphasize very strongly during the next decade. He begins with a homily on the idea that grief and joy, despair and hope, arise not from things but from the "affects" or estimation which the human heart places on things. The Christian passes through all these things, whether good or evil, and locates his hope in God alone.

But then at 162.21 Luther begins a more technical theological approach to the question of the meaning of hope. Hope is a theological virtue only if its sole object is God. And now all of a sudden *promissio* emerges. For God, at least in the eyes of hope, is *defined* as "our good *[bonitas]* and the mercy promised to us" (162.23 f.). And it is only in the Word of God that hope finds the invisible, insensible, incomprehensible promise (163.5-7).

Luther then goes on to develop a lengthy argument against the scholastic view that works or merits are a source of hope, and he insists on the reverse: works arise from hope. The relation of works and faith-hope introduced here will occupy Luther's pen in greater detail in his 1520 *Treatise on Good Works*. A second theme emerges at 172.1: the matter of divine predestination and the doubts it raises against hope. The interesting thing here is that Luther does not make any theological advance, but resorts to a homiletic exhortation to the effect that doubts come from the devil and can lead us to tempt God or to wish to know all things. When in his 1525 *De servo arbitrio* Luther again turns to the question of predestination, election, and necessity, he uses the concept of *promissio*—as he does not here—to explicate the issues.

Luther concludes his excursus with a beautiful summary.

> We must note two things in regard to hope: our merits and the divine promise. Set hope between these two, in order to see that hope depends upon promise and merits come from hope; that while merits are a work of hope, hope is a work of the Word or promise. . . . For God's mercy and His truth, the one graciously promising and the other fulfilling the promise, are the causes of hope. . . . So God, the gracious promising One, or the Word of promise

itself, is the one and only object of faith and hope. . . . For upon this rock of the promise and infallible Word is built the Church of Christ. . . . For in this life we do not grasp righteousness but stretch out toward it, always seeking, always begging to be justified, for sins to be remitted, for the will of our Father in heaven to be done, for His name to be hallowed. And yet it is in just this situation that God reputes us just.[12]

In 1520 Luther was most concerned to establish what he considered the proper relationship between faith, hope, and promise on the one hand, and works on the other. Right from the beginning of his *Treatise on Good Works,* for example, he picks up the theme of the relation of works to faith, "faith" in this context used almost interchangeably with "hope" and "trust." Luther's central argument is that all the commandments are contained in the First Commandment, and that the true and proper "work" fulfilling this commandment is the basic faith, trust, and confidence of the heart in the Word of God. Especially when experience seems to militate against such faith.[13]

In Luther's eyes the most vicious misunderstanding of the relation of faith and works concerns the sacraments. When he turns to this matter in *The Babylonian Captivity of the Church* of 1520, the concept of promise latent in his treatise on works explodes into the text. Luther's task is to attack the notion of the Mass as a work and as a sacrifice.[14] Beginning with the equation of "testament" and "promise," Luther concludes that the only proper access to the Mass (=promise) is faith alone. The substance of the Mass is Christ's Word of promise. The "Babylonian Captivity" in this respect is that no one is permitted to hear the comforting words of promise.

And now Luther generalizes his argument.

For God does not deal, nor has He ever dealt, with man otherwise than through a Word of promise, as I have said. We cannot in turn deal with God otherwise than through faith in the Word of His promise (W 6, 516.30 ff.).

Promise and faith necessarily go together, Luther continues. Since the Mass is a promise, two things follow. First, since a promise demands a personal faith, there can be no Masses for others, especially for the dead. Second, the Mass is a promise made by God. And this is diametrically opposed to the notion that the Mass is a sacrifice made by man.

Many of these arguments again come into play as Luther turns to the Sacrament of Baptism.[15] As with the Lord's Supper, so with Baptism: the chief thing is the Word of promise. In this context Luther's major emphasis is on the certainty of forgiveness of sins that the Christian enjoys when he believes that God is faithful to His promise in the Sacrament. The power of the Sacrament cannot rest in the sign, but rests in the promise. And its efficacy is not broken by human sin, since the Sacrament rests on God's promise and not on man's works. The Sacrament is in fact a sign of the whole Christian life: a life in which the Christian, again and again in his sin and out of his faith, returns to the comforting, nourishing, and guiding promise of God.

In the excursus on hope in the *Operationes* Luther raised the problem of God's predestination and its seemingly vitiating effects on Christian hope. But he did not have recourse to the concept of promise in order to deal with it. In *The Babylonian Captivity* he took occasion on the issue of Baptism to develop the notion that the confidence and certainty of Christian faith rests on the faithfulness of God to His Word of promise. It is in the 1525 work *De servo arbitrio* that the problem and the solution come together.

The new application of *promissio* occurs in connection with what to most scholars has been a problematic theme of *De servo arbitrio:* Luther's so-called "necessitarian" argument. In spite of what his latter-day students say, Luther was convinced that divine foreknowledge and the necessity of events are assertions which the Christian must make. They are moreover pious assertions, for without them the certainty of the conscience vanishes.[16]

When Luther first states his thesis, the concept of promise is not employed. He argues from God's side, as it were. The necessity of events follows from the immutability of God's will and foreknowledge. And God's will and knowledge are immutable because his nature is unchanging.[17] But very soon Luther radically shifts his approach, developing a more evangelical-sounding argument in terms of promise.

> For if you doubt or disdain to know that God foreknows all things, not contingently, but necessarily and immutably, how can you believe his promises and place a sure trust and reliance on them? For when he promises anything, you ought to be certain that he knows and is able and willing to perform what he promises; otherwise you will regard him as neither truthful nor faithful . . . But how will you be certain and sure unless you know that he knows and wills and will do what he promises, certainly, infallibly, immutably, and necessarily? . . . For this is the one supreme consolation of Christians in all adversities, to know that God does not lie, but does all things immutably.[18]

This is the basic theological argument throughout the text. The celebrated instance of Pharoah's "hardening" is highly revealing in this regard. Luther, playing the "fool Reason," first offers an explanation composed of the idea of God's omnipotence remorselessly working through evil instruments.[19] He soon leaves off this exercise, however, and has recourse to the idea of promise. The divine action in Pharoah is meant to show the trustworthiness of God's Word of promise and to bolster the confidence of faith.[20] But then he goes on to *reverse* the argument. Since the Giver of the promise cannot lie, Pharoah was hardened necessarily.[21] And then Luther reverses the argument again![22]

Toward the end of the treatise Luther gives his own personal testimony to this approach. If it comes right down to it, Luther does not want his salvation to rest on the vagaries of his own choice. He feels better knowing that his assurance rests instead on the steadfast promises of God.[23]

It seems then that "the necessity of all things" and "God's faithfulness to His promises" are two related languages or perspectives. Luther's normal course is to argue that, assuming God's foreknowledge, the necessity of events is the *condition for* the confidence of faith in God's fidelity to His Word of promise. Occasionally he can argue the other way: assuming God's foreknowledge, the necessity of events *follows from* the truthfulness of the God of promise. In either case, God's eternal decisions, far from undercutting faith and hope, are in fact the grounds for the surety of the Christian conscience, faith, and hope.

Luther's 1535 *Commentary on Galatians* more than makes good the almost total lack of the use of *promissio* we saw in the 1519 commentary. The sheer volume of references to promise in the later work makes one despair of adequately summarizing it in a few paragraphs. While every aspect and association of promise we have noted so far appears in the text, it is Luther's commentary on Gal. 3:7,10,12,17, and 23 that exhibits his most intense concentration on the subject. A main theme connecting these passages is stated at 3:7: since all the past promises were contained in the promise of the Christ to come, the faith of the patriarchs is the same as our faith. Faith is not temporally determined, therefore. It is out of time.[24]

The close parallel of our faith with the faith of the patriarchs, a hermeneutical theme discovered in the first lectures on the Psalms, occupies Luther's pen again at Gal. 3:10.[25] Paul's citation of Deut. 27:26 gives Luther occasion to treat the issue of Law and works in regard to justification. Unless one looks at the promises made to Abraham, it is impossible to understand what it means to "do the Law." In fact the only way either Abraham or we can be said to do the Law is precisely by faith in the promise or Gospel. Faith in the promise is thus the condition for doing the Law—nay, it is the fulfillment of the Law itself.

At 3:12 Luther begins to concentrate on a more systematic exposition of the relationships among Law, works, faith, and promise, again in the context of the issue of justification.[26] The Law and the promise are radically distinct. Hence works and faith are radically distinct. The Law and works concern man's doing and giving to God. But faith rests wholly and solely on God's promise, and thus consists only in receiving from God. Correspondingly the righteousness of the Law is "do this:" that of the Gospel is "accept this."

At 3:17 Luther continues the more systematic presentation of Law, works, faith, and promise, but moves to a more existential concentration on Law and promise as defining the Christian "time"[27] Luther begins by recasting a theme from *De servo arbitrio*. The promise must be seen to come before the Law, and, concerning justification, to abolish the Law. Otherwise we make God a liar and his promises useless, invalid. It is faith in the promise which destroys the Law in the sense that the Law is no longer able to induce despair and fear into the life of faith.

The Law and the promise are radically separated in time and locus, attitude or function, Luther continues, even though they are extremely close together, joined in the one man. The Law belongs in the flesh, the promise in the conscience—a difficult distinction, Luther concedes, but one which the Christian must make not only in his thinking but more importantly in his life.

Luther's commentary on 3:23 brings the discussion of promise to completion, and in a sense returns us to the theme in the *Dictata* from which we began.[28] The Law is surrounded fore and aft by the promise. It is only by clinging to the prior Word of promise that Abraham, and we, grasp the theological use of the Law. And this use leads us to the fulfillment of the promise in Christ. Our faith is the same as Abraham's, and not simply because we await the second coming of Christ as Abraham awaited the first. Existentially the Christian life is continually a process of living through the Law to the fulfillment of the promise. The Christian life, personally and spiritually, is made up of two "times" in constant alternation: the time of Law and the time of grace. The time of Law is when the Law functions to pound and discipline the flesh, to convict of sin. The time of grace is when the heart is encouraged again by the promise of God's mercy.

Therefore the Christian is divided this way into two times. To the extent he is flesh, he is under the Law; to the extent that he is spirit, he is under the Gospel. . . . The time of Law is not forever;

but it has an end, which is Christ. But the time of grace is forever; for Christ, having died once for all, will never die again. . . . He is eternal; therefore the time of grace is eternal also (26, 342).

The Christian life of faith is the personal, spiritual embodiment of the relation between Law and promise manifest in history. Like Abraham, we experience the Law only in the context of God's promise of salvation in Christ. Like Abraham, we appropriate the Law and valuate it only in terms of God's fulfillment of His promise in Christ. We live in two times. A time of Law, a time which has duration, extention, a locus in experience: the flesh. But this time is finite. Its temporal and existential limit is the time of grace, of Christ, of the promise. And this time is "eternal time." It is no time at all, in the sense that there is no duration, no extension, no locus in experience. It is a time of the spirit, of faith, and the conscience.

2

"No Ground Beneath Our Feet" - "The Concrete Place"

The Christian, Luther said, knows he is a sinner in fact and justified in hope. In order to explicate his understanding of Christian life as a life lived in God's promises, Luther utilized both temporal and spatial metaphors. The two sets of metaphors naturally flow into each other. In the preceding quotation from the *Galatians* commentary, the "times" easily translate into "spaces." The time of the Law is the *extent* of the flesh, and it is finite; the time of the Gospel is a time of the spirit, and it has no space. This time is not said to be infinite but rather eternal. Sinfulness *in re* is always here and now, justification *in spe* always there and then. In the first section we concentrated on Luther's temporal metaphors. His spatial metaphors about Christian self-understanding must now occupy us. They are simply impossible to avoid in any case. The question "Who am I?" immediately becomes "Where am I," or better, "Whence do I receive myself?" God's first word to Adam, recently fallen into an identity crisis, was "Where are you?" (Gen. 3:9).

Language is never neutral, especially the language out of which theology is done. Luther was well aware of the profoundly different approach to theological interpretation that resulted when one began out of the Hebrew rather than the Latin Bible.[29] As the studies of Schwarz and Ozment have shown, Luther made an immensely consequential interpretive decision regarding the meaning of *"substantia"* in the course of his first work on the Psalter.[30] Unlike the philosophers who refer "substance" to the "quiddity" or "essential whatness" of a thing, Luther insists that in the context of Hebraic understanding, *"substantia"* can only be a metaphor. In line with Heb. 10:34 and 11:1, "substance" refers to that on which a man stakes his being. It is the place he makes his stand, the ground of his being. Hence "substance" refers to a qualification of one's existence, the system of values and purposes from which a man takes his identity and his reason for being. "Substance" is a man's locus; it is "where he is at," his *Dasein*. Said God to Adam, "Where are you?"

Exhibiting the same interpretive pattern we have seen in preceding essays, Luther on the one hand sets out the "places" of Christian man and fallen man as mutually exclusive, and on the other hand insists that the Christian alone stands in both places at once. The one place has a duration and extension defined by Law, the flesh, and works, and it is filled with things (. . . *in re*). This place is wholly defined by the ego which is its center, Luther asserts at the start of his commentary on Rom. 8:7-20.[31] The "prudence of the flesh" makes the self the center of the universe of value, and the range of the idolatry of the self is limitless. The objects which compose and define its place, the "goods" to be sought for and disposed of by the god-self, include not merely external goods but also "affectional grace" and "God himself insofar as he is known in his divine attributes" (LCC 15, 225). All of these things are of course good gifts of God. But fallen man twists them so as to define his own place. He puts them in the place of the true God, in that he does not refer them to God (LCC 15, 226). In the place of the true God stands the false god, the idol Self. And all these temporal goods, i.e., everything outside God comprehensible to the senses or the mind, are threatened by death, sin, and the last judgment. Death is the annihilation of the ego's substance. The prudence of the flesh dies, and its place knows it no more.

There is another place, however, for the Christian. It has not duration or extension. It is formed by the Gospel, the spirit, faith, and is filled with hope (. . . *in spe*). This place is wholly defined by God. The "prudence of the spirit" seeks only the common good and common life. Its universe of value centers in the divine valuation, and it has its goods only as they are related to God. The Christian substance is located wholly outside everything available to the senses or mind. In fact the Christian place is an antithesis to everything here and now, the *visibilia*. The Christian substance is outside, in God; it is not only *in re,* but also *in spe*. And it is not founded on the works of the Law, but hangs from faith in the promise. Death is not the threat of annihilation, but a means for securing the Christian place (LCC 15, 228 f.).

93

Having one's substance in God's futurity is not, moreover, only characteristic of Christian man. As Luther reaches Rom. 8:19, his argument culminates in the view that the whole creation is properly defined in this way. He lashes out against virtually the entire philosophical tradition.

> For the philosophers are so deeply engaged in studying the present state of things that they explore only what and of what kind they are, but the apostle turns our attention away from the consideration of things as they are now, and from what they are as to essence and accidents, and directs us to regard them in terms of what they will be. He does not speak of the "essence" of the creature . . . but, using a new and strange theological word, he speaks of "the expectation of the creature.". . . [H]e no longer directs his inquiry toward the creature as such but to what it waits for. But alas, how deeply and painfully we are caught up in categories and quiddities . . . .
>
> So then, you will be the best philosophers and the best explorers of nature if you learn from the apostle to consider the whole creature as it waits, groans, and travails in pain . . . . [T]he fools of philosophers look at God's creature: it is constantly being prepared for the glory that is to come, but they see only what it is in itself and how it is equipped but have no thought whatsoever for the end for which it was created.[32]

Like the rest of creation, Christian man finds his substance only in God. He is restless till he rests in God. The faith which is the substance of Christian man, that from which he receives his identity, can in no way originate either in sense experience or in thought.

By the early 1520s Luther had begun to move away from the language of "hiddenness" and what we could call the "epistemology of the vacuum" developed in the German mystical tradition. But however much the presence of Christ to the Christian, the "for us" and "in us" character of justification, and the clear and objective nature of God's Word might be emphasized, the wholly extrinsic source of Christian self-understanding is a conviction that never weakens. In fact it was just at the time when the hiddenness of faith—the theology of the cross—most occupied Luther's thinking that he began to develop a formulation which he apparently felt both insured epistemological confidence and protected the extrinsic character of theological knowledge. Christian faith, Luther began to emphasize in the *Hebrews* commentary, hangs from the Word and arises *ex auditu*.[33] It seems to me that by speaking of the relation between faith and the Word as one of "hearing," Luther among other things is trying to protect against the notion that faith is something "at hand" or essentially rooted in human experience. The very idea that justification takes place *ex auditu fidei* is foreign to human experience, to the senses, to the flesh. And if in opposition to all he knows or can experience the Christian believes the preached Word, his acceptance itself is not his own act, but is the accomplishment of the Spirit.

Luther's theology is certain (he himself says!) because its substance or ground is the divine Word of promise and not human experience. Usually that experience is in fact opposite to what Christian faith and hope, depending on the Word of promise, takes for certain. Faith, which rests on that which has no palpable grounds, is therefore the most difficult thing imaginable. It is

> . . . torn away and removed from all those things which can be experienced inwardly by the spirit or outwardly by the body and is founded on those things which can be known neither inwardly nor outwardly. Faith is founded on the most high God, the invisible, the incomprehensible.[34]

Now why is faith always faith in things unseen, besides the fact that Heb. 11:1 says so? At one point in *De servo arbitrio* Luther answers the question this way:

> Hence in order that there may be room *[locus]* for faith, it is necessary that everything which is believed should be hidden.

And just following his continuation of how God works under contrary appearances, Luther resumes:

> As it is, since that cannot be comprehended, there is room for the exercise of faith when such things are preached and published . . . .[35]

There must be "room" for faith to "exercise" or extend itself. It would be easy to misinterpret such passages to mean that faith can exist only to the extent that things are *unknown*. But according to Luther faith is not merely another aspect or quality of man, along with knowledge, for example. It is rather the Christian's whole life of absolute trust in the Word of promise. The contrast Luther is expressing is not one between faith and knowledge, but rather between the visible and the hidden Word. Correspondingly the contrast does not concern elements of man's psycho-spiritual constitution, but refers as we shall see to the temporal and historical relationship of God's revelation and man's response.

Although Luther fills his text with assertions or examples of such themes as the hiddenness of faith's object, he rarely attempts a more detailed explanation of his meaning in a different set of metaphors.

But there are at least two such attempts in this case, one in the *Romans* commentary and one in *Galatians*. The language and emphases are different but complementary.

Luther finds occasion to indicate the purpose and function of the hiddenness of the Word in his exegesis of Rom. 9:28, "For the Lord shall consummate His Word and cut it short in righteousness."[36] What do "consummate" and "cut short" mean? Luther, at this point in his career still handy with the Augustinian tradition, begins by construing "consummate" in terms of the polarization "letter-spirit." The Word of righteousness

> . . . must be contracted and shortened so that it can in no wise be extended to the flesh and its wisdom and righteousness, and neither comprehends it nor is comprehended by it (LCC 15, 278).

To explain his meaning, Luther goes on to argue that God's past revelation in signs (in the letter) was, so to speak, extended. It was incomplete, imperfect, and therefore easily intelligible, since it concerned sensible things. The Word of the Spirit, however, the hidden Word of faith, is perfect, nonextensive, and is therefore completely cut off from sensible experience. Luther does not wish to deny sensible experience or the human goods which are the object of that experience. His focus, as usual, is the relation man establishes to these goods. For he goes on to say that it is not the reality manifested by the (extended) Word, but the Word itself, which is cut short. The reason why the "prolonged and extended" Word has to be "shortened" is that it "caused the Spirit to be more and more removed and separated from [man's] goods or from [his] understanding of his goods" (LCC 15, 279). The extended Word tempted man to split up his self-understanding. He wished to have his worldly goods only "according to the flesh," not the spirit. As we have already seen, faith and the spirit concern not a part of man, but the whole man. It is to destroy the false application of the distinction of flesh and spirit that the Word is "cut off." Only the consummated Word gives room for the whole man, including his flesh and his goods, to be affected by the Word (LCC 15, 279).[37]

By moving into a "tropological" application in the corollary, Luther is able to conclude that it is *faith* which is the abridgment of salvation. For the abridged Word is nothing else but faith. Faith is *life* (!), Luther says, and it is the living, abridged Word (LCC 15, 281). And this faith which is the life of the Christian is "cut off" from the present, "consummated" only in its future, since, according to Heb. 11:1, it is the substance of things hoped for (LCC 15, 281).

We have before us an apparently curious situation. As strongly as Luther might emphasize the intimacy of Christ's relationship to Christian *existence* ("faith is life"), he denies the possible inference that the revelation of Christ is in any way present-at-hand for Christian *experience*. Faith, although the existential form of Christian living, has its foundation not in past or present experience available to the senses, but only in the past and future divine Word of promise available only to the ear of faith. Faith is a movement of absolute trust in God's promise. For faith to become, there needs to be "free space" in an epistemological sense. If Christ, the Word and work of God, were simply available for human sensate experience, there would be no room for faith. Sense knowledge would flood our epistemological ground. Faith could only preserve its character as faith in things unseen if it restricted itself to those "objects" which had not—yet—fallen under sense knowledge. In this way faith would get shunted off into a realm of ever-diminishing boundaries. Human knowledge would then pose a threat, and would for its part consider itself autonomous and independent of faith's concerns. The result, according to Luther, is that a false distinction between flesh and spirit is created, or at least reinforced, a distinction based on content rather than on use. And such an anthropology flatly contradicts Luther's conviction that, in regard to the knowledge of God, the whole man is either flesh or spirit, depending on his attitude, and that God's Word to faith is a Word to the whole man, body and soul.

To put it as simply as possible: were God's revelation in Christ "extensive"—recall that Luther characterized the Law this way—it would be *data* just like everything else is data. Knowledge acquired from sense experience would be in direct competition with the revelation received by faith. If in order to avoid the contradictions that are bound to occur you divide the regions of applicability, you fall into the false distinction of a "spiritual realm" and a "carnal realm" essentially unrelated to each other. If, as Luther would insist is in fact the case, you hold that God's Word concerns the whole of human existence, then you are faced with the task of squaring the two "truths" by means of increasingly fine distinctions and casuistic applications. Which would mean, according to Luther, that God's Word would once again be turned into Law, and faith into works.

All these dead ends are avoided, however, if we hold to the proper understanding of faith. Faith is not primarily a content, and has no experienced ground in present fact. It is a mode of life and the form of Christian existence, the life of absolute trust in God's past and future Word, and based on things unseen.

Luther confirms and supplements this interpretation in his exegetical work of the early 1530s. At 3:10 in the *Galatians* commentary, for example, a new set of spatial images appears, again in connection with the concept of *promissio.* Luther is discussing the meaning of faith and works relative to "doing the Law." He says that faith can be considered apart from works. This is an "abstract or absolute" faith. Or it can be considered with works, as a "concrete, composite, or incarnate" faith. And it is only to the latter "incarnate" faith that merits are promised.[38] What Luther is talking about by a concrete, incarnate faith is Christian works of love. At 5:14 he speaks of a "completely bare, meager, and mathematical love, which does not become incarnate, so to speak, and does not go to work."[39]

Christian love is Christian works of love. And therefore it falls under the rubric of Law. This means that love, unlike the righteousness of faith, is "extensive" in character, hence always imperfect. In an exposition of Ps. 45 written in 1532, Luther devotes a long passage to the difference of faith and Christ's kingdom from the Law and works.[40] The Law and morals are an endless casuistic study, he says, because its object is extensive. That is, the Law aims at a "physical and divisible point" which cannot be reduced to a "mathematical and invisible" point. And thus lawyers do satisfactory work if they are able to get within the "circumference," even though they do not touch the "mathematical" or "invisible" center. The righteousness of Christ, on the other hand, is pure, absolute, and mathematical.[41]

We thus have before us two complementary attempts to express the nonextensive character of the object of faith. It can be called an "abbreviated," "consummated," or "abridged" Word in 1515, a "mathematical" or "indivisible" point in the early 1530s. Faith is accordingly "abstract" or "absolute" as contrasted with love, which must be "incarnate." And yet it is only with the *incarnation* of Christ that the Word becomes contracted or abbreviated, becomes an indivisible point for faith. And thus there seems to be something like a sequence of extension, nonextension, and extension. Before the birth of Christ and so long as men hear God's revelation only as Law, the Word is imperfect, extensive, and available as a sense datum to be *misinterpreted* by human experience. With the incarnation, the Word become flesh is perfect, nonextensive, and available only to the hearing of faith. The Word became flesh, that the flesh might become Word. Thus when faith expresses itself in works of love, it again becomes "composite," "extended" or "incarnated," and of course imperfect. We are thus confronted with the idea that God's revelation is first extensive and then nonextensive (from Law- or sign-word to incarnation), and the human response is nonextensive and then extensive (from faith to works of love).

Luther's language—and obviously my attempt to come to terms with it—is somewhat foggy. It will not for an instant stand up to an analysis which looks for a precise system of meanings for the terms employed. But what Luther is trying to get across, it seems to me, is a sense of the Christian existence as a living toward and from faith. The Christian receives his identity, the form of his life and its justification, not from anything actually or potentially within his grasp, but from the "outside." The faith which is his life comes to him from an extrinsic ground which is never available for his disposal. This ground is the promising Word of God. The Christian lives *toward* that promissory Word. His confidence and his hope rest on the absolute faith that God will daily accomplish His promise in Christ in the Christian life of love, just as He accomplished His past promises in Christ on the cross once and for all time. On the basis of these promises the Christian tries to realize or incarnate his received existence in works of love. Works are the living *from* faith. And these works, extended as they are in the flesh, are always liable to judgment, even by man. They are available to human sense. They are imperfect.

The Christian lives in the penultimate, in a double-natured reality. *Coram deo*, in faith and the spirit, his justification is complete, absolute, perfect. *Coram deo et hominibus*, in love, in the whole man, flesh and spirit, however, he knows his sanctification is incomplete, relative, imperfect. The phrases of Bonhoeffer which I used to title this section thus express the dialectical geography of the Christian's identity. His "substance" cannot rest with himself. There is no ground beneath his feet. His justification rests in the promises of God, and he is thus free to respond as a whole man with works of love in the world. Works whose criteria are wholly determined by the need; in Bonhoeffer's language, by the concrete place in which the Christian hears the call of the incarnate Lord, and responds out of the hope that is in him that God will accomplish His Word. Says Luther:

> We have this faint sigh and this tiny faith, which depends only on hearing the sound of the voice of Christ as He promises. According to sense, therefore, this is only the center of the circle; but in fact it is a very large and infinite sphere. What a Christian has is in fact something very large and infinite, but according to his view and sense it is very small and finite. Therefore we must not measure this by human reason and sense; we must measure it by another circle, that is, by the promise of God; just as He is infinite, so His promise is infinite, even though meanwhile it is enclosed in these narrow limits and in what I might call the Word of the center. Now we see the center; eventually we shall see the circumference as well (26, 391 f.).

3

Trucking

As we saw in the first essay, Luther's dialectical associations vary with his shifting perspectives on a subject. When he is most concerned to distinguish redeemed man from fallen man, he will tend to exploit the disjunctive sense of such contrasts as "faith - works" or "faith - Law." But the substance of faith cannot be defined merely in this negative way. In fact the distinction can be made and sustained only if one first establishes the ground of faith in a positive way. When this perspective guides Luther's concerns, his associations will tend to shift to the conjunctive sense of such contrasts as "faith-hope," "faith-promise," or "faith-Christ."

By moving into the perspective of the ground of identity between faith and the incarnate Word of God, Luther's consideration of faith as resting on no sensible or extensive foundation, but rather on the hidden promise, gives his descriptions a tension which can only be viewed as eschatological. Faith takes its identity from its future, but is realized only in present works of love. In this section, which may serve as an introduction to the second half of our study, we must try to gain some appreciation of the eschatological sense pervading not only Luther's understanding of faith but indeed the whole of his thought.

For Luther the word "faith" does not primarily connote a content or name a set of articles for belief. Instead it has the active, verbal sense of "faithfulness" or "fidelity." Faith, Luther emphasizes, is a "living, moving trust in God's grace."[42] Even occurring more frequently is an association of faith with hope. While there are grounds for differentiating faith and hope in terms of function,[43] both are so completely defined in reference to God's promise as to become virtually interchangeable for Luther. It is the Word of promise that gives faith its eschatological character as hope, and hope its firstfruits, its substance, in faith. Hope is, of course, closely associated with things to come, with the future. But Luther maintains that in a sense the man who hopes becomes what he hopes for.[44] And it is the "becoming real" of hope that Luther refers to when he defines faith as the substance, or better in the present connection, the "substantiation" of hope.

This understanding of the relation between faith and hope was developed by Luther just at the moment in the *Romans* commentary when he rediscovered the importance of *promissio* for explicating the "justification of God." In the first attempt to interpret Rom. 3: 4,

Luther employed the analogy of a sick man and a doctor to exemplify the importance of confession. The only way the doctor could be "justified in his words" was for the man to confess he was sick. After Luther's reinterpretation of the passage in terms of promise, however, the same analogy is used again, but in a completely different way. The sick man "justifies" the doctor not by confession but by placing complete faith, hope, and trust in his word. He is thus in a sense well, even though he is sick. He is becoming what he hopes for. Just so, a man

> is at the same time both a sinner and righteous, a sinner in fact but righteous by virtue of the reckoning and the certain promise of God that he will redeem him from sin in order, in the end, to make him perfectly whole and sound. And, therefore, he is perfectly whole in hope, while he is in fact a sinner, but he has already begun to be actually righteous, and he always seeks to become more so, always knowing himself to be unrighteous.[45]

Luther's descriptions of Christian living indicate a shift in emphasis toward the dynamic or "becoming" side of the relationship. This process of becoming is wholly and exclusively defined in reference to Christ: the process is an *ingressus in Christum*. "Faith" and "hope" are terms virtually interchangeable as descriptions of Christian existence just because their one meaning is grounded in Christ: faith that in Christ God has accomplished His promise of salvation for us once for all; hope that in Christ God will accomplish his promise of regeneration in us from day to day.

We need only rephrase this description to expose the fact that the relation "Christian - Christ" is a *reciprocal* process. Faith is possible, it has its substance, only because the Word of God has, in Christ, *entered into* the world of sin to accomplish its salvation. Hope has its substance only because Christ daily *enters into* "this body of sin" to accomplish its regeneration. To say that the Christian enters into Christ and that Christ enters into the Christian is to say exactly the same thing from different perspectives.[46] The unity of Christ and faith is thus to be understood as a reciprocal, dynamic unity of becoming. The Word enters into the flesh, the flesh enters into the Word. We are, Luther said, baked one cake with Christ.

The "beginning of the new creature"—for this is what Luther is describing when he speaks of the mutual process of indwelling—is a beginning that is created and sustained by the Word of promise. The promise is addressed to the individual conscience, to be sure, but it is given only publicly, in preached Word and Sacrament, and only to the conscience which in that moment discovers itself to be part of the community created by the Word.

The becoming of the new creature initiates at Baptism. Baptism, Luther began to emphasize in *The Babylonian Captivity* of 1520, is the first sacrament and the foundation of all the others. And the first thing to consider in Baptism, and its foundation, is the divine Word of promise. Because it is the sign, not of man's promise, but God's promise, the baptismal Word remains more steadfast than the promise in the other sacraments.[47] Correspondingly the Christian conscience remains secure against the temptation to despair in the midst of sin as long as it clings to God's Word in the Sacrament. Inkpots, passed gas, and arguments having proved ineffective, the devil was compelled to leave off his onslaughts only when Luther stood on his baptism!

Baptism is not simply the once-for-all act that begins the renewed life, however. The dying and birthing it indicates is a process characteristic of the whole of Christian existence. The Christian must daily creep back into Baptism, finding therein the promise of God, which he had deserted, steadfast and ready to receive him. The daily baptism of which Luther speaks is the life of repentance. If Baptism is the beginning of the process of faith becoming, repentance is the form in which that process occurs. Luther slowly came to the position during the *Romans* commentary, a position quite consistent with the idea of the nonsensible grounds of faith's self-understanding, that Christian confession is not based on an experience of sin, and thus is not a response of Law or works, a response of fear. It is rather a response of faith and trust in the Word of God.[48] Thus Luther could argue that faith does not reach righteousness and salvation unless it arrives at confession, the "principle work" of faith.[49] In this sense Luther can say that repentance is the medium, the way between unrighteousness, the *terminus a quo,* and righteousness, the *terminus ad quem.*[50]

As repentance is the trusting response of faith to the Word of God, so it is the Word of promise which Luther emphasizes in the forgiveness of sins, the promise which comes to the repentant heart in the Sacrament of the Altar. The Mass is God's new testament, His promise of forgiveness. Correspondingly, we must hold that the only proper access to the Mass is by faith, knowing that

> . . . the beginning of our salvation is a faith which clings to the word of the promising God, who, without any effort on our part, in free and unmerited mercy takes the initiative and offers us the word of his promise.[51]

Faith is life, we heard Luther say earlier. It is a becoming which is created in the Sacrament of Baptism, nourished and renewed in the Sacrament of the Altar, and characterized throughout by repentance. The faith which is the whole life of a Christian is thus a *vita poenitentiae,* indeed a life of continuing repentance, as Luther put it in the very first of his 95 Theses. Because the Word of promise is public, the sacramental life a shared life, the Christian's life of faith is always a common life. It is a life in the living fellowship of those who are always repenting — the church. [52] The church, that hidden *civitas* known only in heaven and defined only by the Word, is born out of the promise and is preserved by the promise. The people of God know that the life to come can be lived only in the Creator, not the creature. It knows its present life is a firstfruits, a beginning of the life to come. The fellowship which Luther describes is never at rest, always moving.[53] Like the Christ on whom its vision is fixed, the church has nowhere to lay its head. The church is always seeking, always trucking, always led by its hope. Its life together is a life which is a time of willing righteousness but not perfecting it in this life.

> The whole life of the new people, the believing people, the spiritual people, is this: with the sigh of the heart, the cry of the deed, and the toil of the body to ask, seek, and pray only for justification, ever and ever again until the hour of death; never to stand still and never to rest in accomplishment; not to regard any works as if they had ended the search for righteousness, but to wait for this end as if it dwelt somewhere ever beyond one's reach; and to know that as long as one lives, he will have his being in sins. . . .
>
> [Christians] confess that they sin and have sinned, but they are sorry for this, hate themselves for it, long to be justified, and under groaning constantly pray to God for righteousness. This is the people of God: it constantly brings the judgment of the cross to bear upon itself.[54]

The life of the Christian people is thus not a life of peace, but one of *passage.* They are always in poverty, in exile; they are runners advanced by the Holy Spirit "who has nothing to do with slow enterprises"![55] They run the royal road, Luther says in the *Romans* commentary, the way of spiritual peace if not earthly peace, the way hedged on one side by the fear of God and on the other side by trust in His mercy. The Christian is *ingressus,* and from this there flows the love whereby others are brought within the becoming of Christ.[56]

In sum, the whole life of the Christian man is a pilgrimage. The earth is his inn, his place a "nachtlager"—a "night's lodging."[57] Life is a *vita viatorum,* and Luther's theology is *theologia viatorum.*

Essay V: *Initium Novae Creaturae*

On Angels and Their Fearful Tread

The relationship of "faith-Christ" is the basic organizing dialectic of Part Two. In the preceding essay, as in the entire first half of the study, my attention was centered on the character of faith as a movement toward Christ, and on the non-experiential epistemological grounds for faith. Such attention was necessary in order to give real meaning to the view of faith as a movement toward Christ.

Yet there must also be experiential grounds for faith. If the othersidedness of it all did not have a manifest this-sidedness, the theologian would quite literally have nothing to say about his subject. Though his *Church Dogmatics* runs to many volumes, it would be as "a tale that is told," and who knows, or could know, whether it be true? Or even relevant?

The Holy Scripture itself can make claim on human life only on the assumption of its authors that the Word of God is not completely alien to the world it meets. Throughout most of history the issue for theologians has not been the *whether,* but the *extent* of the premised mutuality. The matter of a natural theology is a related but different and more complex question. But even on this issue, most thinkers did not reject it on principle but differentiated themselves concerning the status of a hypothesized natural theology within the fallen human estate, its function and limits in Christian consciousness, and the wisdom of its inclusion within the systematic articulation of the faith.

Luther shares this tradition in all its aspects. He had not, after all, had the chance to read Kant and Hume! More importantly for our present consideration, Luther also assumed, along with Scripture and the theological tradition, that the Word of God certified its claims by its experienced or otherwise demonstrable effects in the hearts and lives of those who received it. Appeal to an objective or external "Word of God," more or less identified with the written text, does not suffice to fill an experiential vacuum. Even if it could, to Luther such an appeal indicates bad, i.e., legalistic theology, barren exegesis, and a denial of the Spirit. As important as the appeal to the objectivity of God's Word is in Luther's theology, he never identifies that Word with the written text, and even differentiates, within what he considers God's Word, what is and is not relevant, and under what interpretation (!), to his existential situation. And so in order both to understand Luther's thinking and also to avoid ignoring an important area of his doctrine, we must inquire concerning the ways in which the Christian faith is manifest in experience and demonstrable in works of love.

All this having been said, however, it remains eminently true that the student is entering a most treacherous area when he enters the question of Luther's view of sanctification. Luther was chronically hypersensitive in this region of theology, infinitely suspicious of and implacably opposed to any train of thought which, though admittedly correct in substance and well-intended, might give even the slightest possibility of occasion for the temptation to works-righteousness and Pelagianism. Considering the trends in both the theology and the religion of his time, such a reaction is understandable, indeed justifiable. But combine Luther's well-occasioned fears with his deep appreciation for the almost infinite perversity of the human mind and will, and you have before you a formidable interpretive task. A task requiring the greatest sensitivity of perception and delicacy of expression. The terrain is nearly barren of landmarks. Here and there a vague line or two emerges in a haze which does not, unfortunately, suggest the presence of the Holy Spirit, but rather the shadows of a mind which in most other places did not hesitate to vent itself with full and unshakable assertions.

Expect, at best, to make many mistakes, of fact, of placement and relationship, of valuation. Your colleagues, equally though perhaps differently in error, will be quick to their corrective pens. My own meager attempts will provide sufficient occasion to ponder the limits of human thought, my own as well as Luther's. I can but content myself with the truth that in this world we have no lasting city!

———————

Things are not quite that bad, of course. For Luther not only has a definite vocabulary for describing the new life in Christ, but also provides some directions for assessing the relationship between the grounds for and the expression of faith. From faith in the promise, he says, there immediately follows of itself a stirring of the heart and the initiation of a new and different man. The man has "changed his skin"; he sees everything differently, in fact he reverses all his former judgments.[1] Here we see expressed the complete discontinuity between his own experience and that which is new. There is no way, no method, no extremity whereby man can reach the Word of God. God makes His own way. It is the Holy Spirit who justifies, creates a new heart and new motives, and certifies the reversal of judgments in the heart.[2] The new experience is not man's, in the sense of being from him. It is from God, and a gift to man. The man is passive, as Luther says so often. "Justification" and "the beginning of the new creature" are the same to the Spirit, and the new creature who is beginning is not complete, but partly just, partly sinner. At the same time God does not impute the sin remaining, the sin which will be abolished only with the perfection of the new creature.[3] Dying to the experience of the flesh and living according to the experience of the Spirit is the new creation in Christ. And it is a process of becoming in which consummation is an ever new beginning.

We are thus led to a consideration of the new creature as the place where the actualization of faith's self-understanding is expressed. Under the rubric of "new creature" I have sketched all the topics to be considered in more detail in this essay. The discussion thus shifts focus to the reverse relation of the dialectic "faith - Christ," that is, to the vectorial character of Christ as *ingressus in fidem*. Thereby the eschatological character of Luther's theology will appear as the progressive realization of Christ in the man of faith. The entire second half of the study, which this essay initiates, exactly reverses the perspective of the first half. The first section will include a preliminary evaluation of Law, works, as they form and express the Christian life of love. The second section will concentrate on the relation of this temporal, external process to the nontemporal, internal becoming which, strictly speaking, Luther means by sanctification. The third section will integrate the essay with the anthropology developed earlier, now in terms of the subjective realization of Christ in the man of faith.

1

The Ecstacy of Faith

The themes of human bondage and freedom, and thus of Law and spontaneity, are themes that have been with us throughout the preceding essays and continue to exercise an influence on the discussion of the new creature. Luther says that if Christians had the liberty Paul speaks of, the churches would be closed for lack of attendance within a year because we are still "stinking, lazy sinners."[4] Because of this all-too-obvious fact, Christians need the Law to train the flesh even though the conscience is free. Christian freedom, as opposed to the merely human understanding of freedom, means that man, not Law, is changed.[5] The continued presence of the Law is seen by Luther as a formal presence which, while ending "imputatively" with faith and the remission of sins, ends "expurgatively" only with the perfection of the new creature in grace.[6]

We have thus hit squarely on the problem of the function or use of the Law for the Christian. Christ's righteousness is formal; it is not connected with Law but is in a "new world" above and beyond the Law. And yet the process of transition from an "alien" or formal righteousness to the "proper" righteousness which consists in love to one's neighbor, Luther can describe as a following of Christ's example and a transformation into His likeness. Christ is the form adorning and informing faith. His atoning work, His reign in the believer, are not only done *for* us, but are also meant to be an example *to* us.[7] While Luther may have emphasized this exemplary function of Christ more in the early period, it is not thereby foreign to his mature view of the function or use of the Law. Yet already in the early Luther a certain tension can be seen relative to the obvious presence in the Gospel of Law in what looks like the prescriptive or moral use of the term. For to say that the Christian will "of course" realize or embody Christ in good works is not the same as saying that there is an explicit set of prescriptive laws laid down by Christ which the Christian must follow. And Luther was too sensitive to the matter of works-righteousness lying so close at hand in the latter formulation to ever accept it as the best way of construing the texts in question. Luther's occasionally forced interpretations of the Sermon on the Mount, or in general the themes of Matthew, Luke, Acts, and the pastoral epistles,[8] simply expose and do not resolve this tension.

But Luther does have an approach to what is thus the issue of the relationship between the Christian and works, and of how that relationship is and is not definable by "Law." The Law should be introduced, he says, only when the issue is one of works. But does the Law serve as a guide or directive in reference to the Christian's life of works of love? Luther, seemingly revealing somewhat more idealism on the matter than does Calvin, argues that the true Christian has a "second nature" for works of love.[9] This view, however, is not at all evidence that Luther committed the so-called "error" of Plato — and the Anabaptists! — i.e., the assumption that if you know the good you will do the good. The difference between Luther and Calvin is not over the issue of whether Law is or is not proper to the Christian life, but whether it should be construed as an explicit, positive Law. Luther's position does however, apparently resemble the Platonic view. The reason why enlightened man will, of course, do the good is that in knowing it he knows that Goodness is identical with Being. The equation of knowing and doing is an *ontological* equation. Now Luther for his own part argues that the Christian instinctively knows and does what he ought to do. This position is made possible because of a development in Luther's understanding of the relationship of Law to Christian life. The beginnings are present in the *Romans* commentary, particularly in Luther's struggle with the meaning of Law in chapter two.[10] At 2: 15 Luther made the first connection. He says that "the love shed abroad by the Holy Spirit" is

> . . . the law of Christ and the fulfillment of the law of Moses, or rather, it is a law without law, without measure, without end, without limit, but extended above and beyond everything the law prescribes or can prescribe.[11]

Here we see Luther beginning to interpret Law in other than a prescriptive sense. It is love which is the embodiment or fulfillment of the Law, and which as its perfect expression goes far beyond the reality of the old Law.

But what is the relationship of this "fulfilled" new Law to Christian faith and life? While the answer lay close at hand, Luther did not see it at Rom. 2: 15, for his concern was focused on the issue of how non-Christians could be said to "do the law." In the *Hebrews* commentary, however, the answer clearly emerges. Christian life is a life lived in the Spirit and embodied in works of love. And thus one can say that the Christian instinctively knows what to do, because *the Christian's life is itself the living and fulfilled Law.* This idea, overlooked by many commentators but very important, I think, for interpreting Luther, surfaces at Heb. 7: 12. At this verse Luther is discussing the meaning of a "change" in the Law because of its fulfillment by Christ. The new meaning supplied by Paul in Romans and Galatians, Luther says, is expressed in 1 Tim. 1: 9:

> "The law is not made for a righteous man," i.e., in so far as he is righteous he has all the virtues which the law demands. He is already above the law because he owes nothing to the law: he keeps the law and *his life is the very law itself, living and fulfilled.* . . . But in truth this change (of the law) has not yet been perfected as the first law was, but is being perfected from day to day. . . . because the righteous man to whom no law need be given *does not exist,* for in this life he only makes a beginning to his righteousness.[12]

What Luther has done is to develop his understanding of Law in relation to Christian man in exact systematic parallel to his understanding of Law relative to fallen man. On the latter subject, recall, Luther equated Law with the reality of fallen man and developed his understanding of Law in an existential sense, for which the written or prescribed Law was but a pedagogical reflection or reinforcement. The same is true with the new creature: *Law characterizes his existence before God, and is not basically prescriptive.* [13] We are justified before God because we are covered over by Christ, who is the fulfillment of the Law and the substance of Christian faith. But we are also sinners, and so the New Testament preaching of the Law serves to guide and discipline the Christian way. The so-called second or theological use of the Law is therefore in fact a double use, a doubleness which is not well expressed in the distinction of a "second" and (controverted) "third" use. The Law in its theological function thus exposes a contrast, a relation of identity and difference between the old man and the new man. The identity or continuity lies in the fact that the content of the preached Law remains the same, and is addressed in both cases to one who is a sinner. The difference or discontinuity rests in the fact that in one theological use of the Law man is shown to himself, convicted of sin for this betrayal of the Law, i.e., his betrayal of himself and God. While in the other use of the Law, redeemed man is shown as the living fulfillment of the Law. The Law reflects his new being, guides him into works of love, and encourages him to realize in his life (imperative sense) what he already is (indicative sense).

This line of development culminates in the 1519 *Galatians* commentary with Luther's interpretation of 2: 19: "For I through the Law died to the Law, that I might live to God."[14] Luther begins by reviewing the self-destructive character of the Law, and concludes that there is a twofold sense of "Law." The old law is the law of letters, and is identified with the old man in sin. The new law is related to the old law as the "thing" to the "word," the substance to the sign (27, 235). Referring once again to Rom. 5: 5, Luther says that the new law is the law of the Spirit, which is

> . . . written with no letters at all, published in no words, thought of in no thoughts. On the contrary, it is *the living will itself and the life of experience.* . . . This light of understanding in the mind, I say, and this flame in the heart is the law of faith, the new law, the law of Christ, the law of the Spirit, the law of grace. *It justifies, fulfills everything,* and crucifies the lusts of the flesh (27, 234; emphasis mine).

And Luther then goes on to indicate that what the new Law produces is in fact bodily works of love, bodily incarnations which are spiritual just because they are the expressions of faith (27, 236).

With this "fleshing out"(!), if you will, of his equation of Christian life with the fulfilled law, Luther's understanding of Christian life is, from one perspective on the subject, essentially complete. For in the above passage Luther has opened up the Christian's cognate and volitional experience of himself as a proper means of expressing and veri-fying the self-understanding of faith. Because he sees faith as the mode of Christian existence, Luther is able to affirm that existence, as actually lived and reflected on, as a true though of course imperfect and incomplete extension or incarnation of faith. While faith is a hid-denness, it becomes incarnated, extended in works of love. Christian living — loving — is thus the "standing out" or ecstacy of that faith. As hope is as it were the spiritual ecstacy of faith, so works of love are the bodily ecstacy of that faith. It is how faith becomes incarnate, manifest in the world. It is in this sense, therefore, that Luther can say that faith is the use one makes of what one believes, that it is known from its effects, that it is the principle of all good works.[15]

But right now we are on the very tip of the promontory. One step farther and all is lost! The bottom drops out in at least two direc-tions, and we fall into quagmires that are theologically fatal. We have followed a line of interpretation which culminates in the "working" definition of faith as its expression or realization in works of love. But in the human mind and will, ever ready to turn God's glory into man's glory, this otherwise legitimate conclusion is mercurially unsta-ble. It can lead, with the very slightest shift in center of gravity, to a dreadful reversal in one's attitude toward works of love. Instead of being the *de facto* evidence or natural, spontaneous expression of justification, works of love become the way by which that justification is proved; and then, imperceptibly, the way it is *gained.* Man can seize upon his Christian confidence, seize upon the faith experience which is available to him, and try to turn it to account *coram deo,* to make it "valuable" theologically, and thus turn it, once again, into works-righteousness. In a sense this shift can be seen as a shift from works of love as an epistemological ground of justification to works of love as a methodological tool.[16] It is this danger that was ever before Luther and that made him tread very lightly, and with myriad qualifications, on the truths that love informs faith and that faith with-out works is dead. Luther's uneasiness was not lessened by his oft-repeated and unmistakably clear teaching that works are wholly and exclusively to be directed to the world and not to God; that they are to embody God's righteousness to, for, and in the world, not man's righteousness before God; and that works can be differentiated and valuated only in terms of the world, and not in God's sight.

Such an error is possible because of two interrelated false infer-ences one could make from the line of interpretation we have been following. One false inference is that growth in works of love, a process taking place in time, is identifiable with sanctification. The conclusion is then that the Christian embodies what can be called an "empirical righteousness" or a "progressive sanctification" measureable in time. A little better every day in every way. And then, because of Luther's close association of justification with works of love, the view arises that justification itself is a temporal process begun in Baptism, accruing with and conditionally on works of love, and completed with death and the divine acceptance. As close to Luther as this language apparently is, in fact it is quite alien. First, Luther never identifies works of love with sanctification. Second, while works of love grow in time, the process of sanctification is not a temporal process, but a process of "internal" becoming which expresses itself temporally in outward works of love. And third, Luther in no way makes justification conditional on sanctification, but rather makes sanctification conditional on justification.

A second false inference one can make from Luther's position is that the agent of either or both processes is the Christian *ego,* as though sanctification were a becoming in which *I* am the subject, works of love acts of which *I* am the agent. Against this view Luther raises the Pauline confession, "not I, but Christ dwelling in me." Luther's claim is that sanctification is the becoming of Christ, not of the I; that the I who is the agent of works of love is Christ, not me; and that, in sum, Christ is the true *ego* of the Christian. Luther does not use this "mystical" language as "merely" mystical, as though it expressed the highest and most extraordinary truths of religious experience. He takes it seriously! It is an essential constituent of his theology, and determines everything.

We thus have our tasks before us. The following section concerns sanctification and works of love in relation to time. In the third section we must investigate these subjects in relation to their agent.

2

The Eternal Now

Christian *life* is the living fulfillment of the Law. It is the expression, through and in time, of the works of love which are the incarnation of faith and its showing forth.

Christian *faith,* the law of the Spirit, is "the living will itself and the life of experience, . . . this light of understanding in the mind, this flame in the heart . . . ."

Two statements are before us, and now we repeat the lesson learned in the preceeding section: Christian life *is* Christian faith. We then pick up the "time" theme from the first statement, the "experience" theme from the second, and can combine the two statements

111

as follows: (1)Christian life is the temporal experience of Christian faith; (2)Christian faith is the temporal experience of Christian life. But as soon as we look at the formulations, we realize something is wrong. What Christian life experiences in time is the *world,* and it *expresses* faith to and in that world. And Christian faith does not find its experiential source in life in the world, Christian or not, but rather in the *Word of God.*

Our exercise in sythesis went wrong because we erred in making the simple identification of faith and life. The correct formulation is faith as the *form* or *mode* of Christian life, the way it is articulated, reflected upon, and actualized. One cannot then simply apply, without qualifications, characteristics of one subject to the other. As intimately as living and believing are related, Luther observes distinctions. He says that Christian *life* is temporal, but he calls it an *expression,* not an experience. He says Christian *faith* is an *experience,* but he does not call it temporal.

A better way to state the relationship of the two subjects is to say that faith is the nontemporal experienced form of Christian life and living the temporal expression of Christian faith. We have already introduced Luther's notion of what is expressed in time: works of love. We now have to investigate what is experienced: the eternal presence of God in Christ. Both themes, taken together, define what Luther means by sanctification.

One does not become a theologian by reading or writing theological books, Luther says. Theological knowledge is rather a struggle of the heart, faith's experience of living, dying, being damned and blessed.[17] But this experience of faith is not the result of encounter with the temporal world. It is rather the result of the continuing encounter of the heart with God—with God alone. The Reformation principle of *sola scriptura* insures that it is in God's Word and God's Word alone that the heart finds its theological encounter. And Luther's principle of *fides ex auditu* insures that the heart can only be purely receptive in this encounter, letting itself be formed and informed by the agency of the Holy Spirit through the preached Word. The experience which is faith is thus experience which is formed in the image of God and as a recreation of that image. Unlike the original image of God, hidden so deeply by nature and by sin that it was almost a *res incognita,* the faith which is a recreated image of God is an accessible basis for the heart's feeling for divinity, and is available for providing the normative form of the new creature.[18]

Without prejudicing many other cognate lines of interpretation involved in the subject of the *imago dei,* for our present concerns it is the *eternal* character of that image, and thus of faith, which is important. Since the creation and everything in it, including faith and language, is wholly fixed in temporal terms, Luther finds himself with the ancient problem of expressing the relation of eternity and time. In the *Timaeus* the philosopher said that time was the "moving image" of eternity. Luther will try to express faith as a moving image of God in Christ.

Luther can speak of faith as being united with that which is invisible, unthinkable, and ineffable. These negative statements, he says, express the eternity of their referents.[19] But when he wants to give a more positive description to the nontemporal experiential ground of faith, Luther is forced into the language of time. His descriptions of the existence of the Christian people as an existence *sub specie aeternitatis* could only be descriptions, as we saw at the end of the preceding essay, of an apparently cyclic process in which the end is always the beginning. The Christ who is the object of faith, its beginning, middle, and end, comes spiritually and anew every day to the heart.[20]

The most serviceable expression one can recur to, it seems, is "presence," punning back and forth on its aspects of "eternal," "now," and "gift." As far as I can determine, Meister Eckhart invented the "eternal now" made famous by Paul Tillich.[21] (Sometimes it pays to read the Fathers!) Luther never studied Eckhart, but suggested the same idea in his own way. The God who is essentially outside time is not, according to Luther, eternally preoccupied with past and future like sinful men. All is simply present to Him, His being and activity wholly manifest in His present, in what Luther called God's *"Stündelein,"* God's "hour."[22] The faith that is defined by God's eternal presence in Christ is thus also always a present — a gift, a here, and a now. Man, like God, only has a present.

> We are temporal, or more exactly, a small piece of time. For what we were has departed, and what will be, we are still lacking. So we possess nothing of time except something momentary, what is present.[23]

Because the Christian only has his present, he has no freedom in the human sense. He can only live and move in God's "hour," which means he can only act God's own act, or act not at all. But to act God's act in God's hour is to act apart from the tyranny of time and custom, i.e., it is to act freely.[24]

Christian faith like the rest of creation is thus to be viewed as a present and continuing *recreatio ex nihilo.*[25] Its "substance" cannot be located in what it had, or has, but is rather wholly dependent and waiting on God's creative act in God's hour. When Luther in his com-

113

mentary on Rom. 8 opposes the philosophical consideration of the creature in terms of its "essence" to the theological interpretation according to its "expectancy," he is, in the midst of developing his own ideas of creative process, opposing one way of seeing the creature as temporal, i.e., as an essence undergoing external changes. The theologian sees all life as life in God, who is the eternal source of true life. Created life is a precursor, a beginning, of the life to come. It is a "piece" of eternal life, Luther says; it is the material God will form into true life in His own image.[26] Accordingly all believers are already in heaven, in the restored paradise, at the right hand of God, in eternity.[27]

We have before us an assemblage of passages which can be extended indefinitely, stressing the nontemporal or eternal character of the experience of Christian faith. At the same time Luther consistently describes this experience as an existence in the now which takes its being from God's future, or more exactly, from its future in God. Luther is trying to formulate what he means by Christian *becoming.* The problem is how to express an experienced process of becoming in which one is not *now* what he was *then* and yet also not what he is *to be,* and at the same time to safeguard its character as eternal, not measureable in terms of time and works of love.

It is in the interest of solving this problem that the distinctions between faith and life, experience and expression were introduced as distinguishable but inseparable components of Luther's understanding of sanctification. The eternal becoming which Luther has been describing is the becoming of the new creature, i.e., the "internal" side of sanctification. He does not speak of the process of the becoming of the new creature as a process for which the criterion is a quantitative change in the "attributes" of an existing being, attributes which can be measured in experienced, external, or "public" time. The "expectation" of the creature which constitutes its existence theologically is not to be construed in such time, as we saw. But if Luther is not describing a process that can be viewed in "public" time, how is he using "time"? One could say he is referring to internal or "qualitative" time. This would be correct, if at the same time we do not still continue to measure the process in terms of changes in an existing being. I have spoken throughout the study of the "process of becoming." I do not wish this phrase to be read as the "process of becoming (something)." What I am suggesting is that the process of which Luther speaks is best interpreted as indicating the growth, not of a being which can be shown to be becoming something *else* or something in addition to itself, but the growth or becoming of a being, *period.* "Becoming" is not to be referred to the becoming or growth *of* a being, but the becoming or growth *into* being. The becoming of the creature, to emphasize Luther's position at Rom. 8:19 once more, defines its being theologically. I am taking this view extremely seriously. Of course Luther shares the "substance" view of reality as essences undergoing external changes. But this view is *merely* metaphysical. For Luther it has no currency in theology. *Coram deo,* theologically, what is relevant is the becoming itself. One brings certain faculties, i.e., the conscience, into the becoming of faith, and carries others, e.g., good works, out of it. But the conscience as a criterion for action, and good works as the realization of the action, belong strictly *coram mundo.* They cannot be brought into consideration of who man is before God. Thus sanctification cannot be defined simply as the progressive making holy of existence. That would be a *coram mundo* definition, and it applies to works of love, not to the becoming of the new creature. "The becoming of the new creature" refers to the realization of the divine life in the man of faith, the fruits of which are works of love. The becoming of the new creature is the realization of what was not; it is in the strictest theological sense a *creatio ex nihilo,* a "becoming" which is always best expressed as a "beginning." Since there is growth, duration, sequence, Luther must use the language of public time. But in emphasizing the "eternal now" of the process, he is in effect arguing that such temporal language, though necessary, is inappropriate, at least regarding the experience of faith which is the beginning of the new creature. There is no being in the past, present, or future to provide discernable reference points for measuring the becoming of faith. Only works of love are thus measurable. But both believers and nonbelievers do good works. Both fallen man and the new creature are characterized by "Law," as we saw in section one. The difference is not an external one. There are never any clear grounds for distinguishing the faithful from the unfaithful. The *ingressus* character of the former in no way attentuates their reality as *incurvatus.* The Christian is in the process of becoming real, becoming holy, but is and always is partly sinner, partly flesh. The process of the becoming of the new creature, of faith, is never completed in this life. It is always a beginning. Works of love are visible, bodily, temporal. They are under Law, and cannot therefore become the standard for assessing the theological relationship. The beginning of the new creature, the becoming of which works of love are the temporal expression, is in the profoundest sense hidden from the world.

The becoming of the new creature is the *beginning* of the new creature. Luther expresses the sense of this equation when he says that it is *Baptism* which is the sign for the reality of the Christian faith. And what is signified in Baptism is actual death and resurrection.[28] The outward baptismal sign comes before the inward realization which is dependent upon it. The inward event, faith, is the realization or fulfillment of what Baptism signifies.[29] We are never without the sign or the reality, but its realization is a process incomplete until the last day.

> For our whole life should be baptism, and the fulfilling of the sign or sacrament of baptism, since we have been set free from all else and given over to baptism alone, that is, to death and resurrection.[30]

The realization of the baptismal sign involves the mortification of the flesh and the quickening of the spirit. It is for this that we are set free. Can one then not say that Christian freedom is freedom for becoming real?

The baptismal sign is a Word of promise. And the promise is never in vain, but actually accomplishes what is promised. God's Word would be no word, a false and sterile word, did it not realize itself bodily in Christ. Faith would be no faith, a false and sterile faith, did it not express itself in works of love. The life of Baptism is therefore a process in which the outward sign indicates and initiates the inward realization of the new creature, and this inward realization then expresses itself again in outward signs, works of love. The "beginning of the new creature" cannot be mere verbiage. There will be evidence before the world of what is being wrought by and before God. Baptismal renewal therefore includes a renewal of both mind and body.[31] For the grace of Baptism cannot be understood merely as "favorable disposition." It is a gift. God is favorably disposed and present with the *res,* not merely the *verbum.*[32]

It is just at this point, however, that we get a yellow caution light from Luther. Though the inward becoming of the new creature always manifests itself temporally in the mortification of the flesh and in works of love, one cannot take this fact as evidence that Luther taught simply a "progressive" understanding of sanctification. As throughout Luther's descriptions of Christian life and faith, so here: redeemed man embodies the *"simul."* Christian existence is always both slave and free. The old man, Luther says, is in servitude to sin, free from righteousness. The new man is free from sin, in servitude to righteousness.[33] But the two are always jointly present in the Christian life which is a free fulfillment of the Law of love.

> A person goes from servitude to servitude, from freedom to freedom, that is, from sin to grace, from fear of punishment to love of righteousness, from the Law to the fulfillment of the Law, from the word to reality, from a figure to truth, from a sign to substance,

from Moses to Christ, from the flesh to the spirit, from the world to the Father. All this takes place at the same time.[34]

Luther thus picks up his formulation concerning freedom and servitude, casting it into a description of a process. But this process is not to be understood as a gradual transition, not even as a becoming of one reality into another. Servitude to sin *is* freedom from righteousness; freedom from sin *is* servitude to righteousness. The process from servitude to servitude, freedom to freedom, is not a transition from one entity to another. It is, as Luther explicates it, a process from sign to reality, Law to its fulfillment. A realization of what was not. The becoming of the new creature.

Though there is temporal, incremental growth in works of love, such signs are not to be understood as evidence of what obtains before God. The becoming of the new creature is a process of realization that can only be described as happening *simul*, at once, in God's own hour, in his eternal now. Since God embraces all in his eternal presentness,

> . . . the creature in his eyes in not in time, but everything becomes at once *[omnia simul fiunt]*. Temporal vicissitude relates only to the changing multiplicity of things.[35]

But the creature of course is itself wholly a creature in and of time. How can one then give any real meaning to Luther's assertion that the new creature is in some real respect not in time? The difficulty can be overcome if we now turn to our second task: the matter of the *subject* of this becoming. Not a process which man actualizes and oversees, but one which God actualizes and oversees can be described as taking place in the eternal now. It is not living men, but Christ living in man, who accomplishes the new creature.

3

Yet Not I, but Christ

To say that it is Christ and not the Christian who is the subject of the becoming of the new creature is to broach the issue of the referent of *ego* in Rom. 7. Luther was aware of the long history of exegetical discourse on the matter and found many occasions, especially early in his career, to express his views. His position takes the pattern we have seen exemplified time and again. From one perspective he will say that it is Christ or the spiritual man, and *not* our own psyche or the carnal man, who is the subject. And then from another perspective he will say that *therefore* it is *both* Christ and

I, both the spiritual and the carnal man who is described in the text. "Faith-Christ" is a dialectical relation, and the Christian alone exemplifies both the disjunctive and conjunctive sides of the contrast. The new creature lives both *coram deo* (Christ is the subject, not I) and *coram mundo* (both Christ and I are the subject). In this concluding section to Part Two I will emphasize the first perspective. The second perspective, involving the Christian's life in and for the world, is the basic theme of Part Three.

The descriptions in Rom. 7 lead Luther to conclude that it can only be the spiritual man, the man wholly in agreement with the Law, of whom Paul speaks.[36] Paul is describing a profound struggle, a struggle of spirit with flesh, of the Law of the members with the Law of the mind. And for Luther it is only the spiritual man in whom such a struggle rages. The faithful man is two men, and his faith must struggle against his unfaith. Only the unfaithful man is one with himself. The old man or the flesh is not engaged in a struggle at all, but wholly agrees with the Law of the flesh. He is identical with his flesh.[37]

While the carnal man imagines that he is spiritual, the truly spiritual man knows that he is also carnal. This self-knowledge is theological knowledge. There is just no way it can be experienced or explained except in terms of faith. The antithesis between spiritual man and carnal man is not a "moral" or "metaphysical" antithesis. The metaphysicians refer the *ego* in Rom. 7 to the old man, Luther says, and so pervert everything. They do this because they hold antecedently that there is no sin left after Baptism. Accordingly the *ego* struggling with sin can only be the *ego* prior to baptismal grace. The best the metaphysicians can do with Paul's text is to interpret "flesh" and "spirit" in the sense of two contrary and independent wills.[38] But Paul knows nothing of such things. He does not have two wills, but is one person, one will, living under two "dispensations."[39] The same spiritual man is both flesh and spirit, Luther says, both outward and inward. Or to put it more exactly, without the Spirit the whole man is the old or outward man.[40] When Paul calls the spiritual man carnal, he is using the linguistics of *communicatio idiomatum* (the "transference of proper attributes") to apply descriptions to the whole man of what is actually true only of a part of him. Such a usage is originally applicable to Christ, and is derivatively applicable to the Christian man—but only to the *Christian* man.[41]

Christian faith is true faith, Luther continues, only when it rests wholly in Christ. The Christian lives eternally before God as conscience, and the union with Christ must be so close, Luther claims, that one can say that Christ and the conscience become "one body."[42] Our whole existence is existence in Christ, who also lives in us. And so the righteous man himself does not live, but his life is the living of Christ in him.[43] Faith is so completely defined as trust in Christ as the source of righteousness that it becomes a veritable transformation into the form of Christ.[44] Our righteousness is the righteousness which Christ lives in us, not that which we might claim for our own person.

"Our own person," though obviously *there* in some sense, is an entity to which the Christian whose true self is Christ has no positive spiritual kinship. This self, bound by time and flesh, is to the Christian who lives in the eternal now of Christ and the Spirit, an "alien" or "other" self. Luther sees this other self only negatively, as the "not I." This "not I" is the *ego* of and under the Law, or, in other words, it is the *ego* separate from Christ.[45] From the perspective of our identity in Christ and before God, the life in time and the flesh is an alien life. Luther can call it a physical or natural life which is only a mask, a *larva*. At the same time, and from the antithetical perspective, we are wholly in flesh and time. So it is the natural or physical life which is our "own," while that eternal and spiritual life which Christ lives in us is said to be an "alien" life.[46] The Christian, then, lives two lives, or as Luther put it, in two dispensations. Each life is both his "own" and "alien," depending on the perspective from which it is seen.

But the center of spiritual gravity, if you will, is the I of Christ. The life of the "not I" or old man cannot therefore be viewed independently or in its own terms. Its time and its nature must be defined in terms of God's "hour" and His purposes. The old man is then seen in terms of how it is and needs to be transformed into the new creature. The grace by which Christ covers over the self before God is and must be also a gift, Luther emphasized.[47] Redeemed man is a *new* creature, born, not made, created *ex nihilo* by the efficacy of Christ and the Spirit. "New" and *ex nihilo* are terms that imply a judgment on what is from this viewpoint an "old" and a "nothing." These designations are not designations of time, as I have tried to show throughout this essay. They are designations of value, man as he is seen *coram deo,* in God's hour and for God's purpose. As "new" expresses God's judgment on what is then "old," so the gracious declaration that we are the new creature also implies an imperative, a task or mandate, which we must take up. The "not I" is not simply man, naturally considered. Rather the "not I" is explicated as "the sin that dwells in me, that is, in my body." The sin remaining is real enough, Luther says. In fact it actually becomes real to us only when God's grace is present. But now sin is treated differently than before. No longer is it seen as the grounds for condemnation, but rather as a wound that must be healed.[48] One cannot underestimate this wound or sickness, lest the healing gift of grace become cheap.[49] The becoming of the new creature is a process of healing which involves purification through suffering and the hearing of the preached Word (are they not often coincident?!).[50] God, the good physician, continues to sustain us, sick with sin, and in our hope we look to the health promised us. Because we live in God's present, that health is already ours; because we live in time, it is still in the future. We are *simul* righteous and sinners. Our perfection, like our righteousness, exists *in spe, nondum in re.*[51] We thus live in a continuing process of becoming. We are, concludes Luther, the beginning of God's creature.[52]

————

In Part Two of this study we analyzed the formal relationships of the dialectic "faith - Christ." In the essay on faith and promise we sought to explore the dynamic character of the relation between Christ and faith. What emerged was a picture of faith as a mode of living, a process of becoming into Christ. In the present essay this theme was extended and strengthened. The process began to appear as a process of realization or actualization in which the active subject is Christ. Sanctification thus appeared as a kind of double event: the inward, nontemporal experience of the becoming of Christ in faith, and the overflow of this becoming in external, temporal works of love. This part thus ends thematically as a prolegomenon to Part Three. The new creature embodies both an indicative and an imperative, a gift and a task, the working presence of Christ and the continuing struggle of faith to realize that presence bodily. The new creature thus is the *gift* of Christ's incarnation in faith and the *task* of faith to become incarnate in works of love.

In this essay we could only develop in broad outline Luther's understanding of both the gift and the task. The gift of Christ takes the form of sacrament. The task of faith takes the form of response to God's mandates. The process of realization, in terms of sacrament and mandate, is the theme of Part Three.

PART THREE

God's Body

It would be an interpretive error of the greatest possible magnitude were the student to take Luther's themes of the process of becoming and the self-realization of the divine as evidence of an idealistic world view. The process of becoming we have been discussing is not a movement from carnal and temporal appearance to spiritual and eternal reality. It is in fact the reverse: an eschatological movement from the spirit to the flesh. What this means is that in organizing the topics of Luther's theology the doctrine of creation should be placed at the end rather than near the beginning.

The "platonic" error can easily be made, and the statements in the preceding two sentences appear as a complete puzzle if one assumes an opposition between "carnal," "temporal," and "spiritual," "eternal," and assumes in addition that the first two terms refer to a reality of lesser ontological "purity" than that referred to in the latter pair. Both assumptions are partially true, of course. I have specified the senses in which flesh and spirit are opposed, and in which revelation extended in flesh is impure. But it is also true that Luther argues for a realized unity of flesh and spirit, of time and eternity, and that he experiences saving revelation as the continuing self-revelation in the flesh of the Word of God. Enfleshment, incarnation, is the eternal purpose of divine activity. It is the ultimate purpose of that activity as well, since Christ is the "very heart of God." The unity of flesh and spirit, time and eternity, a unity indicated linguistically by *simul* and later generalized by the phrase *finitum capax infiniti*, "the finite contains the infinite," is the beginning and ending of his theological discourse. It takes as its source the incarnation of the Creator, and as its goal the inspiration of the creature. The unity is a becoming unity: thus its description as a process. The subject of the becoming is God: thus its description as an eschatological process. The eschatological process of incarnation and inspiration is one way

121

of understanding *finitum capax infiniti.* The idea that comes to expression in the title of Part Three is no more daring, and no less so, than that battle cry of Lutheran orthodoxy of which it is the original expression. His denomination neutered and generalized the idea. Its less uptight founder spoke boldly of "God's body."

Part One of this study was devoted to the basically methodological question of how God and man are known in relation to each other. Part Two was essentially epistemological in character, concentrating on the grounds or locus for certifying that relationship. The methodological issues were developed as they variously expressed the dialectical relationship between what we called the "proximate," the reality of fallen man, and the "penultimate," the reality of redeemed man. The epistemological issues were developed through an examination of the dialectical relationship between redeemed man and what we called the "ultimate," the Word of God.

Part Three rests on both of these themes, but sets them within a more ontologically oriented perspective. The basic question of the divine-human relationship thus gains a third element, i.e., the world. The first essay, on the ubiquity of Christ, picks up the theme of the relationship of redeemed man to God's Word, and develops it in terms of creation as sacrament, as the medium in which God gives Himself as a gift, a saving presence, to faith. The second essay, on the "masks" of God, concerns the relation of redeemed man to the fallen world, and examines creation as Word, as the medium in which the man of faith, responding to the divine self-giving, realizes God's mandate to transform the fallen world.

Essay VI: *Ubiquitas Carnalis Christi*

Last Things First

In the tradition of systematic theology it has almost always been simply assumed that the proper organization of subject matter is (1) the natures and general relationship of God and the world; (2) the nature and person of Christ; and (3) Christ's saving work and its relationship to the community of faith. Such an organization seems to make a great deal of sense in an orderly, deductive way. Some theologians such as Schleiermacher were deeply troubled by this organization. It seemed in general to violate, indeed to reverse the order of experience. More importantly it seemed to subordinate what is in reality the primary and definitive fact of Christianity—salvation in Christ. Yet even Schleiermacher ended up bowing to the traditional order, though he did so with a wistful backward glance at what might have been.

Luther did not write a systematic *magnum opus,* however, and although for some purposes we might wish he had, in this respect we benefit from the lack. We are free from the obligation to present Luther in the traditional order of subjects, and are free to reverse it, thereby more accurately reflecting the evangelical reality of things. The necessity and advantages of beginning with Christ's saving work, moving through "formal" Christology, and ending with God and creation, are nowhere more apparent than in Luther's teaching on the Lord's Supper. Luther's thinking always begins from and is rooted in the life of prayer and worship, and in the experience of faith in the saving presence of Christ. Sacramental life in the church is the point of access to the soteriological work of Christ. As we have seen, Luther's characteristic order is to begin with Christ's work and then to develop his understanding of Christ's person and natures in terms of that work. Third, he sees no access to evangelical discourse about God and creation except through the Word of God in Christ. And thus even though the subject of this essay "logically" presupposes an understanding of God's omnipresence, I must make God's omnipresence a generalization from Christ's ubiquity, rather than treat ubiquity as an instance of omnipresence.

The tasks for this essay are then the following. In section one we will examine the function of the Word and that which it mediates in the Lord's Supper. In section two we shall move into a discussion of Luther's Christology as it relates to the issue of ubiquity. In section three we shall begin the generalization to the subject of God's omnipresence.

1

The Doors of Perception

In the second essay I recommended to you Luther's 1526 exposition of *Jonah* as a rich and highly existential, though often overlooked expression of his theology. Once again this work comes before us, this time in a passage we will recur to again and again, a passage that is simply astonishing in the boldness of its formulation. Luther has begun a somewhat autobiographical rumination on Jonah's rather tragicomic attempt to escape God's presence. One both can and cannot escape God's presence, Luther says, because "presence" must be taken in two senses.

> God's being or presence *[wesen odder gegenwertickeyt]* is twofold. In one way it is a natural presence, in another way a spiritual presence. God is naturally everywhere. . . .But spiritually He is there only where He can be known, that is, where His Word, faith, spirit, and worship is. There are His own people, and they alone experience God as a Lord who is omnipotent and omnipresent.[1]

We shall deal with God's natural *wesen* and with its equation with God's presence in later sections. But note that discourse on even God's natural omnipresence is possible only from the viewpoint of the spiritual *wesen* as it is manifest in Word and received in faith.

God's Word is of primary importance for understanding where God is. It is only with the Word that Christ becomes present, by means of the Word that He is joined to faith, and because of the Word that faith benefits from the sacramental union. Although his estimation of the importance of the physical sign varied,[2] Luther always insisted that it was the action of the Word that defined the existence and function of the Sacrament. It is the first element in that "one sacramental reality" which is the Supper. It mediates the presence of Christ to faith, and without the Word Christ's body is of no beneficial use.[3]

Luther's explanations of how the Word functions in the Sacrament have both spatial and temporal overtones. The Word in a sense "opens up" to the use of faith what is otherwise "closed" or not

124

extended to other purposes. In the *Jonah* passage we saw that God's natural omnipresence is not initially or by itself even available, much less theologically significant, apart from the Word. There is a big difference between God's being present and our ability to "touch" Him.[4] God's omnipresence is never a being "present at hand." He is not ever simply available in this way. He is omnipresent, but "present-to-me," present *pro nobis,* only at specified times and places. And the function of the Word is precisely to specify the time and place where God chooses to be present for us, and where faith is to find its object and direction, i.e., in Christ.[5]

When we connect the function of the Word with omnipresence this way, we are able to see precisely what the Word does and does not do. The Word in the Sacrament does not *bring* the divine presence, but rather *reveals,* and reveals only to faith, what is always already *schon da.* Yet in one sense the Word still has a creative function, in that it is *this* place rather than *that* which becomes the locus of the saving presence. We can best imagine this function in terms of a parting of a veil, a light in the darkness, or a window.[6] God's being is already there, but hidden. The Word functions to part the epistemological veil of that hiddenness, to create an opening or a spotlight in which that presence can become a sacramental presence-to-me.

There is a sense, therefore, in which Luther's view of Christ's presence in the Sacrament is more "objective," if you will, than the Roman view. The question of transubstantiation apart, and without any suggestion of "local motion" connoted, we can say that in the Roman view Christ is absent from the elemental locus, and becomes present there only with and because of the words of institution. For Luther, by contrast, Christ is already always present, but His omnipresence in space and time is hidden. The words of institution uncover this presence in the sacramental time and place. In the Roman view the Word makes present what was absent; in the Lutheran view the Word reveals what was hidden. One reason for the impression that the Roman view is the more objective one is that while Luther maintained that Christ is there only for the reception of faith, the Roman view maintains the sacramental presence even apart from the faithful participation in the Supper. Luther in my view could accept this position, but would argue that such a presence, apart from faith, is not a presence-to-me, and thus is irrelevant at best as a subject of theological discourse. As can be seen, there is more than one issue at stake in the Roman-Lutheran discussion of the Sacrament.

Luther's characteristic point of departure, as we are beginning to see, is not the metaphysics of the sacramental presence, but the epistemological function of that presence. This is exactly parallel to his approach to Christology. "What is true in regard to Christ, is true in regard to the sacrament," runs the famous line.[7] It is uttered in defense of the view that Christ is really present in the sacramental elements. "Real presence" is omnipresence *pro me,* omnipresence which is personally and purposefully "centered" in both termini. The sacramental function is an activity *ex deo* in the person of Christ, and *pro me* in the person of faith. Sacramental presence is a gift. Luther is willing, with some conditions, to use any preposition you wish to define the relationship of bread and body.[8] The important thing is that the presence be seen as God's self-giving. The purpose of God's self-giving is the forgiveness of sins. It is accomplished bodily.

Forgiveness of sins is the essence of the Gospel, of faith and of grace. It is the essence of Christ and His work, our true sacrament. The saving presence of God, promised in the Word and realized on the cross, is an activity which judges, pardons, and begins the new creature. But it is an activity which not only originates with the enfleshment of Christ, but also which is wholly directed to our flesh. God's saving presence is conveyed bodily and received bodily. Yet it is a wholly spiritual activity. Once again we are back with Luther's understanding of the relation of flesh and spirit.

Luther, of course, maintains that the real presence of Christ's body is essential for the Sacrament. But he also argues for a bodily benefit from the Sacrament.[9] He denies he is adding anything new to the doctrinal tradition, and insists that the opposition of the "fanatical spirits" is due to their misunderstanding of "flesh" and "spirit." Just as it was useful to contrast Luther with Rome on the issue of how the Word functions in the Supper, on the matter of the means and benefits of that function it is the contrast with Zwingli that is revealing.

The difference between Luther and Zwingli is something of a paradox. The issue is the place of flesh, of bodily functions and senses, in the spiritual knowledge of God. In contrast to Luther, Zwingli makes his central epistemological dialectic "faith-Holy Spirit" and not "faith-Christ."[10] This difference is massive in its consequences. One consequence is that Zwingli will be unable to see any positive sacramental function for Christ's flesh. Christ saves by virtue of His divine nature alone, and salvation concerns our spirit alone. Zwingli makes the realms of the spirit and the flesh mutually exclusive and epistemologically independent.[11] Zwingli thus not only completely devaluates the realm of sense but at the same time gives that sense experience absolute autonomy in its own realm. The realms of the flesh and spirit are radically separated. *Each* is autonomous in its own realm.[12] There is no perceptive door by which the higher realm of the spirit can enter the realm of the flesh. Yet within its own realm the flesh is absolute master and authority. And the senses will not be persuaded of real presence. A "spiritual body" is as incomprehensible to Zwingli as a "bodily mind." A literal presence, he says, must be a perceptible presence. Since it is not perceptible it is therefore not there in the way Luther would have it there.[13]

In Luther the reverse of this valuation takes place. Sense experience is not a lower carnal realm that must therefore be kept out of theology and the realm of the spirit. Yet while he includes it positively in the knowledge of God, he completely deprives sense knowledge of autonomy within its "own" realm. The sacred and the secular just don't relate, or unrelate, that way. They coexist in the one sacramental reality. Luther therefore does maintain that there are perceptive doors through which the Spirit manifests Himself. The senses are integrated into the divine-human relation, but they are kept epistemologically subordinate and thus kept as a proper means for the divine self-presentation. God is not "changed into all things" when He becomes present, but just the reverse. Christ's body, which is spirit, turns us into spirit.[14] The same integration and subordination of bodily sense is evident on the receiving end as well. It is the spiritual eating (believing) that makes the bodily eating useful. The heart alone knows what the mouth eats.[15] The spirit, Luther says, consists in use, not in object. And yet the spirit cannot be present except in material, outward, physical things.[16]

To summarize our results to this point:

In contrast to the Roman view Luther sees Christ as already present everywhere in the world, but hidden. The Word then functions to reveal that presence in a certain place, in the Sacrament, and for a certain time, during the participation in the Supper. In contrast to Zwingli Luther sees the realm of sense as fit for inclusion in the sacramental presence of Christ. Yet the senses are not autonomous, but rather appear as the instruments by which Christ's presence is manifest.

Because of Luther's systematic connection of eucharistic doctrine with Christological doctrine, he saw both the Roman and the Zwinglian views of the Eucharist as opposite Christological heresies. The former, with its notions of the mere "appearance" of bread and wine, was in Luther's eyes Docetic. The latter, with its insistence that Christ was not "really," physically there, appeared to him as Ebionite. Both errors happen because of the same assumption: that the divine and the human cannot coexist in the same place in the same way at the same time. Against this assumption Luther raised his Christological banner: *finitum capax infiniti.* We must therefore now turn to an examination of his Christology in order to give his doctrine of the real presence its sure foundation.

2

A Higher Union

While suggestions of a notion of ubiquity may occur earlier, the first explicit passages do not come before the 1525 tract *Against the Heavenly Prophets,* where the subject is introduced in connection with the theme of the two realms.[17] In the *Sermon on the Sacrament— Against the Fanatics,* of the following year, the idea is even more in evidence, although still lacking the subtlety that will characterize Luther's developed view.[18] It is in *That These Words of Christ . . . Still Stand Firm Against the Fanatics* of 1527 that Luther achieves, in nearly syllogistic form, the bare bones of his complete idea: (1) Christ's body is at the "right hand" of God; (2) the "right hand" or power of God is everywhere; (3) therefore Christ's body is everywhere, and *a fortiori* may be in the bread and wine.[19]

In this treatise Luther is quite clear about the function of his argument, and we will do well to remember it. The task is negative: to prove that ubiquity is not impossible or not inconsistent with Scripture and creed.[20] The *Confession Concerning Christ's Supper* of the following year shows Luther continuing the negatively defended argument, augmenting it with speculative images borrowed from the mystical tradition.[21]

Since Luther sees his task as negative (although he will argue occasionally that ubiquity and the modal presences are indeed Scriptural[22]), and since he knows he is engaging in non-Scriptural speculation, it is difficult to understand why virtually every commentator on this matter begins by denying any speculative tendency in the exercise.[23] Luther does, of course, superficially reinforce the Kantian prejudices of his later students. As he begins to unleash himself in defense of the Real Presence, the first impression is that there will be no "reasonable" discussion, that Luther is going to trample the mind with the dogmas of faith. The chief doctrines of the faith are of themselves scandalous, rationally impossible.[24] But they are not too high for faith, and it is faith alone which grasps "real presence," the external *obiectum fidei.* Luther's famous shift from the "subjective" to the objective side of the sacramental issue was made necessary because he felt that the "fanatics," applying a commonsense or natural reasoning, could make no sense out of any sort of Real Presence, as we have seen. Luther's task is thus to demonstrate a reasoning, indeed a speculative reasoning that begins from faith and the *nova mens,* whereby

128

the ubiquity of Christ, a position Luther felt was entailed in the assertion of Christ's real presence in the Sacrament, could gain some plausibility. Thus even though the discussion of ubiquity is ultimately beyond natural reason, and even though it is to be construed as a basically soteriological issue, still one can expect reasonable discourse on the subject.

What the Word reveals at the table in the present and presence of faith is a reality that is ubiquitous. The only possible way to give even a jot of meaning to the notion of ubiquity is to identify that reality with God. So far I have spoken of the ubiquity or presence of Christ without specifying it as the ubiquity of His body. The reason for this thematic separation is that there are two different doctrinal positions involved. The ubiquity of Christ's divine nature is based on the Trinitarian doctrine, and is more or less agreed to by all parties. The ubiquity of the human nature is based on the Christological doctrine, and it is here controversy starts. But Luther never discusses the doctrines separately in reference to ubiquity, even though he at least implicitly acknowledges the distinction and the logical priority of the Trinitarian doctrine and divine omnipresence.[25]

At first glance there seems to be no cause for disagreement on the omnipresence of the divine in Christ, based as it is on a doctrine of the Trinity presumably shared by all parties. Christ's *wesen*, which constitutes Him one person with God, is to be seen as transcendent and as immanent as is God. Both God and Christ are always very near, though hidden. But when Luther begins to speak of Christ's *body* as sharing the characteristics of the divine omnipresence, he has, to say the least, stimulated a discussion.

At 37, 56 and 61 of his 1527 work Luther says that apart from Christ there is no God. This dictum, applied in many different arguments throughout his writings, is used here to show the absurdity of localizing Christ's presence "on the right hand." Thus far no objection can be raised. But when Luther says "no God apart from Christ," he always means by "Christ" the realized personal union of divinity with flesh and blood. He who dies for us is not the "disembodied God, but the God unified with humanity."[26] When Luther says that Christ is the beginning, middle, and end of all creatures, that he is very close and active, omnipresent but hidden, he is always describing that which is a realized union, even though this reference is often left unstated. This often only implicit meaning reflects Luther's emphasis in Christology. The unity of the humanity and divinity of Christ is the first of four grounds for ubiquity, and the indivisibility of Christ's person is the basis for the possibility of construing ubiquity in terms of the various modal presences.[27]

At 37, 62 Luther argues that because of the personal unity God's presence in Christ is "something different, higher, and greater" than His presence elsewhere, since in Christ God is present not only *wesenlich* but also "bodily." It is now our task to investigate this higher presence of God as it is expressed in Luther's sacramental theory.

Divine omnipresence assumed, the basis of the ubiquity issue is Luther's approach to Christology. Luther does not begin Christology from a consideration of "nature" and "person" and on that basis discuss Christ's work. As we saw in an earlier essay, the organization is in fact the reverse: the soteriological concern is the way of approach, and the questions of natures and person are defined and answered in terms of the work of Christ. The functional approach reflects Luther's view that knowledge of divine things is to be sought in the incarnate Word, and when Luther says that, he means "Jesus crucified." For such knowledge the humanity of Christ is especially relevant, Luther maintains. Christ pursued and overtook human nature when it was fleeing from Him. He assumes, wraps Himself in the clothing and mask of flesh, and in that flesh takes sin into what is then His own body more deeply than any man could. If Christ loses His humanity in our thinking, faith loses its foundation and we our hope.[28] With this emphasis it could only be expected that Luther would be particularly incensed with the dictum of his opponents, "the flesh is of no avail." Luther's response to this position basically concerns the reception of the Sacrament, and not Christology, narrowly defined, but he does have some things to say directly about Christ's flesh. That flesh is different from ordinary flesh. It is not flesh, but spirit, as we have seen. Where that flesh is does not define its character; it is the same flesh whether in the stomach or at the right hand of God. If Christ's flesh is held to be of no *avail,* it cannot be held to *exist* anywhere. Here again we see Luther developing a functional argument for the presence of Christ's human nature.[29] The functions of "spirit" and "flesh" for the moment aside, the difference of Christ's body from ordinary flesh is not that God is bodily present only in *that* body, but that only there is He present physically *pro me.*[30]

Luther also approaches the question of the divine nature soteriologically. It would be a poor and ineffective Christ in whom only the human nature suffered. All Christ suffers He suffers spiritually and as the true Son of God.[31] As we have seen, Luther can even argue for the existence of the divine nature on the basis of the saving function of Christ.

Luther is convinced that he does not confuse the two natures and destroy the integrity of the divine nature by his emphasis on the personal unity. The unity with God is higher than that togetherness of the divine and the creaturely elsewhere.[32] Again we see Luther developing the functional argument, this time on behalf of the unity of the person. Whatever is undergone by man is undergone by God, and vice versa.[33] But Luther goes further. We have seen some of the ways in which Luther sees the Christological union as "something higher and greater" than the union elsewhere. At 37, 219 he begins another train of thought on this matter. In the person of Christ the humanity is more closely united to the divinity than human body and soul. The divinity and humanity of Christ are *coextensive*. If we do not hold this, we would be

> . . . dividing the person and making the humanity merely a pod *[hülfen]*, indeed, a coat which the divinity put on and off according to the availability of place and space. Thus the physical space would have the power to divide the divine person, although neither angels nor all creation can do so.[34]

What we have here is the recurrence of the idea of the nonextensive character of the object of faith which I discussed in the preceding two essays. Luther goes on immediately to appeal to the nonextensiveness of Christ's bodily presence in order to preclude any crass, localized view of the "extension" of God. In the incarnation we have God *in concreto, in extenso,* but also only *in abscondito.* That Christ's body should be both extensive and nonextensive is to say that His presence is *simul totum* immanent and transcendent. Both characteristics are then exhibited in the speculative images Luther borrows from the tradition. Created reality can be viewed as a crystal, in which Christ is the central spark or *Fünkelein* visible from every point on the surface. Luther can then also develop the image into its opposite form, i.e., of the one experiencing the many, in terms of a facial image multiplying in a shattered mirror.[35]

What I think Luther objected to in the "crude" interpretation of Christ's extensiveness is static, substantialist categories of thought, for which the first or local modal presence had affinity. At 37, 214 Luther does argue that the omnipresence of Christ refers to the essences, not the works, of the natures. But what Luther means by "essence" is far from obvious. Note in our opening quotation from *Jonah* that Luther used *Wesen,* a term otherwise difficult to define, interchangeably with "presence." We are at the point where it is necessary to tackle the matter of what Luther means when he consistently speaks of the union of divinity and humanity in Christ as a *wesenlich, persönlich* presence, and speaks of the divine *Wesen* as "presence" understood in the active sense of omnipresent power. What permits the view that Christ's flesh is literally God's body or His incarnation is Luther's stress on the unity of Christ's natures. To keep from appearing to limit God to the "flesh," Luther introduces his view of the multiple modes of presence. He gives us some general directions for where he is going. We know the relation of God and flesh cannot be viewed in terms of abstract natures. In order to give no occasion to such "static" considerations, Luther even spoke of the natures in terms of their actions or functions. The relation of God and flesh is furthermore a personal one. Thus if we are to develop an understanding of this relation, it seems that "personal," "active," and *wesenlich* should be the standards.

If you say that in Christ God and man are one person, Luther maintains, the "good consequence" is the creedal affirmation of true humanity, true divinity, true personal union.[36] As a "consequence of the good consequence," one must accept not merely a linguistic but in fact a real mutual translation of characteristics defining each nature, or else Christ's unity is mere verbiage. Luther thus resurrects an old linguistic form, the *communicatio idiomatum,* to express his emphasis on the personal unity of Christ. He begins with the work or the personal unity of Christ, and the distinction of natures emerges as a consequence. The distinction is somewhat tentative, as we shall see, and is tightly controlled via the use of *communicatio idiomatum.* In a word, Luther maintains, what you say about the person defines what you must say about the natures.[37] This characteristic way of approach may result in, or be the result of, the fact that Luther does not observe any distinctions of referent within the logic of *communicatio.*

As we have already seen, Luther usually begins his discussion with a consideration of Christ's atoning work. And thus he is very much at home with one form of *communicatio,* wherein both natures could be said to participate in the work of atonement on the basis of Christ's personal unity.[38] The more common usage simply applied *idiomata* of one nature to the other on the basis of the personal union, and Luther, of course, found this form helpful.[39]

But Luther's habit of moving from function to existence, from Christ's work to His person to the two natures, led him into a third and more dogmatically problematic form of the *communicatio.* In this usage[40] what is said to be characteristic of one nature is applied to the other, the personal unity in virtue of which the application is made left unstated. In other hands such a usage could lead to various Alexandrian heresies, but we must remember that since Luther argues from person to natures, the personal unity of Christ remains the basis of the *communicatio.* If there is any monist tendency in Luther, it does not originate from a confusion of the natures but from his unwillingness to begin his discussion anywhere but in terms of the personal unity. It is just because he argues from the personal unity, in which there is a real and not merely verbal interchange, that Luther must on his own canon see a real *communicatio* between the natures.[41]

As noted above Luther does not observe distinctions in his kinds of predication. This lack of distinction is most clearly revealed—and we are thereby presented with an insoluble interpretive problem—when he consistently uses the phrase *wesentlich, persönlich* as a technical description of the divine-human union in Christ.[42] At 37, 230 we have a good example of the problem. Luther says that humanity is not God *wesentlich,* but

> . . . because it reaches up above all creation to the essential God
> and is united with him and is wherever God is, it must be at least
> in person God and thus exist everywhere that God is.

Luther is here clearly pushing the personal unity *(genus idiomaticum)* to a *wesentlich* unity *(genus majestaticum).* Since Luther does move from person to natures, we should be correct to argue that Luther at least tends toward a real unity of natures.[43] We may make this claim, however, only so long as we remember that the essential union is no more than the consequence of the personal union.

3

Something New

Speculation! Off the pens of many students that word seems to connote some obscene act: fornication, masturbation, speculation. If Luther's development toward the third form of *communicatio* in his Christological language betrays a speculative interest, we had better learn to live with it. For he has just begun. We have learned provisionally what is unified in the union of divine and human natures. Luther unifies the personal functions of the natures, and therefore, we may venture, he unifies the two natures themselves. Now the question becomes, how? Luther's answer to this question—and he recognizes that both the question and the answer belong to the realm of speculation—is the "modes" of divine presence.

Luther went to the mystical and humanist tradition for his images, to the "old doctors" for the *communicatio,* and now to the "new doctors" for the modes. For he is drawing on his nominalist background not only for the modes themselves but also for the distinction which makes their discussion possible. It is the distinction between God's "ordinate" and "absolute" power that provides the multiplicity of modal presences, and it is also this distinction that gives Luther's discussion its "bracketed" or provisionally speculative character.[44]

Luther introduces the modal presences at 37, 65 and 214 as the fourth ground of ubiquity.[45] In the first or circumscribed mode, both the space and the occupying object are measurably dimensional, and the occupying object is coextensive with the occupied space. Throughout his discussion Luther ridicules all attempts to view ubiquity in this mode, although, as we shall note below, he substitutes his own speculative answer, one which does not involve "stretching" Christ's body in any crude spatial sense.

In the second or "definitive" mode, the occupied space continues to be dimensional, but the occupying object is not coextensive with it. The object is, however, clearly *there:* it is an uncircumscribed presence in a *certain* place. Luther's presentation seems to suggest that the "place" of the uncircumscribed presence is the locus of its activity or its center of interest. This interpretation is strengthened when we read that it is in this mode that Christ is present in the Supper. As we have seen, only in Word and Sacrament is Christ present *pro nobis* as a saving presence.

In the third or "repletive" mode the object is simultaneously and wholly present in all places. The difference between the second and third mode is that in the latter, presence *here* does not preclude presence *there.* At this point in the discussion Luther says the third modal presence belongs to God alone. Following our comparison, this mode appears parallel to Luther's assertion in *Jonah* that God's natural *Wesen* is omnipresence, as distinct from his spiritual *Wesen,* which is a real presence (second mode) for us in Word and Sacrament.

At 37, 216 however, Luther pushes his thinking into a still more controversial position. He begins by defending the possibility of a second modal presence of Christ's body. He asserts that Christ's body is "outside" the realm of creation, and, in a curiously reversed phrasing, says that it is the creature which is "permeable and present to him" (217). Luther will pick up this phrasing again later. But right now he states his thesis, beginning with an assertion we have encountered before.

> But now, since he is a man who is supernaturally one person with God, and apart from this man there is no God, it must follow that according to the third supernatural mode, he is and can be wherever God is . . . even according to his humanity . . . (218, in part).

If you do not allow bodily presence in the third mode, Luther continues, you rupture the personal unity, leaving a "poor sort of Christ," an "isolated" God and a divine person without the humanity.

Luther then defends his view against misinterpretation according to first mode thinking and develops his position further. Christ's bodily existence is in a much higher union than other forms of union. It is in personal union with the Godhead (221) above and beyond all creatures, as he says at the conclusion of the discourse (229). And now, in the midst of a discussion of God's immanence and transcendence, Luther returns to the phrasing we noted above. So far in our presentation it seems as though the creation were inert, so to speak, and that the difference between the second and third modes was a difference in the way *God* was present: *pro nobis* in the second mode, naturally in the third. But now Luther picks up the reverse phrasing and makes the unity of God and the world more intimate.

> Thirdly, since he is one person with God, the divine, heavenly mode, according to which all created things are indeed much more permeable and *present to him* than they are according to the second mode. . . . This exalted third mode, where they cannot measure or circumscribe him but where *they are present to him so that he measures and circumscribes them.* You must place this existence of Christ, which constitutes him one person with God, far, far beyond things created, as far as God transcends them; and on the other hand, place it as deep in and as near to all created things as God is in them. For he is one indivisible person with God, and wherever God is, he must be also, otherwise our faith [!] is false (223, in part; emphasis mine).

And it is with this reversal, from the presence of Christ to creation to the presence of creation to Christ, that Luther returns to a speculative interpretation of how ubiquity is possible even according to the first mode. Even if Christ's body were present only in a single place, i.e., in heaven, yet "all creatures may be present to him and around him there, like the clear, transparent air" (224). And it is to illustrate this idea that Luther develops the images of the crystal and the broken mirror referred to in earlier sections.

Luther offered the various modal presence as a speculative answer to the question of how something could be said to be omnipresent. We must step back now, however, and ask again, exactly what is it that is omnipresent? And when? and where? and whose? We may return to these questions at this point because Luther's discussion of ubiquity has thrown some light on his otherwise problematic ideas of God's "twofold" *Wesen,* his equation of the *Wesen* with presence, and his description of that presence in Christ as a *wesentlich, persönlich* presence.

Let us begin from Luther's equation in *Jonah* of God's *Wesen* and His presence. This means that there is simply no divine *Wesen,* as yet otherwise unspecified, apart from its presence. We cannot raise the question of God's immanence and transcendence here. To do so is both to gainsay the equation and to construe the issue in terms alien to Luther. As we saw in the above quotation, that which is said to be ubiquitous is equally transcendent and immanent. The matter should rather be understood in terms of God *hidden* and *revealed*. The divine *Wesen*-presence is both hidden and revealed. The distinction is at least in part an epistemological one. If Luther's reversal of phrasing is at all significant, we might interpret it as follows. When he says the creation is "present to God," he might be suggesting the hidden presence of the divine *Wesen*. And when he says that God is "present to the creature," he may be suggesting the revealed presence in Word and Sacrament, in Christ.

Be that as it may, it remains true that God's presence is not *either* hidden *or* revealed, but rather both at once. When Luther consistently uses *wesentlich, persönlich* to describe God's presence in Christ, he may again be suggesting the distinction of hidden and revealed presence. So we might read the phrase as meaning that in Christ God's hidden *Wesen* is revealed personally. This would be correct, if we do not conclude that what is *new* in the relationship of God and the world with the incarnation is God's *personal* presence. According to his canon, Luther insists on saying of the natures what he says of the person. A personal presence of God must be an essential, *wesentlich,* presence—and vice versa. When God is essentially present, He is personally present. At 37, 59 and 63 Luther insists that what the incarnation adds is not the personal presence of God. God is essentially and personally present in all things, and it is only because of this personal omnipresence that His personal presence in Christ can happen. Indeed it would not be going too far to say that the personal union in Christ is only an eminent instance of God's personal presence everywhere.

God's *Wesen* is His presence. God is essentially and personally present in all things, and that presence is both hidden and revealed. We might then interpret the "twofold" presence of God Luther introduced in the *Jonah* passage in this way. God's "natural" omnipresence is His essential, personal presence in its hiddenness; God's "spiritual" omnipresence is His essential, personal presence as revealed in Word, Christ, Sacrament.

Then what is new with the incarnation? Sometimes, in the midst of details, we have trouble finding the elephant. But there it is, right in the very word. Luther's entire discussion of Christology, we recall, is a discussion of *bodily* presence in the *Sacrament*. God may always have been essentially, naturally present, but with the incarnation that presence becomes, thenceforth, a *bodily* presence. God may always have been personally, spiritually present, but with the incarnation, or at least the resurrection, that presence becomes a sacramental presence in the Supper (94). The greatest wonder, Luther says at 59, is God's essential, personal omnipresence, and by comparison His bodily presence in Christ is a "trivial" wonder. It then seems obvious to Luther that, since with Christ God's essential, personal relation to creation is now a bodily relation, this body is, being God's, ubiquitous though hidden. And that it is revealed and of sacramental benefit wherever God's Word opens it to faith. Mutual presence—God present bodily in the person of Christ, man present bodily in the person of faith—this is the "one sacramental reality" of which Luther speaks.

It is thus no linguistic trick to speak of "God's body." At 60, for example, Luther moves easily from a consideration of "Christ's flesh" to the immanent and transcendent omnipresence of "God's body." And at 124 f., speaking of Christ's atoning struggle with the tyrant Death, Luther says of Christ's flesh, "God is in this flesh. It is God's flesh, the Spirit's flesh *[Ein Gotts fleisch, Ein geistfleisch]*. It is in God and God is in it."

Must we take this language in a very restrictive sense and hold that Christ's flesh is *alone* God's body? Yes, but only without the implication that there is something or someplace else where that body is not. For Christ's flesh, being God's, is ubiquitous, coextensive in time and space with the creation. Because of the union of Christ with faith, and the derived canon that one says of faith what is said of Christ and vice versa, Luther argues, somewhat impishly, that the *Christian* is omnipresent (235)! And at 42 Luther, playing the fanatic, argues that *all* bodies are "God's." While this argument is clearly sporting, Luther still feels he is not misinterpreting Scripture. Finally at 89 he says that just as the Word says Christ's body is useful, *so* it says the creation is useful. All I have said in this essay about omnipresence has been taken from what Luther said about ubiquity. Many of the features I have concentrated on still have only a provisional formulation, and thus the following essay must be read as a continuation of the present one. In the last reference we saw Luther generalizing from "Christ" and "body" to "God" and "creation." This direction of thought, so characteristic of Luther, is the reason I have begun the consideration of the relation of God and the world from the locus of ubiquity rather than omnipresence. I must now turn to a consideration of omnipresence, in order not only to make ubiquity itself more understandable, but also in order to bring all the themes introduced in this essay in terms of ubiquity to full expression.

Essay VII: *Larvae Dei*

A Living Temple

The discussion of the ubiquity of Christ's body, however far-ranging, still involved basically only one side of what is expressed by *finitum capax infiniti*. The "one sacramental reality" includes not only the infinite, the ultimate, the presence of God in Christ, but also the finite, the penultimate, the physical elements through which that presence is expressed and signified. In the preceding essay the emphasis was on that which Luther held to be present "in, with, and under" the physical elements. Where is this knowledge to be found? In Christ, accordingly, in the Sacrament. What is there? The ubiquitous body of Christ, ubiquitous because the whole man Christ is in personal union with the omnipresent God. Why is it there? Because it is God's will therein to grant forgiveness of sins to those who receive His body in faith, and thereby to begin in them the recreation of the new creature in works of love.

But what of the physical elements? Are they simply *there*—inert, neutral things which, so to speak, God picks out from among the dead mass of the world and sacralizes for His own use in the Supper? And, by implication, is the rest of the world merely secular, dead to God's activity and devoid of signification concerning His will?

We instinctively reject such a conclusion on simple inspection. If a reason need be given, Luther's insistence that God is personally present and active throughout creation, or that Christ's body is the ubiquitous, living organ of divine agency, should be sufficient indications. More important, however, is Luther's claim that it is in Christ and the Sacrament, and only therein, where we can learn what is, by extension, true of the relation of God and creation generally. If we take Luther at his word, we can anticipate his conclusion: the whole physical world is the living organ of God's will and power. It is His act. But, as in the Sacrament and in Christ, this activity is hidden, revealed only to faith. And similarly only faith discerns the ends to which that activity is directed. Creation as God's activity, as the living embodiment of His power and will—this is what Luther means when he speaks of the *larvae dei.* The object of this essay is to understand that image. In other words, the "in, with, and under" of Luther's sacramental theory now occupies our attention.

At the outset, however, we must avoid the tendency to take Luther's images of the "mask," "covering" *(velamen),* "garment" *(indumentum),* or "wrapping" *(involucrum),* in any static, neutral, or falsely naturalistic sense, as though he were speaking of something merely external to God. As we read near the conclusion of the preceding essay, Luther said that the "flesh" was *in* God, and God in it. More directly, to interpret the *larvae* in any neutral and external sense would be an extension of bad Christology. Luther, of course, could not avoid speaking from time to time of Christ's having "put on" the "garment" of humanity. But he went to great lengths to avoid any implied suggestion of Docetic thinking. As we have seen, the flesh is in a functioning, hence real personal union with the divine in Christ. The same must be true in the more generalized relation of God and the world.

In order to achieve this understanding of the masks, we must begin with what Luther sees is manifest in Christ's work. Once again, we must get past the details to the "elephant." What is manifest in Christ's atoning work is the *will* and the *power* of God. In Christ, therefore, Luther sees God *acting.* In the preceding essay we investigated certain aspects of God's *Wesen* as they emerged from the discussion of ubiquity, God's personal presence in Christ. We must now continue the discussion of God's presence, concentrating on its character as personal. That is, we must follow Luther's understanding of how God's will is manifested in the world, and how His power is efficacious in the world. Only then will we be in a position to see the creation as the living organ, the *larva,* of God's action.

1

Luther always insisted that God and man be considered together: men as they stand before God, God as He is active in men. This canon gives Luther's theology its dialectical character. In the first essay I defined "dialectical" as expressing a sustained contrast between the related terms, "contrast" indicating that there were grounds both of identity and of difference between the members. One of our main concerns, especially in the first part of the study, was to locate the source of this contrast. We concluded that in spite of some appearances it was man rather than God who embodied the doubleness. It was because redeemed man was both with and against God that Luther could formulate the relation of God to man as a dialectical contrast.

And because Luther always insisted that God be viewed not *in se* but *in relatione,* his discourse on God always reflected this contrast. We have seen the contrast applied to and expressed in various subjects throughout the study: flesh and spirit, Law and Gospel, old man and new man, bread and body. As we turn now to a consideration of God's will, and in the next section, of God's power, the contrast again emerges. It emerges in a formulation by which in fact Luther often characterized the relationships in all of our earlier subjects: "hidden and revealed." He did this not only regarding other aspects of God's relationship to the world, but also regarding His will and power. Indeed, this is the basis of all the other formulations: God's will and power is *simul absconditus et revelatus.*

Speculation Again

Luther's books always upset a lot of people, usually for the wrong reasons. This was especially true during the second half of the 1520s. Every time something new came off the Wittenberg presses, it seemed, Luther lost a section of support. It was nothing new, therefore, when Luther's sacramental writings alienated most Swiss, French, and English reformers. For Luther had already published one of the most irritating and provocative volumes of his career, a work, according to some lights, that scandalized and betrayed reasonable men everywhere: *De servo arbitrio.*

Yet the basic thesis of the work was not new, not even for Luther. The inability of the human will, apart from grace, to effectively contribute by its choices to man's salvation, was Luther's published teaching from the beginning. It appears in the first 34 theses of the Wittenberg disputation of the summer of 1517, then in the first 28 theses of the Heidelberg disputation in April, 1518. It was a major theme in the Leipzig debates of 1519, and is fully present in what I take to be the watershed of Luther's early development, the *Assertio omnium articulorum* of November, 1520.[1] *De servo arbitrio,* the work forever identified with the teaching, in some respects unfortunately, is largely a defense of positions worked out earlier. The format was dictated by the less-than-adequate treatise of Erasmus, unwillingly wrung from him by king, pope, colleague and opponent alike. Luther's answering treatise, though highly valued by its author, did not present the mind of the writer in its most natural style.

Even those who accept Luther's basic thesis, however, are troubled by what appear to be speculative ventures of Luther in support of it. One of these exercises, concerning the "necessity of all things," we discussed briefly in the essay on promise and faith.[2] There is another related exercise which is even more problematic, however. This is the matter of the supposed "double will" in God, one will relating to God's intention for man, one relating to God's own internal processes, and occasionally in tension, at least, with his "revealed" will.[3] The key passage is held to be LCC 17, 199-202, and 206. Not at all surprisingly, Luther's subject in this passage is the distinction *deus revelatus* and *deus absconditus*. In it we will meet many of the themes we discussed in the previous essay.

Let us begin with a review. God's attributes are misunderstood as metaphysical or apparent, Luther said, because in fact they are hidden under their opposites. This hiddenness was necessary so that faith would have "room" to "extend" or "exercise" itself, as he put it in *De servo arbitrio*.[4] Faith thereby also gains insight into its relation to the world, for "whatever is from God must be crucified in the world." From this principle not even Christ was excepted; Christ is in fact the best example of it.[5] In this statement we see not only that the opposition of God and the sinful worldly realm is unalterable ("must"), but also that in Christ God is both revealed ("from God") and hidden ("crucified"). Not only is the cross the place where this *unio oppositorum* is revealed with ultimate clarity, but as head of the church Christ is the paradigm for an exactly corresponding *unio* in faith.[6] Just as God's attributes are invisible and unknown to the world, so the object which formally defines faith is invisible. Faith unites the soul with the invisible and separates it from all visible things. And since it is faith which defines the Christian ego, not only is the community of faith hidden from the world and from the individual Christian, but Christians are even hidden from themselves.[7] Faith is never a possession whose value one can himself count up. Works of love are hidden in flesh and in sin. Surety rests in Christ and not in man, Christian or otherwise.

We have thus come on two themes: God in His hiddenness revealed only to faith, faith in its hiddenness known only to God. The second theme will be important for section three and for the concluding essay. For now the first governs our attention.

At LCC 17, 200 Luther opens the discussion which leads some students to claim he taught two wills in God. Luther does not, at least in this passage, teach double election. The issue is furthermore developed not as a *premise* but as an *inference* from the obvious fact that some people are touched by Law and grace and some are not. The "hidden, dreadful will of God" is not said to be the source for election to hell or even for double election, but only for election to salvation (200). Luther goes on to say we must discuss God revealed in one way, God hidden in another (200 f.). At this locus at least he means that theology does not discuss God hidden at all.[8] We have here then a distinction which is exactly parallel to that I discussed relative to ubiquity in the preceding essay. God is in everything according to His nature, but not *pro nobis* in everything. He is only there for us where His Word locates Him, namely, in Christ. It is there where it is "clothed and displayed" to us[9] (201).

Then Luther continues, implicitly assuming the distinction *potentiae absoluta et ordinata dei*. The former power is expressed in terms of God hidden in Himself, the latter in terms of God revealed in His Word. And now comes the supposed tension: God in His hidden will wills the death of the sinner, and in His Word He does not (201). But Luther immediately adds a disclaimer: of the hidden will, and thus of the apparent contradiction in God, nothing can be said theologically (201 f.). Apart from God's revealed will for creation and man there is only the naked divine essence, to ponder which is to be consumed. Rather we are to occupy ourselves with the God incarnate (206) who weeps over the secret will of majesty to reprobate some (206 f.). Faith does not live from this secret will, but from the incarnate, revealed, personal Word of promise (207).

Having duly acknowledged this characteristically Lutheran prohibition of speculation and appeal to exclusive concern with God's revealed will in Christ, the student is tempted to drop the subject with what is thus only a statement of the problem and not a solution. But by this point in the study it should not come as a surprise that Luther proceeds with an attempt at a reasonable, even speculative explanation.

The problem as seen by the student of Luther is that his positing of a hidden will in God, unrelated to man's salvation and unavailable as a topic of discourse for Christian thought, seems at odds with his whole evangelical approach. Let us see whether this construction of the problem is correct, and if so, whether it is justified.

The "hidden will" of God, whatever else it is, is in the first place not a supplement, drawn from some other source, to what Luther knows about God from His revealed will. It is important to note that the issue comes up in the context of a *speculative* question concerning God's *actual* dealings with man: why some are touched by the Law and thus led to grace, and others not touched by it (200). In this passive way Luther introduces the distinction of the preached and offered *mercy* of God from the hidden will whereby He ordains some to *receive* this mercy (200). We are thus still wholly within the confines of God's saving activity. But at this point Luther raises Erasmus' question about evil and the problem of God's goodness. And Luther repeats—almost: we talk of the preached *will* of God one way, about God (not "God's will") not preached in another. The most he says is that God may "will to be unknown" (200 f.). Then he pushes further, in the key passage.

> But we have something to do with him insofar as he is clothed and set forth in his Word . . . . In this regard we say, the good God does not deplore the death of his people which he *works* in them, but he deplores the death which he *finds* in his people and desires to remove from them. For it is this that *God as he is preached* is concerned with, namely, that sin and death should be taken away and we should be saved. . . . But *God hidden in his majesty* neither deplores nor takes away death, but works life, death, and all in all. For there he has *not bound himself by his word*, but has *kept himself free over all things.*
>
> Diatribe, however, deceives herself in her ignorance by not making any distinction between *God preached* and *God hidden*, that is, between the *word of God* and *God himself*. . . Thus he does not will the death of a sinner, according to his *word;* but he wills it according to that *inscrutable will* of his (201 in part; emphases mine).

This is as far as Luther goes here. Note that the doubleness of which Luther speaks is a doubleness of God as He is clothed in His Word, as He relates to man. Not once in the phrases emphasized does Luther establish two distinct wills, much less an opposition between them. It is not that God has one hidden will and another revealed will. Rather God's will is both hidden and revealed. The preached Word reveals that God in His mercy wills to save us from sin and death. This is the Gospel: it reveals grace and mercy. But as we saw in the essay on Law and faith, the Gospel also thereby reveals the Law and the wrath from which we are graciously and mercifully saved. And thus faith sees that in the Word there is revealed under the veil of Law and wrath the hidden grace and mercy which is veiled apart from the Word. Only in the Word, and to faith, therefore, is God's will both hidden and revealed. Apart from that Word God's will is simply hidden. Luther is willing to speculate about it, but only on the basis of what is revealed in the Word about the general relationship of God and the world apart from His grace. Now God is unveiled, appearing simply in all His righteousness, transcendent freedom and power, remorselessly and justly working in all things; working the death that He willed consequent upon sin.

All this Luther has said about the *good* God, however. And he has not relieved the intellectual and moral pressure against this affirmation. In fact his discussion has increased it. At the beginning he put the world apart from grace in the passive voice: some men "are not touched." But as Luther began to speak of God's omnipresent active power, this formulation proves insufficient. When the matter of the "secret will" comes up again (206), Luther says those who do not receive Christ are purposely abandoned or hardened and reprobated by the secret will of the divine majesty. The "hardening" of Pharaoh (Ex. 4:21) then becomes the critical case. And it is on this matter that Luther, pitting God's will against the fact of evil, develops his speculative solution further: God is active power, immanent in a world which is His instrument, His evil mask.

The Diatribe robs God of His power of election, Luther begins (228), and so turns Him into the false idol Chance. Like Aristotle, the Diatribe creates a Deist philosophy in which God exercises no wisdom, will, or "present power." The same theme closes the discourse (236). Why does God not cease from His active omnipotence? Because that would mean God would cease to be God; if He ceases His power and activity, He ceases to be good.

Set within these terms comes Luther's speculative answer to the question of how the good God can be said to work evil (232 ff.). It reflects a simple acknowledgement of the fact of evil, combined with a completely active definition of God's omnipotence. Evil is located in the will; but it is the will of the *fallen creature,* turned in on itself, that is the subject, not God's will. Concerning God, Luther only speaks of *omnipotence.* God's power is incessantly active in every creature. If the creature is an evil instrument, its will curved in on itself, the resulting "hardening" is due to the instrument, not the power moving it. God exploits the self-destructiveness He finds. In sum, God cannot alter His omnipotence on account of evil, the evil instrument cannot alter its incurvedness, and thus hardening is incessant and evil inevitable.

Yet even now, Luther continues (237 f), the evil result is, behind the veil, shown to be good. If only one could see through to it. And the hardening of Pharaoh is shown, in God's Word and to faith, as a demonstration of God's willingness and ability to accomplish His promise of mercy in His people. And thus even God's "secret will" is revealed, when it is revealed, only in relation to salvation.

God's good will is hidden—under its *opposite.* To be able to say this implies, of course, that God's good will is also *revealed* under its opposite. *That* is the whole point of including the fallen world, sinful man, the tyrants, and the devil as masks of God, instruments of his power. Luther asserts here, as he does elsewhere, that God can order the devil, His servant and mask, to tempt man.[10] God and the devil in fact wear each other's mask. God wants to be recognized under the devil's mask, and wants the devil condemned under the

144

mask of God.[11] The source of temptation is thus always ambiguous: "white Devil"? or, perhaps, "black God"?

The only thing faith can do in this situation—and it must do it—is to "pierce on through and appeal against God to God."[12] This quotation comes from the year following the publication of *De servo arbitrio,* in the commentary on *Jonah* containing the statement about the "twofold" *Wesen* or presence of God. What are the referents of "God" in *"widder Gott zu Gott"?* Clearly, in this context, the appeal is from the God who is masked in His wrath, in the devil, to the God of mercy, to the heart of God as it is both masked and unmasked in Christ.

By approaching the issue of God's attributes in terms of the questions of divine goodness and the evil instruments through which God's power and will work, we have gained another important characteristic of Luther's doctrine of God's presence in the world. Luther did not even attempt to resolve the mystery of divine election in *De servo arbitrio.* So just forget about *that* matter. But he was willing to speak about God's will apart from the Word in 1525, about God's *Wesen* apart from the Word in 1526, and about Christ's body apart from the Word in 1527—8. In every instance, however, that which is discussed is never theologically neutral. Because the world is corrupt, God apart from Word and faith appears malevolent. Thus God in the hiddenness of His will works evil. God's natural *Wesen* is a tyrant hounding Jonah around the earth. And Christ's body, apart from its reception in faith, is eaten to death and destruction.

On each subject Luther has developed a speculative exercise. From the viewpoint of redeemed man the relationship of God and the world is a contrast, one side enmity, the other reconciliation. The grounds for the enmity lie in the evil world. And so Luther speculates, abstracts from the contrast, developing only one side of what to faith is really two-sided. The consequence is not a very pleasant sight. It is hell, a moral and intellectual scandal, a consuming fire. But that is what you get into, Luther says, when you wander away from God clothed in His Word. Forewarned is forearmed.

2

Misplaced Concreteness

When Luther was discussing the masks in connection with evil, a subtle shift took place in the referents of "power" and "will." The objection raised by Erasmus was that, if *man* has no *power, God's will* must in part be malevolent. But as Luther responded with his speculative solution, the subjects became transposed: *God's power* works through *man's evil will.* It is man's will that is evil; and it is God who has power.

This transposition of subjects gives us a new insight into the function of the masks. We heard Luther say that it was fatal to look at God apart from His Word. Why is the mask necessary, after all? Is it that God is *really* an all-consuming fire, but is made to *appear* loving and merciful in the mask of His Word? It cannot be. For Luther insisted that Law, wrath, and the devil were the outward masks of God, and that God's "heart," as revealed in Christ, was pure love and mercy.

If God appears evil in the mask, it is because the mask reveals *human* evil. It is human nature, Luther says, that is too depraved to see God without a cover. God must reveal Himself under a veil if sinful men are to know Him at all.[13] The veil belongs to creation, and when man carried himself and the rest of creation into sin, the veil could not but corrupt and distort what it revealed. What is God's mandate in creation becomes God's Law in the Fall. The mandate directed man in God's will; the Law convicts him of sin. Sinful man could not bear such a naked vision of God's righteousness, however, and so that revelation is masked in the voice of Moses and the commandments.[14] But in this necessary mask the Law increases sin. For sinful man, trapped in his flesh and without the spirit, can only see the flesh, the letter, and not the spirit, the intent, of the Law. He assumes the Law concerns civic morality, but he is constantly driven back *coram deo,* the impossible demands of the Law leading him finally into terror of conscience, despair of himself and hatred of God.

There is only one way to get past this deceptive, destructive veil. One must look beyond the Law to Christ and the Gospel, to God clothed in the joyful and reassuring mask of His promising Word. *Christ* is the mediator. He is not only the pleasant mask of God, but has embodied Himself in the mask of sinful flesh in order to fulfill the demands of the naked Law. Thus the *Christian* lives constantly under the "curtain" of Christ's flesh.[15] That curtain or garment is Baptism. If we depart from it, we once again enter a spaceless, timeless void, a nothing. We once again find ourselves before the naked, outraged essence of God.[16]

So it is that Luther, in *De servo arbitrio,* directs our inquiry concerning good and evil wills to its proper locus of discussion: God's self-revelation in Christ. It is there we find our own assessments inverted, or rather reestablished in their true valuation: God's will is good, man's evil. But the inquiry concerning the character of will is in fact inseparably bound up with the inquiry concerning the status of power. In *De servo arbitrio* Luther, as we saw, construes the issue of the moral freedom of the will in terms of the actual efficacy of power. In fact, he says throughout the text, any consideration of wills, God's or man's, that is not founded on an assessment of powers, God's and man's, is an empty, specious verbal exercise in compounded error. And Christ reveals not only God's will as alone good, but also God's power as alone efficacious.

Let us then turn to a consideration of power. Once again we will recognize familiar themes in a new form and application.

Power Politics

As we have seen in earlier essays, Luther's religion begins, as he put it, at the bottom. His approach to the knowledge of Christ is a functional approach. Christ's attributes are seen in terms of His works in His people.

> Christ's reign consists in truth, righteousness, equity, peace, and wisdom, not because He alone is these things, but because through Him His faithful are also true, just, equitable, peaceful and wise.[17]

Christ's divinity is "proved" by considering His saving activity: no mere man, but only a god, could do what Christ did. And thus Luther not only sees the relationship of man to Christ in terms of efficacious power, but sees Christ's relationship to God in the same way. Christ is the only sure place for a true knowledge of God because only in Christ do we see God's will manifested in act and power. One of Luther's key evangelical breakthroughs was the discovery that God's attributes must be seen as "his works in his people." God's righteousness is not that wherein He is *in se* righteous, but that whereby He makes us righteous. The same holds for all the divine attributes. Many things could be mentioned as having prepared Luther for this shift in approach, but I think the key was his exposure to the Hebrew language and the mode of thinking it expresses. At the end of *De servo arbitrio* Luther clearly indicates the importance of the change in language for his approach to discourse about God.[18]

It is this functional, one might say operational understanding of God that defines the issues of *De servo arbitrio*. If one is ignorant of God's works and powers, Luther says, he is ignorant of God.[19] As with the other attributes, so with God's power: it is not that whereby God is powerful in Himself, but that whereby He empowers us. And we are, therefore, apart from God's active power, merely passive, of no power. It is because Luther always defines God in relation to man that God's power must be defined in relation to man's power. When the relationship is discussed on its disjunctive side, that is, God in relation to sinful men, the issue is formulated in terms of *competitive* power. This feature is already clearly evident in the *Romans* commentary. The power of God is distinguished from the power of man, the latter annulled on the cross in order that God may give us His power, which works by the spirit and not the flesh. Luther goes on to formulate the competitive aspect even more sharply: human symbols of power, or at least the desire for them, must be destroyed or else God's power will not be in us.[20]

We can take this statement as the programme for the development of Luther's teaching in *De servo arbitrio*. As we have seen, Luther from the beginning of his treatise insists that the question is not really the existence of free choice, but rather its power to influence salvation.[21] Human power is a contradiction to divine power. You therefore cannot logically (theologically!) affirm that both God and man have power. To retreat and say, as does Erasmus, that human power is ineffective, is nonsense. "Ineffective power" is a contradiction in terms; it is no power at all.[22] An effective *free will*, then, can only be predicated of God.[23] And this means that human "free" will, because ineffective, is no free will at all. If on the other hand you predicate free will of man in regard to salvation, you rob God of His elective wisdom and power, and He is no longer God.[24] Luther must see the powers of God and man in this mutually exclusive way because he defines power, like everything else, as an *act*. And God's omnipotence, Luther says, must be understood as the active power by which He works all in all.[25]

It would be a very interesting pursuit, but one which we cannot make here, to investigate the extent to which Luther associates power more closely with the essence of divinity than either love or justice.[26] The question is relevant in our connection because Luther never speaks of God's power as though it were just another attribute. The relational character of his theology insures that divine power will always be understood as it affects man, i.e., as present and active power. On the other side of the relation, Luther involves power as intimately with the divine essence as he does with creation. This insures that power will always be understood as omnipotence. Early in the 1527 treatise on the Sacrament, Luther achieved the identification of power and the divine nature. Luther's opponents had dissociated divine power from the divine nature, insisting that the latter could be in one locus while the former was omnipresent. In *De servo arbitrio* Luther's argument was that if you remove God's active power, you remove God. Here we have the other side: wherever God's active power is, there is God. Luther's response is quite clear.

> We know, however, that God's power, arm, hand, nature, face,
> Spirit, wisdom, etc., are all one thing; for apart from the creation

there is nothing but the one simple Deity himself. And thus, if before the creation of the universe there doubtless existed *the power and hand of God, God's nature itself,* then it did not become something else after the creation of the universe.

Luther continues, associating the second and third persons of the Trinity with the divine *Wesen*-power.

Indeed, he makes and does nothing except through *his Word,* . . . *i.e., his power.* And his power is not an ax . . . with which he works, but *is himself.* Then if *his power and Spirit* are present everywhere . . . then his divine right hand, nature, and majesty must also be everywhere.[27]

Luther thus uses the term "power" to designate the divine *Wesen.* As we saw in the *Jonah* commentary, Luther had used the term "presence" interchangeably with *Wesen.* It is because God's essence is His presence that God's power, His essence, must also be seen as presence. Omnipotence is omnipresence, and vice versa. But we saw that God's presence was "twofold." God's "natural" presence was hidden, His "spiritual" presence was both hidden and revealed in the Word. An exactly parallel formulation obtains with respect to God's power. It is a transcendent power, hidden from the world. And it is an immanent power, both hidden and revealed in the Word. "Power" and "presence" are not, therefore, two different subjects; the locus for theological discourse on them is the same. It is Christ who is the revelation of the power and presence of God. God's efficacious presence in Christ and the Sacrament is possible, we recall, only because of God's efficacious presence throughout creation. And it is only on the basis of what we know about the relationship of Christ and the sacramental elements that we can generalize to the relationship of God and creation.

It is Christ the Word, the *involucrum* of God, who provides to the new creature a way of entrance into the knowledge of God present and active in the *larvae* of creation. In Christ we do not have a knowledge of God different from that given in creation, but rather in Christ we have a clarification of creation.[28] Creation then is a medium for God's self-disclosure. It is His sacrament, His body.[29] Since the creatures are of God, Luther agrees that it is possible to reason discursively from creature to Creator. Speculation again, and in the *Galatians* commentary of all places! But speculation that is carefully qualified and applied. For Luther goes on to argue that the ground for such discourse is not the mask but that which the mask bears: God's "ordinance," His will, Word, or mandate in the creature.[30]

By concentrating on the Word in the mask rather than the mask itself, Luther insists, we also avoid a misapplication of inferential reasoning. In his commentary on Genesis Luther criticized the old doctors for their bad habit of arguing "from natural effects to supernatural."[31] The difficulty as he saw it was that the doctors began by assessing immanent cause-effect relationships, then abstracted and transposed their conclusions to the relationship between God and the world. Whatever may have been well- or ill-said concerning God, Luther insisted there was a bad misunderstanding of creation. As he had said already in the *Romans* commentary, we will be the best philosophers of nature if we drop the habit of considering creation *in se* and see it instead from the beginning exclusively in relation to God. We go wrong from the start when, restricting ourselves to the immanent order, we speak of the creature as "cause." Luther begins, not with what we might call the "horizontal causal" relationships within the immanent order, but with the "vertical dependence" relationship between the transcendent Creator and the creature in which He is immanent. There is no purely immanent order, therefore, if we mean to connote by "immanent" relationships that are in some, even in severely qualified senses, autonomous. Nothing in creation can then be considered a "cause." The existence of and relationships among creatures are the immediate effects of God's active, present power and will. And that will and power, as we have seen throughout Part Three, are not bound by the world. In fact it is the world which is bound to God's purposes. It is the instrument of His power, the *larva* of His will. It is His Word.

Instead of a delicately adjusted schema of transcendent and immanent causation, therefore, we get in Luther a discussion of God's omnipresent power hidden and revealed in a creation which is wholly and in every part immediately dependent on Him.

All life is in God, Luther says. Life is a good *creature* of God.[32] But to be a creature means to be wholly dependent. The difference between Creator and creature is just that: only God creates.[33] And this means He creates *ex nihilo.* Here is one reason why we cannot argue "from natural effects." Every new being is a new creation *ex nihilo,* or as Luther puts it in a beautifully trinitarian passage reminiscent of Augustine, a new creation out of the "nothings" of non-being, falsehood, and evil.[34] Creation is continuous, so continuously a *nova creatio ex nihilo* that in order to preclude deistic viewpoints Luther almost defines creation in terms of preservation.[35] God's power is within the world, ceaselessly ordering, sustaining, and recreating the creation according to His will. In the German Bible Luther gave his strongest expression of the immediacy of God's power. There is no axle, pin, rack, strap, or trace that God in His spirit does not drive from within. Yet Luther continues: the firmament is the saddle cloth, over it is the saddle, God's throne, and on the throne sits Christ.[36]

In the midst of a statement of what we take to be God's radical immanence, a statement of His radical transcendence! Something else is working here, something which the distinction "transcendent-immanent" does not adequately express by itself. The distinction is too amenable to the crudities of "first mode" thinking.

> But this is not the way we speak. We say that God is no such extended, long, broad, thick, high, deep being. He is a supernatural, inscrutable being who exists *at the same time* in every little seed, *whole and entire,* and yet also in all and above all and outside all created things. There is no need to enclose him here . . . for a body is much, much too wide for the Godhead; it could contain many thousand Godheads. On the other hand, it is also far, far too narrow to contain one Godhead. Nothing is so small but God is still smaller, nothing so large but God is still larger. . . . He is an inexpressible being, above and beyond all that can be described or imagined. . . . But here, where we are dealing not with body but spirit—indeed, who knows what this is that we call God? He is above body, above spirit, above everything man can say or hear or think: how *at one and the same time* can such a being be *completely and entirely present* in every single body, every creature and object everywhere, and on the other hand, must and can be *nowhere,* beyond and above all creatures and objects, as our Creed and the Scriptures confess both truths about God? Here reason must conclude without further ado: Oh, surely this is utter nonsense and can be nothing but nonsense.[37]

These passages, so representative of Luther's speculative thinking, occur in his arguments for the ubiquity of Christ. In the maddening but expected oscillation of his logic, Luther treats God's omnipresence in creation now as the premise for, now as the conclusion from, Christ's ubiquity in the Sacrament. Notice how the "immanent-transcendent" issues which appear in speculative reasoning about God and creation are transformed when developed in connection with Christ and the Sacrament. In the former case one has the task of discovering where, along the "great chain of being," to make the slash between God's immanence/ and his /transcendence. To put it most crudely, the issue was how much of God is in how much of the causal nexus?

From the Christological and sacramental concern, Luther brings forward the perspectives which represent the experience of faith and are therefore a scandal to reason. In place of the *partim* language of reason we get the *simul* language of faith. God is *at once*—and here comes the scandal—*wholly* immanent and *wholly* transcendent, the emphasis falling on God's immanence, as in the above text. The force of the Christological and sacramental concerns not only provides this emphasis on immanence, but also begins to change the formulation to which *simul* is applied. For what might begin as a discussion of God's *being* as transcendent and immanent is continued as a discussion of God's *presence:* God is at once both wholly *there,* and also not there. And because what is manifest about God in Christ and in Sacrament is manifest only to faith, Luther will go on to transpose further, changing what in other hands might be an ontological statement into an epistemological one. "God both wholly there and not there" becomes "God both revealed and hidden."

We are back to the eternal problem for Christian theologians: how to proceed, given the twin centers of gravity, God and Christ. As we have developed the problem in this section, there is, at one locus, God's being as it is both transcendent of and immanent in creation. At the other locus, Christ as the embodiment of God's presence, both hidden and revealed in the Sacrament. Though he can work the other way, Luther prefers to keep his discourse located in Christ. This is the only way, to his mind, that faith can be distinguished from reason, the only way it can gain sure truth. God is both wholly revealed and wholly hidden in Christ. Wholly hidden, otherwise unredeemed reason could by itself gain saving knowledge of God, faith thereby becoming a second-rate or at best supplemental mode. Wholly revealed, otherwise faith has no ultimate confidence, no ultimate truth, and Christ loses His place as the final and complete revelation of God to men.

Only on the sure and exclusive basis of Christ and faith can one then proceed with any theological skill to speak about God and creation. The new creature sees creation in terms of God's self-revelation in Christ, i.e., as a sign of His promise of salvation and restoration. And the new creature sees not only that God uses creation to accomplish salvation for man, but also he himself is to be a cooperating instrument of God's saving will for the creation. Everything created is thus a Word of God. The creature, the mask, cannot be taken as something in and for itself, *incurvatus in se.* It must be seen as the living vehicle for the divine Word, the means for God's *egressus ad nos,* and thereby also the means for our *ingressus in deum.* The Christian sees God's power and will in the mask of creation, but only in Christ does he know how to distinguish the worldly mask from the divine Word it bears. Christ, the personal union of Creator and creature, is the paradigm. The perfect *larva dei,* and thus the ground for understanding how to distinguish God from the mask. Distinguishing God's will in and from the mask is in fact the chief mandate of Christian life and faith. It is to the creation as mandate that we now turn our attention.

3

The Royal Road

Luther just didn't relate very much to the issues in the Book of Job. In that book the chief issue is God's *absence* and how one gets sucked into filling that vacuum with bad theological systems. Luther felt very much at home with the Book of Jonah, however. There the issue is God's *presence* and the tragicomic lengths one will go to in order to escape the pressure of that presence. God's presence was the eminent fact of Luther's religious experience, and of all his discourse about God. It is because of this fact that our characterizations of God's power as "immanent and transcendent" or of His will as "internal and external" are at best provisional. There is, of course, a doubleness about God's relation to the world, but these distinctions not only cut the cake the wrong way, but also violate Luther's guiding theological canon. God must always be considered only in relation to man. But these distinctions suggest there are senses in which God is free from the world, balanced by senses in which He is said to be related to the world.

For Luther, as we have seen, there is a much better language for expressing *the fact* about God - His presence - in its doubleness. That linguistic form is the distinction "hidden and revealed." And Luther will always try to express the prior distinctions in these terms. God is completely free from the world because His presence is wholly hidden. God is completely related to the world because His presence is wholly revealed. It is only with this kind of language that one can avoid the "quantitative" or "first mode" thinking so near at hand in alternate formulations. And this is also why Luther used the metaphors of *larva, velamen,* and so on, to describe that in which God is present. Just like the "symbol" in the Tillichian meaning, the *larva* both does and does not participate in its *res*. It hides what it reveals.

Outside the theological circle of faith, only one side of the contrast appears. God's power is ruthlessly neutral, His will inscrutable. For men of whom it can be said merely that they are sinners, God in His righteousness can become the idol Chance or Fortune. But Luther insists that God must be seen from within the circle of faith, among men of whom it is said that they are both sinners and saved. Only here does the conjunctive side of the contrast appear to complement the disjunctive side. Only here can we speak of *larvae dei.* Now God appears in His mercy, His power a normative, directive, facilitating power, His will guiding man His *cooperator* in works of love. Such an emphasis means that God cannot become the idol Fate or Necessity.

This is the "royal road" of which Luther speaks in the *Romans* commentary and elsewhere. Neither the despair of a wrongly placed sense of human bondage, nor the confidence borne of a wrongly placed sense of human freedom. On the one side, God as a motor, the world as an inflexible machine. On the other, God a thrower of dice, the world a table of statistical odds. In Christ, God as loving Father, the world a *larva dei*, the living organ of His saving will and power. Only the Christian knows wherein his freedom lies, where he must become responsible, not despairing. Only the Christian knows where that freedom ends, where he gives himself up, not to unconcern but to trust. The Christian life is a process, ever new, of discovering the distinction between God and man, between the Word and the work. It is because God reveals Himself only under *larvae* that faith is mandated to make the distinctions; and it is to the *larvae* that the consequent decisions are applied.

Both Sides Now

God always gives corporal signs where He is to be found, such as the water, the bread, the wine of the sacraments. God always presents Himself ("presents himself"—that is an excellent way of putting it!), presents Himself in corporal signs, eminently in Christ, but also everywhere else all the time, veiled in His Word of promise. The sign or *larva* is not, however, to be identified with its contents. It is an ambiguous sign because it belongs to the world which is fallen, *incurvatus in se.* The sign is necessary for us creatures of sense, because we also participate in this fallenness. Only the new creature, in whom spirit is not identical with flesh, is capable on that account of making the necessary distinction between the external sign perceived by the eye and the spiritual content perceived by the heart. Only the new creature, therefore, is able to assess correctly the presence of God in the creation without identifying the creation with God, thereby making idols of both.

Bread and wine are *larvae dei.* As such they indicate that wherever God works, He works in love. The Sacrament as a sign of the activity of God is different in referent than the mere words that accompany its administration. The latter have no reference beyond their immediate meaning.[38] But the sacramental sign refers beyond itself, not only to the gift of God's self-realization in Christ, but also to the Christian's task of realizing God's activity in creation. Our whole life is to be a baptism, a kind of sacrament or sign which we fulfill, realize, by faith. Yet we must understand that this process of realization is not a movement from appearance to reality, but rather from the human experience of reality to God's reality.

The creature, says Luther, is the material out of which God shapes His own glorious future.[39] Since the new creature lives out of his future as the work of God's hands, one must be quite careful in the status or valuation he gives to human activity. The most natural activities of the creature are *in* the nature of the creature, but their *source* is the Holy Spirit. Nature is thus the place, the instrument, but not the origin, of the activity.[40] Only when the creature is conceptually held in this status can it be kept penultimate and not made falsely ultimate. But the result of this strictly subordinate valuation is that the new creature cannot be distinguished, publicly or privately, from the rest of the fallen world. If the creature is only the instrument and not the source of reconciliation, then there are simply no grounds in the creature for distinguishing it as a special place or form of divine agency. While the Christian could not be more different from others, Luther says, according to appearances he is indistinguishable from others. The new creature is a man without name, species, difference.[41] Bread remains bread, whether it nourishes the body or the soul; flesh remains flesh, whether it belongs to the old man or the new man. Only faith knows where and when the Word becomes flesh; only God knows where and when flesh becomes Word. The hiddenness can be expressed, therefore, from both sides of the relationship between God and man. Only faith can speak of *larvae,* and something becomes a *larva* only when it acts for God.[42]

All human powers, says Luther, are thus *larvae dei,* where they are controlled by faith and the Word of God.[43] Whether these powers are operative in the religious, social, or political spheres, they are *orders* established by God for the realization of His purposes. The *estates* are, of course, rooted in natural fact, but even so the interrelationships of men, indeed their very existence, are concrete expressions of God *mandates.*[44] These orders are orders of preservation. They are the means whereby God sustains and orders His creation, and are therefore mandates given to men, directing them in the same task. All these *stations*[45] are therefore creatures of God, sacramental forms for the directive Word. Since the orders have been established by God, they are masks which must be respected though not divinized. God has ordained rank in the worldly realm. *Coram mundo,* therefore, respect must be maintained for the grades of order, lest confusion and chaos result, God's preservation of creation threatened. *Coram deo,* or theologically, however, differential rank is not to obtain: before

God all is equal.[46] Holiness and salvation are two different things, Luther says. The orders, including faith, are not means of salvation. Only Christ saves. But they are means for becoming holy, for becoming God's means for realizing His purposes.[47]

It is just at this point that there emerges the same danger we encountered in the essay on the new creature: mistaking the New Testament directives as Law. The orders would once again be mistaken as ultimate, would cease to be "creatures of God," if they were taken as laws or requirements rather than as mandates, directives. Above all orders, Luther says, stands Christian love.[48] The natural law, the written Law, and the "Law" of the Gospel do not differ in content. They all come together in love. Each mask is an embodied mandate, a creature of God, whether it be in natural or written form. It is not a human principle. Only expressed in concrete form, as mandate, is Law useful to the new creature. But there is no absoluteness about it. The mandates, since they have only concrete existence, change as the context changes, as God's "hour" is manifest with its own exegencies. One may be mandated to give the cup of water in one "hour," to withhold it in the next. To make the mandate into a general principle is precisely to deny the creaturely status God gives the mandate. Only the love that is above Law knows what it is to do where and when. Christian action is not action in time, but in eternity, in God's own "hour," and the action is God's own action. It is at once both bound and free: free from the abstract rules of law, bound to God's concrete act. Often enough the mandated act is the opposite of what man would judge is needed or just. Luther can define "inequity" as failing obligations in the name of what seems right, and "equity" as fulfilling obligations regardless of what seems right.[49] The "right of private judgment," it has been argued, is a pretty fair translation of what Luther meant by "original sin"! What fulfills the mandate is not your best ethical judgment, but faith. As we can now reemphasize, faith is not primarily intellectual assent, but an act of commitment. Commitment is not, of course, the reason or goal of faith's act. Faith's act, its existence, is its becoming conformed to Christ. It is faith which is obedient to God's Word. It is in fact nothing else than the obedience of the spirit, and the most telling opposition to faith is disobedience.[50] Belief and action are not identical, of course. *Coram deo* belief is receptive, and the believer does not say, "What must I do to be saved?" But in the present context the subject is God's mandate to faith for the fallen world. The Christian's relation to the world is conditioned by his relation to God. He is not two consciences, two persons. That is precisely the wrong way to distinguish the realms, the consequence being an unavoidable schizophrenia of divine ordinance and Christian ego. *Coram deo,* only faith and not action is the appropriate response to God's gift. *Coram mundo,* which also means *coram deo* when God's task is before us, it is true, to borrow a theme from Bonhoeffer, that only he who is obedient believes, and only he who believes is obedient.

But how then is the distinction to be made? Luther says that God's work in creation is to lead to the fear and praise and worship of God.[51] There is correspondingly a *bodily* command in the *Third* Commandment: We must drop everything and betake our bodies to the place where the Word can be heard.[52] The civil mandates are bodily and have a purpose for the spirit; the religious mandate is spiritual and involves a bodily command! The Christian is flesh and spirit. As flesh and spirit have mutually influential functions in the reception of God's gift of Himself in the Sacrament, so flesh and spirit are mutually related in fulfilling God's purpose in the world through the mandates. But the distinction of "flesh and spirit" is not the way in which to distinguish the mandate in the mask, and it is not the way to assess the arenas in which the Christian exercises freedom or submits to bondage. For Luther often says that the conscience is free and the body unfree; but he also says, no less often, that the will is free in things below but unfree in things above. When God's mandates are in view the whole man, flesh and spirit, is involved, and the whole man is both bound and free. The distinction Luther utilizes in this context is "person - office."

The man of faith knows in general the whence and the whither of his activity. He knows it is God's outgoing, the becoming flesh of the Word, that creates and empowers his own outgoing, the becoming of Word out of flesh. He also knows that his task is the restoration of the creation, including man, to the life for which they were created. But when it gets down to concrete cases, the whence and whither of his relation to God and the world becomes highly ambiguous. Faith is faced with the task of trusting itself not to the *larvae,* but to the Word under the *larvae.* And this is an extraordinarily difficult decision to make.[53] Christian good is always hidden under its opposite. Even though the spirit chooses the common good for the common life, and even though its only concern is God and what is related to His will, still the decision about what is good and evil is never obvious. The best judgment, as we noted above, is often the reverse of what the ego feels. My good is often the neighbor's evil, and vice versa. The natural ego is only a mask.[54] And while man judges only according to the mask or *persona,* unjustly, God judges according to the *cor,* justly.[55]

The ambiguity that thus characterizes the experienced source, application, and nature of the mandate, originates in the fact that the mandate is the theological task of the man of faith, who is both *incurvatus* and *ingressus*. Man is duplex, says Luther; the blessing and curse on him is therefore duplex.[56]

We are beginning to feel the press of two related themes. On the one hand, the question of the meaning of "person," especially as related to the meaning of "office" or "work." We must pursue this matter before the issue of God's mandates can be clarified. Related to the "person - work" polarization, possibly as its generalized formulation, is the question of the two realms. The ambiguity that is involved in God's revelation under *larvae*, of the good hidden under *larvae*, of the Christian activity under *larvae*, leads Luther to insist very strongly on a clear and correct distinction of the realms.[57] The problem here is not with what obtains *in regno dei, coram deo*. The mandate is to be fulfilled *in regno mundi*, and it is the worldly realm which is shown to be ambiguous, or as we learned much earlier in this study, shown to be a self-contradiction. The world taken by itself and for itself is fallen, it is unambiguously one thing. Only with the presence of the ultimate is the world seen by the man of faith as ambiguous. Only with this presence does dialectical language become the possible, indeed the necessary theological language. And because the presence of God is an eschatological presence — a becoming of presentness — the man of faith discovers the distinction of realms not only as a fact, but also as a task. He must be able in his conscience to distinguish correctly his person from his work, and he must be able in the *larvae* to distinguish correctly the realms of God and the world. He must realize in the world and for the world what is already God's fact. Thus the task, the mandate, which stands above every particular mandate, is the distinction of the two realms. And the realization of every particular mandate is at the same time the distinguishing of the two realms.

The concluding essay must then be given over to the dialectic, *regnum mundi - regnum dei*.

Conclusion

Essay VIII: *Regnum Dei - Regnum Mundi*

The "doctrine" of the two realms is not just one doctrine among others in Luther's theology. In fact it is not a doctrine at all, and even if it is, it does not directly concern social ethics. As the other themes I have considered in the study, the theme of the two kingdoms is a perspective, with its own emphases, on the whole divine-human encounter as Luther sees it. The sequence of themes in this study indicates a shifting focus of attention. We began with a concern for method, form, sign, and gradually moved to a concern with things, power, flesh. With the essay on the new creature the process of becoming which the various themes described became formally eschatological, that is, what was being described was the becoming of Christ into the man of faith. As the subject of God's realization in the world began to dominate our interest, the description and analysis began to be channeled increasingly into the discussion of power. Not simply power considered abstractly, but power with a purpose; directed, organized, valuated power. We then have three features or characteristics of the process before us. The process is a process of becoming, or realization; it is to be formulated in terms of power; and it appears as eschatological in the incarnation of Christ. These characteristics emerge variously in all the themes we have considered, but it is in Luther's *regnum* language, as we indicated in the opening essay, that these features are expressed most clearly.

The "two realms" thus has a far more general importance than appears from its problematic association with the subject of social ethics. It is possible to describe Luther's ethical teaching just as well in other terms, for example, the polarizations *coram deo - coram mundo* or "faith - Law." Because of the long-established connection between the "two realms" doctrine and Christian ethics, in which scholarly tradition both matters have often been badly misinterpreted, it would in fact be better to avoid the "kingdoms" approach to ethics and the ethical approach to the kingdoms—at least for a while, until the Pavlovian conditioning has been broken and we can see the real though limited connection between the subjects.

This is the strategy I shall follow. You should be advised therefore that the essay does not *basically* concern itself with Luther's thoughts on vocation, social ethics, and related matters. When these subjects are introduced, they are to be considered illustrations or applications of the basic theme of the essay. If this relationship can be kept in mind, the discussion following will be less liable to misunderstanding.

The reason why the ethical application should not be the first response to the "two realms" is that in the first place there are *not two* realms. There is only the kingdom of God. Only when the kingdom of God becomes present and active does something begin to appear as something *else*. And the something else is only then shown as a kingdom which is not the kingdom of God, and which, as a kingdom of the world, is not only opposed to the kingdom of God but also contradicts itself. The "two kingdoms" is a *judgment* of God and is therefore a statement that can only be made by faith. The "two kingdoms" is not a given, natural fact, the basis for what then becomes a dualistic ethics which appeals to the fact. The "two kingdoms" is a consequence of a divine judgment. It is God's exposure to faith of the fallenness in which faith lives, and of the scandal which faith is mandated to overcome.

In this essay the task is first to discuss the becoming of the kingdom of God and to investigate why it presents itself as a kingdom. In the second section we shall see how the kingdom of God accomplishes its purposes in the world and how faith is properly to view its relation to God and to the world. In the third section the issue will be the becoming of faith in the midst of and by means of the distinction of the kingdoms. Throughout the essay all of the themes I have already discussed will again come to expression. The *regnum dei - regnum mundi* dialectic not only epitomizes the theology of Luther, but is therefore also an excellent way to conclude this study.

1

Raising Political Consciousness

In the introduction to Part Three I said that one cannot according to Luther simply begin talking about the nature of God, His attributes or creating work, but that what is first necessary is to consider Christ. The same epistemological principle holds true for the subject of the kingdom of God. It is not immediately present at hand for theological discourse. To interpret it correctly, we must go to the place where it is interpreted to us. That means our point of departure is the *regnum Christi.*

Exhibiting the same paradoxical conjunction of temporal and non-temporal language that we saw in his statements about the new creature, Luther says that the *eternal* kingdom of Christ *begins* with the preaching of John the Baptist.[1] The new kingdom affects man's body, mind, and will. His body is being renewed, and he is gaining both a true knowledge of God and a new disposition. This renewal, complete only with death, is the ongoing task of the Holy Spirit,[2] who, as Luther defines in a neat piece of demythologizing, is "something beyond your thought."[3] As a new kingdom, the kingdom of Christ brings renewal. The renewal can be described as "eschatological" in that it is both already accomplished *for* us by Christ and is also therefore still to be accomplished *in* us by Christ. At the same time the renewal can be described as "restitutionist," for its norm is the undamaged, unified relationship among God, man, and the world that obtained before the fall.[4] As I argued in the essay on the new creature, "new" not only reflects the gift of God but also His judgment on the "old." The kingdom of Christ is always associated in the Scriptures with "righteousness" and "judgment," because Christ justifies the new man and judges the old man. When *iustitia* is given, the kingdom is given with it. And the kingdom consists in the humiliating judgment that we are sinners.[5]

We have seen in the preceding essays that not only God's attributes, but also those of Christ were defined and understood as acts. Thus it should be no surprise that here also the togetherness of Christ and faith is discussed in terms of Christ's action in the new creature. Correspondingly the *kingdom* of Christ must be understood in reference to His new *people.* In fact one must not say that the kingdom *brings* a renewal, but rather that the kingdom *is* Christ's work of renewal in His people.[6] The new people in whom Christ works and who exhibit their oneness with Him insofar as they exhibit the work and the working of Christ, is the church, the *communio sanctorum,* the bride of Christ, the spiritual body whose head is Christ.[7] The church, Luther says, is created, born, nourished, and preserved by the faith it sustains in the Word of promise.[8] Being defined by the promise, the church is thus the embodiment of God; it has God as He really is. And the reality created by the presence of God in His promise is the eschatological reality of faith. It is an eschatological life of faith in which the church lives from its future hope and not from its present experience. All who believe, says Luther, though they still live in the flesh, are at the same time in faith, in the Word, in heaven. They are what they are becoming.[9]

Notice how Luther's language is changing. What began as a univocal description of the kingdom of Christ has already become bivocal or dialectical. The kingdom of Christ involves righteousness and judgment; the church lives from faith and the future, not from its present experience; it is in heaven, not really in the flesh. Luther continues to express the reality of the kingdom in other polarities. The spiritual realm shows "how one must live before God above and beyond the external."[10] One of the more frequently occurring polarities is the contrast of the kingdom with the Law - the Law one of the "externals."

> Although they were there first, there is no law or mandate in the kingdom of Christ, but rather in grace we are all receiving - God us and we God. We are not libertarians, but the true kingdom exists in the inward heart, in which there can be no mandate, or else it is not in the kingdom of Christ.[11]

The Law, says Luther, enjoins many external works, while the Gospel enjoins only one internal work, which is faith. Expressing the functional equation of Law with flesh as contrasted to the equation of faith with spirit, Luther says the things of the old Law pertain to the flesh, those of the new Law to the spirit or conscience.[12] The kingdom is preserved against sinners not by the Law of love, says Luther, but by Word, faith, and the Spirit.[13]

I said at the beginning that the two realms was not a theological given, that one could not proceed immediately to applications presupposing that distinction. As Gerhard Ebeling has so well indicated, the first theological task is to discover the *necessity* for the distinction.[14] The kingdom of Christ is both a soteriological and an eschatological reality, as we have seen. But this means that its proclamation is intended to serve a need, to clarify and resolve a problem which not only cannot be solved otherwise, but also which is not even recognized as a problem until the proclamation of the kingdom of Christ reveals it. This function comes to expression in Luther's language about the kingdom of Christ. The situation to which the proclamation is addressed is the confusion of divine and human functions in the matter of salvation, the reversal of relationships, and the consequent self-contradiction of the world when it constitutes itself a kingdom. The proclamation of the reality of Christ as a kingdom is precisely the exposure of this self-contradiction.

Luther insists on a radical distinction of the two realms. The distinction is necessary, he says, in order to preserve the Gospel and true faith.[15] Here we see that the distinction is being made for the sake of the spiritual realm; later we shall see that it is made for the sake of the world as well. Luther can define the "spiritual realm" as being *coram deo*, in contrast to the "physical realm" which thus by implication belongs *coram hominibus.* One must not take what belongs to the world and bring it before God.[16] The realms thus indicate the *"coram"* dialectic we have discussed earlier, with its connotations of man existing in competitive *fora.* If the realms or *fora* are not kept distinct, not only will their mixture be of no beneficial consequence, but it will in fact produce only evil and confusion.[17] Part of the source of the confusion lies in that fact that, in regard to the effects and meaning of evil, the worldly realm is more ambiguous than the spiritual realm, which has a clear mandate in regard to the First Table of the Law. There are no such prescriptive standards for works of love, as we have already seen. Thus, even though the kingdom of Christ is clearly manifest in Christ's preaching of God's will, it is still very hard, especially in the midst of the greatest evil, death, to distinguish the righteousness of the Law from that of Christ.[18]

It is human reason, says Luther (not unexpectedly), that wants to confuse and reverse the realms. The "reversal" is the important point. We heard Luther say above that the things belonging *coram hominibus* should not be brought *coram deo.* But reason, which cannot help but think according to Law, insists on bringing its own reality before God. It confuses the Law and the Gospel by holding that Law is a means, along with the Gospel, to be sure, of justification. But this means the Gospel itself becomes simply another form of Law. What is happening is that reason makes what is normative before men normative before God, in the forum of conscience. Luther seldom becomes more enraged than when he hears righteousness and love discussed as inherent forms, virtues, or qualities, and distinctions made which assume that these are virtues which belong to the world.[19] The source of the mixing, confusion, and reversal of function or realms is the world.

It is not difficult to understand why the confusion of realms can happen. *Christ* also rules the *worldly* realm. Life is a good creature *of God.* It can be defined theologically in terms of its becoming *ingressus in deum.* Its ordinances and estates, rooted in physical birth, are divine mandates. One can even reason discursively from creature to Creator if this is done properly. "Properly" is of course the key. What happens is that when reason overvaluates the creation, the creation not only becomes "vain" as far as knowledge of God is concerned, but also by remaining *incurvatus in se,* reason corrupts itself and everything around it.[20] The world becomes evil; it becomes *subject* to the devil, becomes a demonic *regnum* which in its supreme smugness (*securissime*) discounts the activity of God.[21] Instead of remaining dependent on its Creator, the creation seizes on the mandates and order within it and attempts to unify and absolutize them into laws and a kingdom. It attempts to reach the "mathematical point" that belongs to the kingdom of God alone.[22] It cannot do this unless it denies ultimacy to the kingdom of God. Thus we get the reversal: "Man cannot naturally wish God to be God; indeed he wishes himself to be God and God not to be God."[23]

And thus is expressed the self-contradiction of *regnum mundi.* As we saw in Part Three, the creation is God's gift. It was intended to lift up and enlighten man, but once it was corrupted by human sin, the creation contradicted its intended purpose by blinding and crippling man. If the sinful man loves the creature, he therefore cannot love the Creator. In the self-contradiction of *regnum mundi* love of one excludes love of the other. The Law was given to establish the "external spiritual regiment." But its implied mandates, as we have seen, changed character in the Fall. The mandate was a creative Word giving what it commanded; it is now a Law of sin and death. We have already seen that while human nature can be defined in terms of Law, human nature at the same time hates the Law. The peace and joy of the world, Luther says, seem to be its life, but are rather the sign of its death. And death is the greatest self-contradiction of all, since man was created for life.[24] The world both agrees and disagrees with the judgment of God. We are found to be sinners both before the world and before God, but the reasons for the judgments are exactly opposite.[25] The contradiction is shown with ultimate clarity in Christ. "Whatever is from God"—and the *world itself* is from God— "must be crucified in the world," we heard Luther say in the *Romans* commentary. Christ, the highest righteousness and truth, embodies the contradiction because He is at the same time the highest sin and lie. This kind of language, so common in Luther's descriptions of the atonement, indicates that the contradictions which are embodied in Christ are self-destructive. In Christ the world's Law, sin, freedom, slavery, good, evil, etc., do away with themselves. The devil is destroyed by the devil, sin by sin, Law by Law.[26]

This self-contradiction is not self-evident; in fact it cannot be discovered at all, but rather the opposite appears to be the case. Only when God reveals Himself are the claims to ultimacy of the world revealed to faith as false and the "reality" which makes such claims revealed as a self-contradiction. We have seen in a preliminary way what the kingdom of God is. We have seen why it has come and why it comes as a kingdom. Now we must investigate how the kingdom of God accomplishes its purpose, and how the proper relationship of the realms is to be viewed.

164

2

War of the Worlds

The contradiction of which I have spoken can be formulated as that involved in the creature denying its createdness. In the preceding section, reflecting Part One of the study, my concern was to point out the implicit struggle for power that results when the world denies its contingency and becomes a "pretender to the throne." The struggle is only implicit, however, until by its activity the kingdom of God exposes the pretensions of a world which insists it is a self-contained, self-derived, self-sustaining kingdom. The *aseity* of the Godhead is finally what the world claims for itself when it proclaims itself a kingdom. As we saw in Part One, the fallen world defines God in its own categories; now it is shown to define itself in divine categories.

This section reflects Part Two of the study. Its subject is the Word of God as it acts to expose the contradiction, and thus the *absconditus sub contrario* in which faith finds itself.

Luther argues that when opposites are placed next to each other the contrast better exposes the essential natures of the contrasted elements.[27] This sharpening is one of the functions of Luther's dialectical language. Thus God's glory is better revealed when we are humbled, His truth, when we are exposed as liars, and so forth. This function is not limited to characteristics of the divine and human natures, but can be applied to the economy of salvation as well: the reprobate are made worse, the elect better, by the Word.[28] With the coming of the Word the realities or ultimate concerns of the two realms are exposed to each other. The essential character of each realm is seen in the criticism it levels against the other. The world and the Gospel condemn each others ways, Luther says. The world condemns the Gospel for *lawlessness,* and the Gospel condemns the world for *idolatry.* The world is ultimately concerned with maintaining its own order, maintaining itself as a kingdom. The Gospel is ultimately concerned with letting God be God, with keeping the creation from becoming idolized.[29] Lawlessness or true religion; order or idolatry! I cannot think of a more precise way to formulate the contrasting concerns of the two realms than Luther has done in the *Galatians* commentary.

As we saw in the essay on Law and faith, one of the "twofold" functions of the Gospel is the revelation of sin, the task which the Law by itself cannot accomplish. People blame the evils of the world on the Gospel, Luther insists, but the Gospel rather exposes the world's evil. Without the Gospel the world remains in darkness, ignorant of itself. When Luther is speaking of the *regnum dei* rather than specifically of the *evangelium dei,* the twofold function can be construed in terms of the "kingdoms" of Christ's humanity and divinity. The kingdom of humanity or flesh conforms us to itself. It turns us proud gods into true men, that is, into miserable sinners, and thereby gives us true knowledge of ourselves. The distinction of the realms, therefore, is not only made for the sake of the kingdom of God. It is also made for the sake of the world whose reconstruction is the purpose of the kingdom of God. Just as the Gospel cannot maintain its purity unless it is distinguished from Law, the Law cannot be recognized in its proper use unless it is distinguished from the Gospel. The world cannot recover the truth about itself until and unless the kingdom of God is revealed to it. The kingdom of God thus realizes the purpose of the Law. It reveals the old birth, the kingdom of the devil, and thus prepares for the new birth via faith in Christ.[30]

How does the exposure of a contrast between the realms become the struggle of the realms? The Gospel, the kingdom of God and of Christ, has two functions: judging and justifying. Man's character as *incurvatus* must be exposed, judged, and in principle overcome before it can become *ingressus.* But we do not freely lend ourselves to the destruction that the process of reconstruction presumes. A war must be fought and won.

The Word of God, Luther says, throws the world into confusion. It had thought God's truth was the same as its truth, that nothing within its *regnum*-structure was at issue, and that still outstanding difficulties were only a matter of minor adjustment. But the Word of God does not present itself in order to criticize *flaws;* the Sermon on the Mount is not technical advice for running the world. *Everything* in the world, Luther insists, especially the constituted secular and spiritual authorities at its center, must absolutely *oppose* God.[31] What opposes God is not a disorganized collection, but an organized unity, a kingdom. Luther argues that apart from faith all doctrines and all life separate and disunite mankind. But when Christ comes with the Gospel, the various religions conspire and unite themselves to suppress Christ's kingdom.[32] I said earlier that the world cannot be exposed as sinful until Christ comes, that the opposition to God was only implicit, that the character of fallen man as *lex* was not apparent until the coming of the Gospel. Thus the coming of the Gospel as a *regnum* crystalizes or precipitates what is otherwise only latent. Only with the coming of the kingdom of God is the heretofore unexamined, unknown, unsuspected nature of the fallen world exposed as a false kingdom whose chief characteristics are law and opposition to God.

The world and its god, the law, cannot bear to hear this Word and the true God; the true God will not be silent. The result is war.[33]

The office of Christ is to begin the kingdom of life, and to do this He must destroy the kingdom of death, the power of the world, the flesh, and the devil.[34] To wish to stop this war is to wish to impede the Word of God, whose purpose it is to change and renew the world. It is God who initiates the conflict, and the war is not over until He crushes all opposition. The knowledge of these two warring kingdoms is by itself enough to refute the doctrine of free will.[35] The battle cannot be decided *by* man, and furthermore it is not even decided *in* man. To assert the former would deny the atonement and evoke the objection we heard Luther utter much earlier in the study, "Of what need then is Christ?" To assert the latter would contradict the anthropology of the new creature and the understanding of the process of sanctification Luther holds. The battle is decided by Christ, and in Christ. And what is at issue is not how the kingdom of the world shall be *administered.* The struggle is not over the *Second* Table but over the *First.* It is in fact a struggle over the First Commandment: whose righteousness shall be ultimate?[36]

The kingdom of Christ is also a *fait accompli.* It is the proclamation that the struggle over the First Commandment has been decided. It is a proclamation that the contradiction of *regnum mundi* is ended, that the kingdom can now once again become creation.

Let me rephrase. To proclaim the kingdom of God is to proclaim that *bondage* to the kingdom of the world is ended. For the worldly kingdom is not ended as a fact of life by Christ's work. Rather by that work we can affirm the kingdom of the world in its proper sense. But are we not thus involved in a difficulty? If *regnum mundi* is a self-contradiction, and if the kingdom of God has come to expose and overcome that self-contradiction, how then can the Christian find in the proclamation of the *regnum dei* a mandate to affirm the world as a kingdom?

It is just at this point that Luther distinguished himself socially and politically from reformers of the "left wing." To deny the continuing reality of the worldly kingdom is not only to deny the obvious facts of life, but is also to do bad theology. The kingdom of God does not bring its citizens out of the unity of the world's sin into the unity of divine perfection. The change is not from life in *faith* to life in *God.* The kingdom of God creates faith, and only in faith is the double judgment possible. Theology is not a discourse from the realm of sin, nor is it a discourse from the realm of perfect righteousness. It is discourse from the realm of faith. The kingdom of God frees man from simple bondage to *sin* and places him in the life of *faith.* That means the Christian can now embody the double judgment. The worldly kingdom continues for the Christian because the Christian too is characterized by sin. The difference is that the Christian can recognize sin for what it is. He embodies the contradiction within himself and experiences its pain—as did Christ. And he tries to do what he can, given the requirements of the moment, to overcome the contradiction in fact as Christ has overcome it in principle and is overcoming it in fact. He knows what is to be brought before whom and why. He knows how to distinguish the two realms. He has this knowledge because he is in the kingdom of God and not in the kingdom of the world. And the proclamation of the kingdom of God is itself the proclamation of the distinction of the two realms.

The distinction of realms is not a worldly separation of man and God into "spheres of influence." The distinction is made by God, and it is He who allots each realm. The distinction can be formulated in a number of ways by Luther: as the kingdoms of Christ and the world, of Christ and the devil, of the heavenly and earthly righteousnesses, of faith and unfaith, of the Word and the sword.[37] Regardless of the formulation, the distinction is exhaustive, covering all human relationships. There is no middle ground between the realms; each includes the whole man. As we have seen, it is the world's false understanding of itself as a kingdom which makes it opposed to the kingdom of God. The distinction as it is made from the latter, however, does not imply such an opposition. The worldly realm is external, the spiritual realm internal. It is the Word which makes this distinction, and within the spiritual realm the Word does not distinguish the external person, time, and place as does the worldly realm.[38] The multiplicity of relations, the hierarchy of values that obtains in the physical realm, are not in opposition to the unity of the spiritual realm; they are simply not relevant to it.[39] When Luther says the Word does not consider the external person, he is using "person" in the sense of *persona*, mask. The worldly realm is "below" the spiritual realm; it is God's creature, thus His instrument, the means of His mediated immediacy. As a *larva dei*, the worldly realm is intended to instruct man in God's will. It directs him "below himself," that is, from himself *coram deo* to himself *coram mundo*. It should therefore be a symbol, a mask, of true salvation.[40] Now we are once again meeting the important theme of Part Three, the masks as expressions of the eschatological unity of the finite and the infinite. The worldly kingdom is the instrument of the infinite God, but is itself a creature. It is finite, it has boundaries.[41] As we heard earlier, the creature, though it is the locus and means of the divine power, cannot on these accounts distinguish itself as divine, or necessary to the divine working. The kingdom of God prevails everywhere Christ is, in all instruments and powers, but the power of the kingdom is not dependent on the instruments. It receives nothing from them the way the worldly kingdom does from its instruments.

The distinction of the realms, as it is made from the *regnum dei*, does not lead to mutual exclusion, therefore, but rather affords a contrast, and thus gives the Christian a distinction which he can sustain while at the same time retain his personal unity. But the fallen world continues its own false self-understanding of the *regnum mundi*, and because the Christian is also involved in this fallenness, he continues to share this view and to experience its disruptive effects. As we know, only the Christian knows he lives in both realms; only he experiences and recognizes the dialectical situation of faith. What distinguishes the Christian from the natural man is that the Christian suffers. He suffers the radical distinction of the realms, the mutual opposition of the realms which is created by sin: God's grace and peace only along with the world's wrath and discord; worldly grace and peace only along with the wrath and turmoil of God.[42] In fact it seems that it is the devil's citizens who are at peace, and only the citizens of God's realm afflicted. The Christian must suffer the completely opposite judgments of the two realms. As we saw in Part Two, he must experience the bondage of his flesh to sin and Law, the freedom of his conscience from sin and Law; the bondage of his conscience to God, and the freedom of his flesh regarding works of love. In sum, the Christian is wholly in both realms, and partly in both. To pray "Thy kingdom come," says Luther, is to admit we are partly in the kingdom of Satan and partly in the kingdom of God. And once again we must emphasize that the dialectic is a dynamic one. Just as the relation of the old man and the new man we discussed in Part Two, the Christian in the two realms is involved in a continuing process—a "cross, a shift, a passage, a being led" from one realm into the other.[43] And as with the matter of sanctification, so also the process of becoming into the kingdom of God is not a simple progression, but a movement in which the end is the beginning. Not the growth of the political or social power of the Gospel, but the growing realization of faith in worldly works of love. Not the increasing separation of the person from the office, but the increasing realization of the person in the office. Not the progressive escape from the world into God, but the progressive becoming of Christ into the world.

3

Person and Work

The Christian is said to be in two realms because he is in the process of becoming. The first half of this essay was concerned with the explication of the what, why, and how of divine becoming. The last part of the preceding section shifted focus to the how of Christian becoming as a response to God's activity. This final section, reflecting Part Three of the study, must assess the why, the purpose, of constructing Christian life as a life in two realms, and conclude with a summary of what it is that is thus revealed about the nature of Christian reality.

The fall into sin had the effect of producing a form of definiteness which, while it could be seen by the man of faith as a fatal entrapment, an *incurvatus in se*, a self-contradiction, yet appeared to itself as an internally consistent, univocal, and objectively verifiable kingdom. No such form of definiteness characterizes the Christian, just because faith is not this or that definable entity, but is rather, in Luther's description, a relation. And so long as he lives in the flesh, the Christian is always in the process of realizing his faith. But he never completes the process; his identity, his salvation, is fulfilled *in spe, nondum in re.*

Because the process of Christian becoming is taking place in the midst of sin, the Christian is not simply hidden, but is hidden *sub contrario.* Faith is the reconciliation of opposites. The kingdom of God to external appearances looks like death, ignorance—the opposite of what it is. This is so because the wisdom and power of God, which order and sustain the kingdom, are hidden under their opposites. There are no extrinsic, extensive grounds for the showing forth of faith, as we have seen. The kingdom of grace is and remains secret, concealed from the world, maintained in Word and faith until the time of its final revelation. The Christian people cannot be seen. They are known as a city, as a kingdom, only in heaven. As we saw in the essay on the new creature, the Christian is indistinguishable to others, and cannot distinguish himself from others, even though there is in fact the greatest possible difference. But this hiddenness is his joy. Says Luther in a passage most revealing of both his piety and his theology, "O what a great thing it is to be a Christian [and] have a hidden life . . . in the invisible God himself."[44]

But this hiddenness is not all that can be said. In fact one must emphasize the divine mandate to faith to realize itself in the creation if one is not to construe Luther's statements on faith's hiddenness as a world-escaping mysticism. God rules both realms and gives faith mandates for each. Thus the Christian life of becoming, when it is constructed as a life in two realms, must not be seen as a becoming out of the created and sinful world into the realm of uncreated divine perfection, but the becoming from the kingdom of God, from faith before God, into the worldly kingdom, into works of love before and for the world. It is in this sense that Luther can affirm as a mandate the Christian existence in two realms, even as he earlier uses the "two realms" as evidence of sin.[45] The believer is above all, yet subject to all; like Christ, he is "twin-born," having two forms.[46] He is both under the Law, and without the Law. The Christian is described as being under law and government, not because of sin, but because it is God's good will for the creation. The government is outward, yet binds faith because of the Word it contains. Government is a divine order, a *religious* institution, holy, founded on the Word and contained in it. We are subject to this order not for its own sake—it is only a creature—but because of God's will.[47]

Luther gives existential point to both emphases in describing the double relation in terms of the distinction between "person" and "office" or "work." We have seen him use "person" in the sense of *persona,* mask. It is in this connection that we must understand Luther's statements about *two* persons. He can, for example, make the distinction between office and person, but then go on to explicate it in terms of two persons in one man: the one person we are born under, the natural person, and the other, the divine person whom God makes us into. And then, in explication of this latter person, Luther can again revert to the earlier distinction and define the divine person as holding a divinely appointed office.[48] Later on he says that the "two persons" are lived simultaneously, defining them as the "Christian" and the "secular" persons. But he then goes on to use *persona* in the sense of *larva,* and says that the *offices* are distinct, combined in *one* person, yet contradictory. And *then* he concludes with a description of *two* persons, one for self or before God, the other for other men.[49]

This apparent confusion stems in part from the two ways *larva* can be taken. The *larva* is on the one hand purely the external form. When "person" is explicated in this sense of *larva,* I think Luther is simply indicating that the Christian appears externally to others in a different way, as a different person, than he is known to God. But there is another sense of *larva,* one in which the sense of "external mask" is retained, but also in which the divine instrumentality is meant. And it is with this latter, double meaning of *larva* that the distinction "person-office" is expressed. The Christian is person both before the world and before God, but with differing senses of "person." Before God he is the person of his conscience; before the world he is the person of his work. Before God there are not two persons. There is only the person of faith which is created by the personal presence of Christ. It is in regard to the world that the ambiguity arises. The world mistakenly takes the work for the person; faith keeps the person before God, and correctly interprets that which is before the world as the work or office.

I said above that the process of Christian becoming as expressed in his life in two realms was to be construed as a movement from the *regnum dei* to the *regnum mundi*. The discussion of the distinction "person-work" explicates this direction of movement. One does not make his work before the world the qualification of or the credentials for the status of his person before God. Rather it is the person *coram deo* that qualifies the work *coram mundo*. As Luther says innumerable times, usually in criticism of Aristotle and the educational theory based on his views, theologically it is the person that makes the work, and not the work that makes the person. And for "person-work" one can just as correctly substitute "conscience-body," "faith-love," "Gospel-Law," or *regnum dei-regnum mundi*.

The Christian thus stands in a double relationship, or perhaps better, he sees himself in reference both to his whence and his whither. He has a holy pride, a contemplative and active life. His faith is both external and internal; his justification is twofold: between God and him and between himself and others.[50] But sin continues, continues in the world where he exercises his office, and continues in himself, in his person before God. The believer is thus still always involved in a contradiction while he is involved in living. He is held righteous before God and a sinner before the world. He has no peace but by way of the cross; he is on earth and not on earth. His life is a pilgrimage.[51] But we have learned that this pilgrimage is not from the world to God, but from God to the world. It begins from faith and ends with love.

The extension of faith to works of love can be called the "ecstacy" of faith. If, as I have suggested, the creation is in some sense a constituent of God's presence or essence, then the Christian's *ingressus in deum* is thereby also his *ingressus in creationem*. This is so because the Christian in his work is God's *larva;* because the need to which the work is called is God's *larva;* and because the mandate which relates the work to the need is God's *larva.*

God, as Luther says so often, is all in all.

A Retrospective Look Forward

The discussions in the last three or four sections of this study have concerned the themes of the masks of God and the two realms. These are *generalizing* themes. They incorporate everything we have discussed throughout the text.

With the interpretation of the two realms in which the Christian lives as a process of becoming from the kingdom of God into the kingdom of the world, this study is formally complete. The doctrine of the two realms, thus interpreted, reflects the same eschatological process of becoming we have seen expressed in the other dialectics controlling this study. *Regnum dei-regnum mundi* seems to me to be the most comprehensive dialectical perspective, including within it all of the themes we have discussed earlier. The struggle of the kingdom of God with the false self-understanding of the worldly kingdom reflects the themes of the second and third essays. The establishment of the kingdom of God as the true forum from which the Christian receives his identity reflects the themes considered in the fourth and fifth essays. The mandate given in the kingdom of God for the realization of the divine will in the kingdom of the world reflects the themes considered in the sixth and seventh essays.

In this concluding essay on the dialectic *regnum dei-regnum mundi,* one of the most important and pervasive interpretive tools was the dialectic *coram deo-coram mundo*—the theme of the introductory essay. We should have to interpret this *coram* language itself in order to fully understand the *regnum* language. And thus we seem to have come full circle. As I noted in the beginning, Luther leads you 'round and 'round. The *coram* pattern finds its complete explication in the *regnum* pattern, and the latter again finds its explication in the former. The two languages interpret each other. The two dialectical patterns are related in this way because they are both related to, and are expressions of, the third dialectical pattern, "Christ-faith." The *coram* pattern, which was more dominant in the first half of the study, explicates the meaning of faith as an *ingressus in Christum.* The *regnum* pattern, which was more dominant in the second half of the study, explicates the meaning of Christ as *ingressus in fidem.* It is the dialectic "Christ-faith" which provides the reason, in both a philosophical and a theological sense, for Luther's discourse. This dialectic—and we might recall here that it is a *hermeneutical* instrument—gives Luther's theology its systematic character. Because the relation of Christ and faith is a highly dynamic one, in both directions, the dialectic provides the unity characterizing Luther's theology—an internally interconnected whole in which one formulation or theme finds its full explication only in all the others, and at the same time is itself an explication of all the others.

In the first half of the study my general purpose was the presentation, through various themes, of the relation of God and man as a process. In the second half, the general task was the specification of this process as eschatological, that the subject of this process was God. There are no internal reasons for this order of presentation: the themes and the language form one circuit of thought. But one

173

must begin somewhere. My presentation of each topic was, moreover, not exhaustive, nor was that the intent. What I intended to do was to develop a very general outline or organization for interpreting Luther. I do feel that I have developed an organization which not only brings into view certain teachings, and certain characteristics of all Luther's teachings, which have been overlooked or underestimated by many students, but which give the beginning student (we are all beginning students!) some serviceable tools for getting into the man. Perhaps the most important task before me was that of evoking a feeling in you for Luther's way of approach to theological issues, all the while investigating the effective relationships among some of his major subjects. To this end I approached the issues from a series of interrelated, interdependent, and mutually enhancing thematic perspectives. Each theme is highly metaphorical. The metaphors which served to title each essay also served as perspectives for expressing the central motif and as means for uncovering it. There were, in addition, other formulations which served the same purposes. The schema I developed in the first essay, "proximate-penultimate-ultimate," was a preliminary formulation of the central motif, and provided the logic for organizing the study. The *coram, regnum,* and "Christ-faith" dialectics, all highly metaphorical, are alternate ways of expressing and uncovering the motif. So is *finitum capax infiniti,* an idea which does not appear in quite that form in Luther (cf. W 39 II, 112.15-19), but which is a very adequate general expression of that eschatological motif.

Among all of these mutually enhancing and qualifying expressions there appeared, especially in the second half of the study, variations on the idea of "the divine self-realization in creation." That idea is the guiding formulation of this study. In some respects it is the most problematic. The concluding discussion should then be given over to the meaning and use of this idea.

The Process of Divine Self-Realization in Creation

This phrase is a generalized expression of the eschatological motif which I have sought to expose in this study. It is important first of all to note that I have always used the word "eschatological" rather than "eschatology." The latter term includes a traditional set of topics concerning the "last things," and of course Luther writes about them too. But they were not the subject of this study. Many students, however, refer to the "eschatological" character of this or that topic in Luther, or of his theology in general. And these topics are at best only very marginally related to those subsumed under "eschatology." "Eschatological," as seen by these students, myself included, is a

174

term applicable to *all* of Luther's topics. Thus one cannot look for *one* locus in which to anchor the discussion of whatever is meant by the term. Rather the task is to seek it everywhere, to expose its partial, varied, supplementary and often contrasting expressions in the language of each topic, and especially to study the relationships among all the topics as the most fruitful means of formulating the definition of the motif. What all this means, of course, is that it is impossible to distinguish the motif either as a direct conclusion from the data, or as a purely interpretive means of selecting and formulating the data. In the following discussion of "the process of divine self-realization in creation," both the deductions and the inductions which make up the motif will be examined.

The phrase is an attempt to express the relations among the topics investigated in this study. Its center is the dynamic, becoming unity of Christ and faith, which was presented in the essays *Promissio et Fides* and *Initium Creaturae Novae*. The mutual ingression of faith and Christ can be construed as both "justification" and "sanctification," depending on which side of the becoming is in view. In the essay on the new creature this process was discovered to be a process of realization. The discussion indicated that this process was hidden. It could not therefore be formulated in any way that would suggest an external change—in Luther's terms, the process did not belong to the category of "works." Thus the process was defined as one of becoming, of realization. Since Christ is the subject, it was further defined as the process of Christ's self-realization in faith.

In the same two essays I presented the view that faith will always become incarnate, will necessarily realize itself in works of love. The essays in Part Three developed the view that this realization of faith was a realization in creation. It was a realization in which the Christian, living under the mask of Christ's flesh, responded to the divine mandate as given definitively in the *larva* of Christ and then in the *larvae* of creation. Because that in which the mandate is given is related to God as His self-disclosure, it is now to be termed "creation," not "world." This distinction has been utilized throughout the study, especially in Part One and Part Two. As Christ realizes Himself in faith, and faith correspondingly realizes itself in creation, it is possible to summarize these two sets of relationships by referring to "Christ's self-realization in creation."

Now let us turn to the other development from the central meaning, that is, to the application to God of what was said of Christ. This matter is more complex and subtle. In fact the tension between the doctrines of God and of Christ has never been resolved. Luther couldn't, and neither can we. Two related issues present themselves.

175

One is the extent to which we can predicate of God what is said of Christ; the other is the extent to which we can say of God's "nature" what is said of His relation to the world. Both of these issues are specific formulations of the same general question raised in the study of Luther: what is the relation between ontology and epistemology in Luther's thought? And this question cannot be answered satisfactorily, because Luther does not recognize the distinction!

We know first of all that for Luther there is no God apart from Christ, and apart, therefore, from faith. This is clearly an epistemological claim, but let us see whether it is more than that. To ask the question of method will help: *how* is God manifest in Christ? As we have seen, the divine in Christ is consistently proved by His work, i.e., it is an inference from Luther's analysis of function. We also saw that Luther develops his view of the divine nature from what he holds about the person, and that he understands the person in terms of the function. We can summarize by saying that, at least insofar as Luther's Christology is indicative, he understands "nature" in terms of "work" or function.

We need not limit this conclusion by the qualification, however, for Luther in many contexts speaks of God without expressly limiting his discourse to Christological statements. There is first of all the evangelical discovery that the divine attributes shall refer not to God's "nature," but to His active relations with the world. Then we have the passages in which God's *Wesen* is defined functionally, as an active relation to the world, as active power. We have the oft-occurring statement that God is *wesentlich, persönlich* present in Christ—an idea which renders ambiguous, and is in turn rendered ambiguous by, the idea expressed in *Jonah* which identifies *Wesen* with "presence," and construes the latter in two senses. No clean distinction between ontology and epistemology can be made, and even the reference to Christ will not help. The Christological relation is after all only *one* of *four* grounds for ubiquity, for example. God's presence, His *Wesen*, is on the one hand grounded in the discussion of the "multiple modes," but on the other hand Christ's omnipresence is only a "trivial instance" of God's omnipresence. Yet the modes themselves are developed as forms of the *bodily* presence of *God*, i.e., of the *personal* presence of *Christ*. Once again we are faced with the inseparability of language about God and about Christ.

Thus we are faced with the situation that Luther can distinguish his discourse as referring to God or to Christ, but that he says nothing about God that is not first true of Christ. In fact even when he is speaking about God "alone," we must keep in mind his Christological perspective.

To answer the question posed earlier as best I can out of the Christological perspective:

—Discourse on God's relations with the world must be considered discourse on God's *Wesen,* or else the full *unity* of Christ is in doubt;

—Discourse about Christ must be considered discourse about God, or else the full *divinity* of Christ is in doubt; and

—Discourse on God's relations with the world must be considered discourse on God's real incarnation in flesh, else the full *humanity* of Christ is in doubt.

These then are the grounds in Luther which allow the extension to "God" of what is said of "Christ." And thereby the full expression of the motif, "the process of divine self-realization in creation," is achieved.

I have not allowed myself to develop a further idea which this material makes possible. This is the idea that the Trinity is involved in change, is affected by the world. Such is the scandalous conclusion entailed when you emphasize the unity of God with flesh. Luther assumed that the doctrine of the Trinity was not in question, and thus did not apply his creative energies to its reformulation, even though his Christological concerns exerted tremendous pressure on the inherited doctrine of divine aseity. The reproach of many of his contemporaries that Luther did not sufficiently protect the divine glory from involvement in the dirty business of worldly existence, is fairly well-founded. But while Zwingli, for example, took this as an indication of Luther's theological incompetence, there are today theological circles in which this characteristic of Luther's thought would be celebrated. But that is the subject of another book.

177

Notes

Most references are to the American Edition of Luther's works. I will cite by volume and page. References prefaced by the designation "LCC" are to the Library of Christian Classics volumes on Luther. References to material not included in either the American Edition or the Library of Christian Classics series will be to the standard critical edition of Luther's works. These citations will be prefaced by the designation "W," followed by volume, page, and line.

Notes to Essay I

Coram Deo-Coram Mundo

1. See for example W 7, 137. 18-24: both the disjunctive *"partim . . . partim"* and the conjunctive *"simul . . . simul"* are used to explicate the relation of sin and righteousness.
2. Dietrich Bonhoeffer, *Creation and Fall,* trans. John Fletcher (New York: The Macmillan Co., 1961), p. 37.
3. LCC 15, 236.
4. Emmanuel Hirsch, *Lutherstudien,* vol. 1 (Gütersloh: C. Bertelsmann, 1954), is still the best general treatment of this subject. Cf. in this context pp. 127, 134.
5. The material is found in 12, 311. I am only using the passage to establish an outline for the study, and therefore will document only the most important references.
6. 12, 308; the critical edition has a slightly different reading.
7. 12, 311.
8. I am indebted to Gerhard Ebeling for this very fruitful idea. Cf. his *Word and Faith,* trans. James W. Leitch (Philadelphia: Fortress Press, 1963), p. 390.
9. 12, 311.
10. 21, 109.
11. The following material is based on Dietrich Bonhoeffer, *Ethics,* ed., Eberhard Bethge, trans. Neville H. Smith (New York: The Macmillan Co., 1962), pp. 79-100.
12. W 5, 163, 28 f.
13. 12, 311.

Notes to Essay II

Homo Incurvatus-Homo Ingressus

1. 27, 363.
2. 27, 367.
3. 37, 92.
4. 27, 249.
5. 37, 92 ff.
6. Cf. St. Augustine, *The City of God,* Book XI, ch. xvi; Book XIX, chs. iv-xiii.
7. W 5, 661. 10-22; my translation.
8. LCC 17, 259; W 10, 1A, 204. 16 ff.
9. W 10, 1A, 203. 3 ff.
10. LCC 16, 33.

11. W 10, 1A, 188. 18 ff.
12. 26, 120.
13. W 1, 225. 1 f.; my translation.
14. 1, 172 f.
15. The following discussion is based on the passage, LCC 15, 25-27.
16. LCC 16, 83.
17. 26, 296; LCC 15, 23 f.
18. 26, 28; 292.
19. W 1, 224. 34 f.
20. 25, 61.
21. The following is based on LCC 15, 225 f.
22. Cf. Ludwig Feuerbach, *The Essence of Faith According to Luther,* trans. Melvin Cherno (New York: Harper & Row, 1967).
23. Cf. for example W 19, 210. 5 ff.; 214. 25 ff.
24. W 19, 193. 24 ff.; 203. 1 ff.
25. W 19, 209. 15 ff.
26. W 19, 215. 23 ff.
27. 13, 94.
28. Cf. Gustav Aulen, *Christus Victor,* Trans. A. G. Hebert (New York: The Macmillan Co., 1961). His view has been criticized by many. Cf. Paul Althaus, *Die Theologie Martin Luthers* (Gütersloh: Gütersloher Verlagshaus Gerd Mohn, 1963), pp. 191ff. David Löfgren, *Die Theologie der Schöpfung bei Luther* (Göttingven: Vandenhoeck & Ruprecht, 1960), pp. 125 ff., and Kjell Nilsson, *Simul* (Göttingen: Vandenhoeck & Ruprecht, 1966), pp. 193 ff., both attempt to reformulate the "classic" theory in response.
29. 26, 31; 282.
30. 51, 278 f; 26, 132.
31. 26, 37 ff.
32. Note in comparison the validity and the limitations of Bonhoeffer's famous definition of Christ as "the man for others."
33. This line of interpretation is taken by Lauri Haikola, *Studien zu Luther und zum Luthertum,* "Uppsala Universitets Arsskrift," 2: (Uppsala: A.-B. Lundequistska Bokhandeln, 1958), p. 114. Cf. also Karin Bornkamm, *Luthers Auslegungen des Galaterbriefs von 1519 und 1531,* ("Arbeiten zur Kirchengeschichte," 35; Berlin: Walter de Gruyter & Co., 1963), p. 136.
34. W 5, 602, 32 ff.
35. 26, 164.
36. 26, 159 f.
37. LCC 15, 43.
38. LCC 16, 349 f.
39. LCC 15, 205; 207; 27, 367.
40. 37, 95 f.
41. LCC 15, 205.
42. LCC 15, 204.
43. LCC 16, 196 f.; 26, 64.
44. LCC 15, 16; 27, 65.
45. Recall in this connection Luther's use of the traditional analogy of man the beast ridden either by God or the devil.
46. 27, 364.
47. 26, 349.

Notes to Essay III

Lex et Fides

1. LCC 16, 95 f.
2. LCC 15, 61.
3. W 10, 1A, 193, 9-22.

4. LCC 17, 210 f.; 213.
5. The best single source for Luther's developed views on this issue is his 1535 *Lectures on Galatians,* especially on chapter three.
6. LCC 15, 278-280
7. W 39, 1, 387. 1-4, et al.
8. 22, 150 ff.; LCC 16, 348; LCC 17, 131.
9. 37, 134 f.; LCC 15, 299 f.
10. This theme begins to emerge in Luther's 1517 *Lectures on the Epistle to the Hebrews* and 1519 *Lectures on Galatians.* Cf. LCC 15, 301 f.; LCC 16, 74 f.; 194 f.; 27, 249.
11. 22, 21 f.; 14, 70; 25, 39 f.
12. This thesis is evident already in the *Lectures on Romans,* and finds its richest exposition in Luther's 1535 commentary on Galatians, chapter three.
13. LCC 15, 298; LCC 17, 129 ff.; 172; 14, 335.
14. 26, 301 f.; 27, 197.
15. 26, 299 f.
16. 26, 54; 64.
17. 26, 72; 115; W 39, 1, 361.4-6.
18. 26, 91; 116 f.; 142; 144; 208.
19. 26, 402.
20. 22, 141 f. This theme is most in evidence in Luther's exchange with Erasmus of 1525.
21. 26, 307; 343.
22. A distinction of Kjell Nilsson, *Simul,* (Göttingen: Vandenhoeck & Ruprecht, 1966).
23. 26, 326; W 7, 114. 25 ff.
24. W 1, 227. 26 ff.; 14, 295.
25. For the following discussion cf. LCC 15, 45 ff.
26. Cf. LCC 16, 272 f.
27. 27, 235.
28. 26, 80; 362; 22, 145.
29. W 39, 1, 348. 27-30; 354. 17 ff.; 374.18-20, et al.
30. W 39, 1, 345. 20 f.; 361. 19 ff.; 369. 13; 404. 16 f.
31. W 39, 1, 477. 1 ff.; cf. 361. 30; 353. 37 f. Cf. also Martin Schloemann, *Natürliches and Gepredigtes Gesetz bei Luther* (Berlin: Verlag Alfred Töpelmann, 1961), pp. 92 f., 127, on the "already there" character of the Law.
32. 26, 348.
33. 22, 165; my translation. The more literal translation better preserves the sense of Luther's urgency.
34. Cf. Paul Althaus, *Die Ethik Martin Luthers* (Gütersloh: Gütersloher Verlagshaus Gerd Mohn, 1965), p. 22; Lauri Haikola, *Usus Legis,* "Uppsala Universitets Arsskrift," 3: (Uppsala: A.-B. Lundequistska Bokhandeln, 1958), p. 128; Schloemann, *op. cit.,* pp. 50 ff.
35. Gerhard Ebeling, *Word and Faith,* trans. James W. Leitch (Philadelphia: Fortress Press, 1963), p. 75; cf. p. 278.
36. 26, 150; 312 f.
37. W 39, 1, 424. 4-6; 425. 2-4; 542. 12-14.
38. 27, 221; 354; 26, 260; W 7, 115. 5-20.
39. LCC 16, 139 f.
40. 26, 365; 27, 17; LCC 17, 126 ff.
41. W 39, 1, 460. 17-22.
42. W 7, 51. 17; 26, 294.
43. Some students have suggested this interpretation of Luther. Cf. Paul Althaus, *Die Theologie Martin Luthers* (Gütersloh: Gütersloher Verlagshaus Gerd Mohn, 1963), p. 153; B. A. Gerrish, *Grace and Reason* (Oxford: Clarendon Press, 1962), pp. 58, 82; Reinhard Schwarz, *Fides, Spes, und Caritas beim Jungen Luther* ("Arbeiten zur Kirchengeschichte," 34; Berlin: Walter de Gruyter & Co., 1962), p. 150; Vilmos Vajta, *Die Theologie des Gottesdienstes bei Luther* (Stockholm: Svenska Kyrkans

Diakonistyrelses Bökforlag, 1952), p. 15; Gustav Wingren, *Luther on Vocation* (Philadelphia: Muhlenberg Press, 1957), p. 200.
44. 27, 197.
45. 27, 219 ff.
46. Cf. for example 26, 86; 88; 113 ff.; 142 ff.; 271; 300; 343.
47. For the following cf. 26, 4-12.
48. Cf. Ebeling, *op. cit.,* p. 279; Haikola, *op. cit.,* p. 68, n. 36.
49. 26, 229 ff.; 44, 31 f.; W 5, 396. 31 ff.
50. 27, 175; W 19, 200. 30-32.
51. 26, 82; 27, 259; 264; LCC 15, 145; 154.
52. Cf. John Loeschen, "The Function of *Promissio* in Luther's *Commentary on Romans,"* Harvard Theological Review, Vol. 60, n. 4 (October, 1967), pp. 476-82.
53. LCC 15, 78 f.; 81.
54. LCC 15, 79 f.
55. LCC 15, 124 f., in part.
56. LCC 15, 208; 26, 232.
57. LCC 15, 127 ff.; 135.
58. W 39, 1, 542. 5-9; 544. 10 f.; 561. 11; 652. 10 f.; 26, 349.
59. 51, 281; 27, 203; 236; 37, 249; LCC 15, 108; 123.
60. W 5, 119. 14 f.; 176. 1-11.
61. W 2, 146. 29-147. 23; 12, 357; 27, 252.
62. W 39, 1, 93. 8-12; 200. 9-11; 226. 14-17.
63. LCC 15, 322 f.

Notes to Essay IV

Promissio et Fides

1. Cf. the studies of Schwarz, Wingren, Wolf, Grundmann, Nilsson, Borsch, Iwand, von Loewenich, and Bandt, listed in the bibliography. These studies, though given primarily to other subjects, reflect the growing place given to the concept of *promissio* for interpreting Luther.
2. James S. Preus, *From Shadow to Promise* (Cambridge: Harvard University Press, 1969); Stephen Ozment, *Homo Spiritualis* (Leiden: E. J. Brill, 1969).
3. Cf. John Loeschen, "The Function of *Promissio* in Luther's *Commentary on Romans,"* Harvard Theological Review, Vol. 60, n. 4 (October, 1967).
4. Preus, *op. cit.,* p. 179, n. 9.
5. Ozment, *op. cit.,* pp. 105 ff.; cf. Reinhard Schwarz, *Fides, Spes, und Caritas beim Jungen Luther* (Berlin: Walter de Gruyter & Co., 1962), pp. 158 ff. I shall return to Ozment's valuable conclusions in section two.
6. LCC 15, 4 f.; 12.
7. 25, 24 f.; LCC 15, 61 f.
8. The following is a summary of Loeschen, *op. cit.*
9. LCC 15, 235 f.; I shall return to this passage in section two.
10. 27, 377.
11. The excursus is found in W 5, 158.4-177.27.
12. W 5, 175. 11-37, in part.
13. 44, 30 ff.
14. The following is a summary of the argument from 36, 35-57.
15. The following is a summary of 36, 57-74.
16. LCC 17, 117; cf. John Loeschen, "Promise and Necessity in Luther's *De servo arbitrio," The Lutheran Quarterly* (August, 1971).
17. LCC 17, 118.
18. LCC 17, 122 f., in part.
19. LCC 17, 232 ff.
20. LCC 17, 237 f.
21. LCC 17, 239.

22. LCC 17, 240.
23. LCC 17, 328 f.
24. 26, 239.
25. Summarizing 26, 251-256.
26. Summarizing 26, 271 f.
27. Summarizing 26, 299-302.
28. Summarizing 26, 340-42.
29. Cf. for example LCC 17, 309.
30. For the following, cf. Schwarz, *op. cit.*, pp. 158 ff.; and Ozment, *op. cit.*, pp. 105 ff.
31. For the following, cf. LCC 15, 225-38.
32. LCC 15, 235 f., in part; cf. 322 f.
33. LCC 16, 74 f.; 194; LCC 15, 301 f.
34. LCC 16, 75; cf. W 5, 96. 30 f.
35. LCC 17, 138, in part.
36. For the following, cf. LCC 15, 278 ff.
37. As is normal in this commentary, Luther's language tends to shift away from traditional usages. As he continues the discussion, the "letter-spirit" contrast is replaced first by "Law-spirit," then by "Law-Gospel."
38. 26, 264 f.
39. 27, 52.
40. For the following, cf. 12, 238 f.; 242.
41. For a discussion of the "divine mathematics," cf. Werner Elert, *The Structure of Lutheranism* (St. Louis: Concordia Publishing House, 1962), pp. 82 ff.; and Ole Modalski, *Das Gericht Nach den Werken* (Göttingen: Vandenhoeck & Ruprecht, 1963), p. 128.
42. W, DB 7, 10. 16 f.
43. Cf. the discussion of Luther's *Operationes in psalmos* in the first section; cf. Schwarz, *op. cit.*, for the most complete general treatment.
44. 27, 333; LCC 17, 214; LCC 15, 239 f.
45. LCC 15, 127 f.
46. The former perspective has been the guiding motif of the first half of our study; the latter will guide the second half.
47. 36, 58; cf. 44.
48. LCC 15, 78; 151.
49. LCC 15, 294.
50. LCC 15, 322.
51. 36, 39.
52. W 46, 583.
53. LCC 15, 321 f.
54. LCC 15, 118 ff.
55. 27, 32.
56. W 5, 408. 1-13.
57. 30, 35.

Notes to Essay V

Initium Novae Creaturae

1. 36, 40 f.; 27, 140; W 10, 1A, 233. 7 ff.
2. 26, 380; 27, 140; LCC 17, 304 f.
3. W 7, 109. 24-30; cf. W 5, 302. 36 f.
4. LCC 15, 387; cf. 26, 7.
5. 27, 326.
6. W 39, 1, 431. 10 ff.
7. LCC 16, 45 f.; LCC 15, 230.
8. Cf. 21, 72. The sermon is indeed addressed to Christians, but concerns doctrine, not life or morals, 27, 184; LCC 17, 210: Law in the Gospels is either "interpretation" or "remedies."

9. 44, 25; cf. W 4, 213. 19-21.
10. I discussed this struggle in the third essay.
11. LCC 15, 52.
12. LCC 16, 139 f., in part; emphasis mine.
13. Cf. Gerhard Ebeling, *Word and Faith,* trans. James W. Leitch (Philadelphia: Fortress Press, 1963), p. 71; Reinhard Schwarz, *Fides, Spes, und Caritas beim Jungen Luther* (Berlin: Walter de Gruyter & Co., 1962), pp. 171, 247; and Lauri Haikola, *Usus Legis,* "Uppsala Universitets Arsskrift," 3 (Uppsala: A.-B. Lundequistska Bokhandeln, 1958), pp. 104 ff., 134, 144, for interpretations of "Law" which approximate my own.
14. The following summarizes 27, 232-36.
15. 36, 335; W 39, 1, 114. 28-30; W 39, 2, 248. 11 ff.
16. At LCC 15, 123 Luther indicates something similar to this distinction.
17. 14, 298; W 5, 107. 14 ff.; 163. 28.
18. W 1, 186. 25-29; W 5, 118. 1-3; 26, 8 f., among many other passages affirming the existence and function of a recreated *imago dei.*
19. LCC 15, 180; LCC 16, 75 f.
20. 22, 28; 26, 360 f., among many other passages.
21. So also with Tillich's "ground of being," and "shaking of the foundations."
22. Cf. Luther's notes on Ecclesiastes, 15, 49 ff., and his sermons on the Gospel of John, W 33, 400 ff., for material on this theme. The most valuable secondary presentation is found in Johann Haar, *Initium Creaturae Dei* (Gütersloh: C. Bertelsmann, 1939), pp. 14 ff.
23. 12, 52 f.
24. 15, 49 ff.
25. 22, 28 f. Cf. Karin Bornkamm, *Luthers Auslegungen des Galaterbriefs von 1519 und 1531* (Berlin: Walter de Gruyter & Co., 1963), p. 343: justification is also for Luther a continuous *creatio ex nihilo.*
26. W 10, 1A, 200. 3 ff.; 203. 3 ff.; 34, 139 f.
27. W 5, 465. 38-40; W 10, 1A, 208. 17 ff.
28. 36, 124; LCC 15, 181; 26, 352.
29. 36, 66.
30. 36, 70.
31. 27, 140.
32. 27, 252; 349.
33. 27, 325.
34. 27, 349.
35. W 9, 58. 15-18.
36. LCC 16, 358. Most of the relevant sources for this section are found in the *Lectures on Romans* and the treatise *Against Latomus,* with additional material from the 1519 and 1535 commentaries on Gal. 2:20.
37. LCC 15, 201; 204; 207.
38. LCC 15, 213 f.
39. LCC 16, 358.
40. LCC 15, 205; 207.
41. LCC 15, 204 f.
42. LCC 16, 355; 26, 166.
43. 26, 166 f.; 27, 238.
44. LCC 16, 354.
45. 26, 167 f.
46. 26, 170; 27, 239.
47. LCC 16, 350.
48. LCC 16, 350 f.; LCC 15, 212 f.
49. LCC 16, 356; W 7, 110. 36-38.
50. 30, 17; 27, 290.
51. LCC 15, 125; 208.
52. LCC 15, 214.

Notes to Essay VI

Ubiquitas Carnalis Christi

1. W 19, 197. 18-32, in part.
2. Cf. Paul Althaus, *Die Theologie Martin Luthers* (Gütersloh: Gütersloher Verlagshaus Gerd Mohn, 1963), p. 320 f.; Ekkehard Börsch, *Geber-Gabe-Aufgabe* (München: Chr. Kaiser Verlag, 1958), pp. 50 ff.; Hans Grass, *Die Abendmahlslehre bei Luther und Calvin* (Gütersloh: C. Bertelsmann Verlag, 1954), pp. 22 ff.
3. 37, 88 f.; 133; 338.
4. 37, 68.
5. 37, 68 f.
6. The first image suggests Luther's understanding of God's *larvae;* the second was given classic formulation by St. Augustine. On the Word as "window," cf. Vilmos Vajta, *Die Theologie des Gottesdienstes bei Luther* (Stockholm: Svenska Kyrkans Diakonistyrelses Bokförlag, 1952), p. 195.
7. 36, 35.
8. 37, 65; 184; 187; 230.
9. Luther touched on the matter at 37, 71, but began to concentrate on it only at 37, 115.
10. Cf. his *Commentary on True and False Religion,* in *Sämtliche Werke (Corpus Reformatorum,* 90: Berlin: C. A. Schwetscke, 1905—), pp. 764 ff.
11. Cf. his *On the Clarity and Certainty of the Word of God,* in *Sämtliche Werke (Corpus Reformatorum,* 88), pp. 366. 30 ff.; 369. 25 ff.
12. *Commentary,* 786. 31 ff.
13. Ibid., 786. 31 ff.; 792. 24 ff.; 817. 32 ff. Luther at 37, 51 recognizes this criterion as the operative one for the fanatics.
14. 37, 64; 85; 87; 100.
15. 37, 87.
16. 37, 95. By relating the realms in this way Luther is suggesting a significantly different interpretation of how God relates to the world than obtained in the Western philosophical tradition. Cf. the fine work of Erwin Metzke, *Sakrament und Metaphysik* (Stuttgart: Kreuz-Verlag, 1948), especially p. 20, in this regard.
17. 40, 216 ff.
18. 36, 338 ff.
19. 37, 63 f.
20. 37, 55; 69.
21. 37, 224.
22. 37, 217.
23. Cf. Albrecht Peters, *Realpräsenz* (Berlin: Lutherisches Verlagshaus, 1960), p. 62; Regin Prenter, *Spiritus Creator* (Philadelphia: Muhlenberg Press, 1953), pp. 299 ff.; Philip Watson, *Let God Be God!* (Philadelphia: Fortress Press, 1947), p. 162. Only the work of Metzke, *op. cit.,* is at home with Luther on this matter. But his fine monograph has largely been ignored.
24. 37, 51; 62; 210; 297.
25. 37, 63.
26. 37, 218 f.; W 50, 589. 25-28; W 45, 298. 16-20; 299. 26 ff.
27. 37, 214 f.; 218, et al.
28. LCC 16, 65; 26, 277.
29. 37, 84. Cf. 48 f.; 59; 61; 64 for the same kind of argument on related issues.
30. 37, 62; 68.
31. 37, 209, et al.
32. 37, 228 f.
33. 37, 212 f.; 218 f.; 222.
34. 37, 219; cf. 229.
35. 37, 224 ff.
36. 41, 96 ff.; cf. 101 f.
37. 41, 102 f.

38. Later orthodoxy named this form the *genus apotelesmaticum*. Cf. Kjell Nilsson, *Simul* (Göttingen: Vandenhoeck & Ruprecht, 1966), p. 240, for a discussion of the various *genera*.
39. The *genus idiomaticum*. Cf. 37, 62 f.; 210, *et al*.
40. The *genus majestaticum*.
41. Cf. Nilsson, *op. cit.*, pp. 232, 247 ff., for passages.
42. 37, 61 f.; 218.
43. Cf. Nilsson, ibid., p. 245.
44. Cf. 37, 47; 94; 140; 207; 223 f. Cf. Hans Grass, *Die Abendsmahlslehre bei Luther und Calvin* (Gütersloh: C. Bertelsmann Verlag, 1954), p. 58; David Löfgren, *Die Theologie der Schöpfung bei* Luther (Göttingen: Vandenhoeck & Ruprecht, 1960), p. 234; Hermann Sasse, *This Is My Body* (Minneapolis: Augsburg Publishing House, 1959), p. 157.
45. Let me simply note here that the fourth ground is based on the prior three: the doctrine of Christ, the doctrine of God, and the doctrine of the Word.

Notes to Essay VII

Larvae Dei

1. LCC 16, 266 ff.; 276 ff.; W 7, 91-152.
2. For an expanded consideration of the matter, cf. John Loeschen, "Promise and Necessity in Luther's *De servo arbitrio,*" *The Lutheran Quarterly* (August, 1971).
3. Cf. Paul Althaus, *Die Theologie Martin Luthers* (Gütersloh: Gütersloher Verlagshaus Gerd Mohn, 1963), pp. 240 ff.; David Löfgren, *Die Theologie der Schöpfung bei Luther* (Göttingen: Vandenhoeck & Ruprecht, 1960), p. 128 f.; Gordon Rupp, *The Righteousness of God* (London: Rodder and Stoughton, 1953), p. 282 f.; and Hans Vorster, *Das Freiheitsverständnis bei Thomas von Aquin und Martin Luther* (Göttingen: Vandenhoeck & Ruprecht, 1965), p. 308, for differing views on the supposed tension.
4. LCC 17, 138.
5. LCC 15, 43; cf. 17.
6. Luther explicitly develops the "wondrous exchange" aspect of this tropological application of *communicatio idiomatum* at W 5, 219 f.
7. 26, 5.
8. Cf. 5, 43 f.: "A distinction must be made when one deals with the knowledge, or rather the subject, of the divinity. For one must debate either about the hidden God or about the revealed God. With regard to God, insofar as He has not been revealed, there is no faith, no knowledge, and no understanding."
9. Cf. 1, 13: It is insane to argue about God apart from His Word or covering. We ought to keep to the "forms, signs, and coverings of the Godhead . . . which are His Word and His works."
10. LCC 15, 27. Cf. Kjell Nilsson, *Simul* (Göttingen: Vandenhoeck & Ruprecht, 1966), pp. 98, 165 f.; Gottfried Forck, *Die Königsherrschaft Jesu Christi bei Luther* (Berlin: Evangelische Verlagsanstalt, 1959), p. 43.
11. 27, 43. 14, 31 contains the best, or the worst, example of Luther's paradoxical extremes I have encountered.
12. W 19, 223. 12-16.
13. 1, 11; 12, 21 ff.
14. 26, 323.
15. 26, 232.
16. 1, 11.
17. W 5, 301. 24-26; cf. 14-17.
18. LCC 17, 309.
19. LCC 17, 117.
20. LCC 15, 16.
21. LCC 17, 116 f.
22. LCC 17, 141.

23. LCC 17, 141 f.; 170.
24. LCC 17, 228; 236.
25. LCC 17, 244.
26. These terms as Trinitarian references is an idea of Paul Tillich, *Love, Power, and Justice* (New York: Oxford University Press, 1960).
27. 37, 61, in part; emphasis mine.
28. Cf. Kenneth Cauthen's excellent article, "Christology as the Clarification of Creation," *The Journal of Bible and Religion,* XXXIII (January, 1965, n. 1).
29. Cf. B. A. Gerrish, *Grace and Reason* (Oxford: Clarendon Press, 1962), p. 103, and Nilsson, *op. cit.,* p. 274.
30. 26, 246 f.
31. W 43, 28. 25.
32. 13, 101.
33. 22, 28.
34. W 4, 595-602.
35. 22, 28 f.; cf. W 42, 14. 32 ff.: 57. 9 ff.: W 22, 444. 20 ff.
36. W, DB 11, 1, 396. 7-15.
37. 37, 228; 60, conflated; emphasis mine.
38. 37, 274.
39. 34, 139 ff.; cf. Johann Haar, *Initium Creaturae Dei* (Gütersloh: C. Bertelsmann, 1939), pp. 93, 98.
40. 26, 171.
41. 26, 171.
42. Cf. Gustav Wingren, *Luther on Vocation* (Philadelphia: Muhlenberg Press, 1957), pp. 137, 180; Vorster, *op. cit.,* pp. 380 ff.
43. 9, 41.
44. 22, 93; cf. Nilsson, *op. cit.,* p. 38.
45. The terms "order," "estate," "mandate," and "station," have subtle differences in nuance. I have chosen to work with the term "mandate" because of its connections with "law" and "freedom."
46. 26, 95 f.
47. 30, 73 f.
48. 37, 365.
49. LCC 15, 34 f. W 56, 186. 31.
50. LCC 15, 286; 332.
51. 1, 39; 109; 131.
52. 44, 72.
53. 9, 41; 203; 26, 95; LCC 15, 84 f.
54. 26, 170.
55. 27, 206.
56. 27, 261 f.
57. 13, 193 ff.

Notes to Essay VIII

Regnum Dei-Regnum Mundi

1. 22, 38.
2. 13, 290 f.; 299.
3. LCC 15, 242.
4. 13, 289; cf. W, DB 11, 1, 402. 15-38.
5. W 5, 294. 4-7; LCC 17, 309 f.; LCC 15, 81.
6. W 5, 301. 14-17.
7. 37, 365 f.
8. 36, 107.
9. 12, 25; cf. Johann Haar, *Initium Creaturae Dei* (Gütersloh: C. Bertelsmann, 1939), pp. 50, 89 f., 98.
10. 21, 12.

11. W 15, 725. 7-10.
12. LCC 16, 45; 166.
13. 27, 114.
14. Gerhard Ebeling, *Word and Faith,* trans. James W. Leitch (Philadelphia: Fortress Press, 1963), p. 386 f.
15. 22, 225.
16. 26, 174.
17. 22, 226; 13, 194 f.; LCC 15, 359 f.
18. 12, 42; 26, 10.
19. 26, 127; 27, 52; LCC 15, 293; 329.
20. LCC 15, 238; W 10, 1A, 203. 8 ff.
21. 26, 39 f.; 27, 59.
22. 12, 238 f.
23. LCC 16, 267.
24. LCC 15, 204; 12, 215.
25. W 5, 661. 10 ff. Ebeling, *op. cit.,* pp. 390 ff., and Wilfried Jöest, *Gesetz und Freiheit* (Göttingen: Vandenhoeck & Ruprecht, 1961), pp. 29 f., 41 ff., are the best discussions of this self-contradiction.
26. 27, 232 f.; LCC 16, 60; 26, 159 ff.
27. LCC 15, 357.
28. LCC 17, 229.
29. 26, 13.
30. 26, 351.
31. 13, 249.
32. 13, 7; 12, 19.
33. LCC 17, 129; W, DB 11, 1, 402. 15-28.
34. 13, 13; LCC 17, 129.
35. LCC 17, 129.
36. 12, 19.
37. 26, 8; 42; W 5, 301. 14 ff.; 30, 75.
38. 30, 20; 76.
39. 22, 94.
40. 13, 197 f.
41. 26, 173.
42. 27, 170.
43. W 5, 128. 29 ff. Cf. Gerhard Ebeling, *Luther: Einfuhrung in Sein Denken* (Tübingen: J. C. B. Mohr, 1964), pp. 181 ff.; Jöest, *op. cit.,* pp. 63, 69 f.
44. LCC 16, 182.
45. 37, 281: LCC 15, 398 f.; LCC 16, 31.
46. LCC 15, 359.
47. 30, 73 f.; 37, 364.
48. 21, 23; cf. 109.
49. 21, 21; 110.
50. 26, 287; 27, 30; 377; 34, 162; W 39, 1, 208. 9-11; 226. 14-17.
51. W 5, 418. 33 ff.; 30, 24 f.; 9, 184 f.; 37, 283.

Bibliography

Althaus, Paul. *Die Ethik Martin Luthers*. Gütersloh: Gütersloher Verlagshaus Gerd Mohn. 1965.

———. *Die Theologie Martin Luthers*. Gütersloh: Gütersloher Verlagshaus Gerd Mohn. 1963.

Aulen, Gustav. *Christus Victor*. An Historical Study of the Three Main Types of the Idea of the Atonement. Trans. A. G. Hebert. New York: The Macmillan Co. 1961.

Bandt. Helmut. *Luthers Lehre vom Verborgenen Gott*. Eine Untersuchung zu dem offenbarungsgeschichtlichen Ansatz seiner Theologie. Theologische Arbeiten, ed. H. Urner, Bd. VIII. Berlin: Evangelische Verlagsanstalt. 1958.

Börsch, Ekkehard. *Geber-Gabe-Aufgabe*. Luthers Prophetie in den Entscheidungsjahren seiner Reformation 1520—1525. Forschungen zur Geschichte und Lehre des Protestantismus, Bd. XIII. München: Chr. Kaiser Verlag. 1958.

Bonhoeffer, Dietrich. *Creation and Fall*. Trans. John Fletcher. New York: The Macmillan Co. 1961.

———. *Ethics*. Ed. Eberhard Bethge, trans. Neville Horton Smith. New York: The Macmillan Co. 1962.

Bornkamm, Karin. *Luthers Auslegungen des Galaterbriefs von 1519 und 1531*. Arbeiten zur Kirchengeschichte, 35. Berlin: Walter de Gruyter & Co. 1963.

Cauthen, Kenneth. "Christology as the Clarification of Creation," *The Journal of Bible and Religion,* XXXIII, no. 1 (January, 1965), 34—41.

Ebeling, Gerhard. *Luther*. Einführung in Sein Denken. Tübingen: J. C. B. Mohr. 1964.

———. *Word and Faith.* Trans. James W. Leitch. Philadelphia: Fortress Press. 1963.

Elert, Werner. *The Structure of Lutheranism*. Trans. W. Hansen. St. Louis: Concordia Publishing House. 1962.

Feuerbach, Ludwig. *The Essence of Faith According to Luther*. Trans. Melvin Cherno. New York: Harper & Row. 1967.

Forck, Gottfried. *Die Königsherrschaft Jesu Christi bei Luther*. Theologische Arbeiten, Bd. XII. Berlin: Evangelische Verlagsanstalt. 1959.

Gerdes, Hayo. *Luthers Streit mit den Schwärmern um das Rechte Verständnis des Gesetzes Mose*. Göttingen: Göttinger Verlagsanstalt. 1955.

Gerrish, B. A. *Grace and Reason*. A Study in the Theology of Luther. Oxford: Clarendon Press. 1962.

Grane, Leif. *Contra Gabrielem.* Luthers Auseinandersetzung mit Gabriel Biel in der Disputatio Contra Scholasticam Theologiam 1517. Übers. E. Pump. Acta Theologica Danica, vol. IV. Copenhagen: Gyldendal. 1962.

Grass, Hans. *Die Abendsmahlslehre bei Luther und Calvin.* Beiträge zur Forderung Christlicher Theologie, Bd. 47. Gütersloh: C. Bertelsmann Verlag. 1954.

Grundmann, Walter. *Der Römerbrief des Apostels Paulus und seine Auslegung durch Martin Luther.* Weimar: Hermann Böhlaus Nachfolger. 1964.

Gyllenkrok, Axel. *Rechtfertigung und Heiligung in der Früher Evangelischen Theologie Luther.* Uppsala Universitets Arsskrift, 1952: 2. Uppsala & Weisbaden: A.-B. Lundequistska Bokhandeln. 1952.

Haar, Johann. *Initium Creaturae Dei.* Eine Untersuchung über Luthers Begriff der "neuen Creatur" im Zusammenhang mit seinem Verständnis von Jakobus 1: 18 und mit seinem "Zeit"-Denken. Gütersloh: C. Bertelsmann. 1939.

Hägglund, Bengt. *Theologie und Philosophie bei Luther und in der Occamistischen Tradition.* Lunds Universitets Arsskrift, Bd. 51, n. 4. Lund: C. W.-K. Gleerup. 1955.

Haikola, Lauri. *Studien zu Luther und zum Luthertum.* Uppsala Universitets Arsskrift, 1958: 2. Uppsala: A.-B. Lundequistska Bokhandeln. 1958.

———. *Usus Legis.* Uppsala Universitets Arsskrift, 1958: 3. Uppsala: A.-B. Lundequistska Bokhandeln. 1958.

Heintze, Gerhard. *Luthers Predigt von Gesetz und Evangelium.* Forschungen zur Geschichte und Lehre des Protestantismus, Bd. XI. München: Chr. Kaiser Verlag. 1958.

Hermann, Rudolf. *Luthers These "Gerecht und Sünder Zugleish."* Gütersloh: Gütersloher Verlagshaus Gerd Mohn. 1960.

Hillerdal, Gunner. *Gehorsam Gegen Gott und Mensch.* Luthers Lehre von der Obrigkeit und die moderne evangelische Staatsethik. Lund: Hakan Ohlssons Boktryckeri. 1954.

Hirsch, Emmanuel. *Lutherstudien I.* Gütersloh: C. Bertelsmann. 1954.

Iwand, Hans. *Rechtfertigungslehre und Christusglaube.* München: Chr. Kaiser Verlag. 1961.

Jöest, Wilfried. *Gesetz und Freiheit.* Das Problem des tertius usus legis bei Luther und die neutestamentlich Parainäse. Göttingen: Vandenhoeck & Ruprecht. 1961.

Löfgren, David. *Die Theologie der Schöpfung bei Luther.* Forschungen zur Kirchen- und Dogmengeschichte, Bd. 10. Göttingen: Vandenhoeck & Ruprecht. 1960.

Loeschen, John. "The Function of *Promissio* in Luther's *Commentary on Romans,*" *Harvard Theological Review,* vol. 60, n. 4 (October, 1967), 476—483.

———. "Promise and Necessity in Luther's *De servo arbitrio,*" *The Lutheran Quarterly,* vol. XXIII, n. 3 (August, 1971), 257—268.

von Loewenich, Walter. *Luther's Theologia Crucis.* München: Chr. Kaiser Verlag. 1954.

Lohse, Bernhard. *Ratio und Fides.* Eine Untersuchung über die ratio in der

Theologie Luthers. Forschungen zur Kirchen- und Dogmengeschichte, Bd. 8. Göttingen: Vandenhoeck & Ruprecht. 1958.

Luther, Martin. *Luther: Early Theological Works.* Ed., trans. James Atkinson. *The Library of Christian Classics,* vol. XVI. Philadelphia: The Westminster Press. 1962.

————. *Luther and Erasmus: Free Will and Salvation.* Ed., trans. E. Gordon Rupp, Philip S. Watson. *The Library of Christian Classics,* vol. XVII. Philadelphia: The Westminster Press. 1969.

————. *Luther: Lectures on Romans.* Ed., trans. Wilhelm Pauck. *The Library of Christian Classics,* vol. XV. Philadelphia: The Westminister Press. 1961.

————. *Werke: Kritische Gesammtausgabe.* Weimar: H. Böhlau. 1883—.

————. *Luther's Works.* American Edition. Eds. Jaroslav Pelikan, Helmut Lehman. 55 vols. St. Louis: Concordia Publishing House. Philadelphia: Fortress Press. 1955—.

Metzke, Erwin. *Sakrament und Metaphysik.* Eine Lutherstudie über das Verhältnis des christlichen Denkens zum Leiblich-Materiellen. Schriftenreihe Lebendige Wissenschaft, H. 9. Stuttgart: Kreuz-Verlag. 1948.

Modalski, Ole. *Das Gericht nach den Werken.* Ein Beitrag zu Luthers Lehre vom Gesetz. Forschungen zur Kirchen- und Dogmengeschichte, Bd. 13 Göttingen: Vandenhoeck & Ruprecht. 1963.

Nilsson, Kjell Ove. *Simul.* Das Miteinander von Göttlichem und Menschlichem in Luthers Theologie. Forschungen zur Kirchen- und Dogmengeschichte, Bd. 17. Göttingen: Vandenhoeck & Ruprecht. 1966.

Ozment, Steven E. *Homo Spiritualis.* A Comparative Study of the Anthropology of Johannes Tauler, Jean Gerson and Martin Luther (1509—16) in the Context of Their Theological Thought. Studies in Medieval and Reformation Thought, 6. Leiden: E. J. Brill. 1969.

Peters, Albrecht. *Realpräsenz.* Luthers Zeugnis von Christi Gengenwart im Abendmahl. Arbeiten zur Geschichte und Theologie des Luthertums, Bd. 5. Berlin: Lutherisches Verlagshaus. 1960.

Preus, James Samuel. *From Shadow to Promise.* Old Testament Interpretation from Augustine to the Young Luther. Cambridge: Harvard University Press. 1969.

Prenter, Regin. *Spiritus Creator.* Trans. John M. Jensen. Philadelphia: Muhlenberg Press. 1953.

Rupp, Gordon. *The Righteousness of God.* Luther Studies. London: Rodder & Stoughton. 1953.

Sasse, Hermann. *This Is My Body.* Luther's Contention for the Real Presence in the Sacrament of the Altar. Minneapolis: Augsburg Publishing House. 1959.

Schloemann, Martin. *Natürliches und Gepredigtes Gesetz bei Luther.* Berlin: Verlag Alfred Töpelmann. 1961.

Schwarz, Reinhard. *Fides, Spes, und Caritas beim Jungen Luther.* Arbeiten zur Kirchengeschichte, 34. Berlin: Walter de Gruyter & Co. 1962.

Seils, Martin. *Der Gedanke vom Zusammenwirken Gottes und des Menschen in Luthers Theologie.* Beiträge zur Forderung Christlicher Theologie,

Bd. 50. Gütersloh: Gütersloher Verlagshaus Gerd Mohn. 1962.

Stange, Carl. *Luthers Gedanken über die Todesfurcht.* Berlin: Walter de Gruyter & Co. 1932.

Tillich, Paul. *Love, Power, and Justice.* New York: Oxford University Press. 1960.

Törnvall, Gustav. *Geistliches und Weltliches Regiment bei Luther.* Forschungen zur Geschichte und Lehre des Protestantismus, Bd. II. München: Chr. Kaiser Verlag. 1947.

Vajta, Vilmos. *Die Theologie des Gottesdienstes bei Luther.* Stockholm: Svenska Kyrkans Diakonistyrelses Bokförlag. 1952.

Vorster, Hans. *Das Freiheitsverständnis bei Thomas von Aquin und Martin Luther.* Kirche und Konfession, Bd. 8. Göttingen: Vandenhoeck & Ruprecht. 1965.

Watson, Philip. *Let God Be God!* An Interpretation of the Theology of Martin Luther. Philadelphia: Fortress Press. 1947.

Wingren, Gustaf. *Luther on Vocation.* Philadelphia: Muhlenberg Press. 1957.

Zwingli, Hulrich. *Sämtliche Werke.* Corpus Reformatorum, vols. 88, 90. Berlin: C. A. Schwetscke. 1905—.

191

INDEX

Abelard 53

Abraham 90-91, 92

Anabaptists 32, 107, 128, 167

Anselm 53

Anthropology: bondage of man 52-53, 54; of Christian man 57-58; of flesh-spirit 45, 46-47, 56-57; *incurvatus* 48, 52; and image of God 47; and Law 69-70, 83; psychology 44-45; relational nature of 45-46; and systems of value 50-51; and tyrants 59, 61. *See also* Bondage of the will; Conscience; Flesh and spirit; Image of God; Knowledge of God; Knowledge of man; Law; Person-work; Sin

Aristotle 144, 172

Atonement 54; Christ's divinity proved by 53-54, 130, 132; dialectical language of 17; *pro nobis* character of 56; theories of 53; and tyrants 54-56. *See also* Christology; Tyrants

Augustine, St. 10, 43, 46, 50, 67-68, 96

Author's method 9-10, 17, 28, 30, 37, 59, 66, 123, 160, 173-174; outlines 37-39, 41, 43-44, 81, 84, 106, 122, 124, 139, 160; periodization 12, 13-14; selection of data 12-13; summaries 26-27, 28-29, 58, 68-69, 72, 74-75, 83, 104, 120, 122, 127, 133, 139-140, 159, 172-173, 175

Baptism and confession 102; and hope 89; and masks 146; and promise 88-89, 102, 116; as sign of faith 115-116. *See also* Forgiveness of sins; Promise; Sacraments

Bondage of the will: as anthropological definition 52-53; in *De servo arbitrio* 140; and double will in God 141-145; and hope 89; and necessity of events 89-90, 140-141; and power 144-145, 146-147, 147-148; to sin 53-54; and struggle of realms 166-167, 167. *See also* Anthropology; Erasmus

Bonhoeffer, D. 9, 18, 30, 33, 99, 157. *See also* Schema

Calvin, J. 20, 107

Camus, A. 55

Catholic theology 32, 125, 127. *See also* Lord's Supper; Scholasticism

Christ: and Christian life 101, 117-120; and creation 146, 152-153; and knowledge of God, man 52, 54-55, 141; modal presence 133-135, 136-137; place in Luther's theology 173; and real presence 125-127, 127-128, 130; and sanctification 106, 175; and Scripture 62, 63-64; and struggle of realms 166-167; and ubiquity 128-129; and Word 124. *See also* Faith; Knowledge of God; Knowledge of man

Christian life 111, 112; and church 102-103; dialectical character of 29-30, 34-35, 57-58, 71, 73-74, 76, 169, 170-171, 172; as ingressive 34, 35, 37-38, 52, 58, 77, 86, 101, 106, 114-115, 152; and masks 154; and promise 99; as spatial and temporal 91-92, 92, 93, 96, 97-98, 111-112, 112-115, 117, 156-157. *See also* Church; Eschatology; Hope; New Creature; Promise; Sanctification

Christology 175-177; and atonement 53-54; and *communicatio idiomatum* 132, 132-133, 133; and incarnation 121-122, 131-132, 136, 136-137, 139; and sacraments 125-126, 127; and ubiquity 129, 130-131, 134. *See also* Atonement; *Communicatio idiomatum;* God's body; Lord's Supper; Tyrants

Church 103, 161, 170. *See also* Christian life

Communicatio idiomatum 132, 133. *See also* Christology; Lord's Supper; Ubiquity

Conscience 101, 171; as anthropological definition 19, 19-20, 23; certainty of 89, 90; and law 71, 91, 114-115; and values 45-46, 47. *See also* Anthropology; Person-work

Creation: expectancy of 19, 86; Fall of 49-51; as mask 146, 149-151, 152, 154, 155-156, 175; mandates in 26, 35-36, 149, 152, 156-157, 164; orders 49, 155-157, 163-164, 170-171; as realm 25-26, 28-29, 165, 170-171; sacramental theory 133-135, 138-139; substance 92-93, 94, 113-115. *See also* Eschatology; God's body; Hope; Masks; New creature

192

David, King 21, 22, 25

Ebeling, G. 70, 162
Eckhart, Meister 113
Erasmus, D. 140, 142, 144, 145, 148
Eschatology 18, 30, 31, 100, 106, 121-122, 159, 161, 168, 173, 174-175. *See also* Author's method; Christian life; Creation; Hope; New creature; Structure of Luther's theology

Faith and experience 111-112; and Gospel 63-64; hiddenness of 33-34, 45-46, 47, 86, 95, 98-99, 113, 114-115, 141, 155, 157, 165, 170, 172; and hope 100; and justification 75-76; and Law 38, 60-61, 64, 65-66, 72-75, 75-76, 83; and promise 90; and Word 94-95, 96, 97; and works 60-61, 88, 91, 97-98, 110, 156-157. *See also* Christ; Christian life; Hope; Justification; Law; Promise; Works
Fanatics *see* Anabaptists
Feuerbach, L. 51
Finitum capax infiniti 121-122, 127, 138, 174. *See also* Creation
Flesh and spirit 44-47, 56-58, 74, 126-127, 157. *See also* Anthropology
Forgiveness of sins 22, 25, 102, 125-126. *See also* Baptism

God, attributes of 141, 143-144, 150-151, 153; hidden and revealed 95-96, 131, 135-136, 139-140, 140-141, 141-142, 143, 144, 146, 149, 150, 151-152, 153; omnipresence 123; power 142, 145-146, 146-147, 147-149, 159; presence 124-125, 131-132, 133, 134, 135-136, 137, 139, 145, 149. *See also* Knowledge of God; Masks; Theology; Scripture
God's body 121-122, 131, 137, 149. *See also* Christology; Creation
Gospel 63; and Law 38, 59-61, 64-65, 70-71, 163. *See also* Law; Promise; Revelation; Scripture
Grace 22, 64-65, 83-84, 91-92, 116, 119-120, 140, 142. *See also* Holy Spirit; Works

Heidegger, M. 45
Holy Spirit 57-58, 69, 70, 105-106, 126-127. *See also* Grace; New creature
Hope 86, 87-88, 100-101. *See also* Grace; Holy Spirit; New creature
Hume, D. 104

Idolatry 25, 48-52, 165. *See also* Knowledge of God; Sin
Image of God 47, 112-113. *See also* Anthropology

Jonah 51-52, 145. *See also* Tyrants
Justification 64-66, 72-74, 75-77, 85-86, 91, 100-101, 110-111. *See also* Faith; Luther Research; Sanctification

Kant, E. 11, 104, 128. *See also* Luther Research; Speculation
Knowledge of God 20, 21, 29, 43, 47-48, 50-51, 53-54, 63. *See also* Anthropology; Christ; Idolatry; Knowledge of man; Masks; Revelation; Theology; Word and Sacrament
Knowledge of man 20-21, 43-44, 50-51, 53-54, 63. *See also* Anthropology; Christ; Knowledge of God; Theology

Larvae Dei see Masks
Law 52, 59-61, 66-70, 90, 146, 162; and Christian man 106-109; and human nature 66-70, 72. *See also* Anthropology; Faith; Gospel; Justification; Promise; Works
"Left-wing" Reformers *see* Anabaptists
Lord's Supper 102, 126-127, 127, 138. *See also* Christology; *Communicatio idiomatum;* Mass; Sacraments; Ubiquity; Zwingli
Luther research 10-11, 75, 84-85, 128, 159. *See also* Justification; Kant

Masks 39, 50, 138-139, 143-144, 144, 145-146, 149-150, 152-155, 157, 158, 168, 171, 172. *See also* Creation; Knowledge of God; God, attributes of
Mandates *see* Creation
Mass 88, 102. *See also* Lord's Supper; Sacraments
Melanchthon, P. 86
Moses 69, 146

New creature 101, 105-106, 114-116, 117, 120, 154-155, 161. *See also* Christian life; Creation; Eschatology; Hope; Holy Spirit; Sanctification

Paul, St. 19, 43, 44, 53, 57, 67, 71, 73, 85, 86, 90, 106, 108, 111, 118
Penultimate *see* Schema
Person-work 111, 117-120, 156-158, 168, 171-172. *See also* Anthropology; Conscience; Works
Plato 107, 113, 121
Process philosophers 11
Promise 62, 64, 84-92, 99, 100-101, 116. *See also* Baptism; Christian life; Eschatology; Faith; Gospel; Hope; Law
Proximate *see* Schema

Realms 159, 160, 162-163, 164, 165-166, 167-168; of Christ 160-162, 162, 163, 166, 167; contradiction in worldly 25-26, 28-29,

33, 46-47, 48, 55-56, 158, 160, 162, 164, 165; life in two 29-30, 46-47, 167-169, 170-171; opposition between 24-26, 28-29, 45-47, 165, 166-167, 168; worldly 24, 25-26, 162-163, 165

Reason 20, 43, 47, 128-129, 149-150, 152, 163. *See also* Speculation; Ubiquity

Revelation 50, 63, 64; and Word of God 61-63, 63-64, 69-70, 72, 96, 143, 145, 166. *See also* Gospel; Knowledge of God; Scripture

Sacraments 125, 138-139, 151-152, 154-155. *See also* Baptism; Lord's Supper; Mass; Word and Sacrament

Sanctification 35, 75, 77, 105, 110-111, 114-115, 116, 119-120. *See also* Christian life; Justification; New creature; Sin; Works

Schema 30; penultimate 29-30, 31, 32-37; proximate 29, 30, 32-36, 37; ultimate 30, 31-32, 36-37. *See also* Bonhoeffer, D.

Schleiermacher, F. 123

Scholasticism 20, 22, 25, 133, 150. *See also* Catholic theology; Reason

Scripture 61-62, 91-92, 104-105, 107, 147. *See also* Gospel; Knowledge of God; Theology

Sin 21, 22, 25, 48-49, 52-53, 59, 66-67, 69. *See also* Anthropology; Idolatry; Sanctification; Tyrants

Speculation 128-129, 131, 133-134, 135, 142-144, 145, 149, 151. *See also* Kant; Reason; Ubiquity

Structure of Luther's theology 15, 100, 121, 147-148; contrasts in 16-17, 23, 34, 37,

139-140; dialectical form of 15-16, 17, 18-19, 23-24, 29-30, 37, 56-58, 139-140; epistemology 83-84, 94-95, 97, 110, 125-126, 126-127, 135-136, 160, 176; method 26-27, 129-131; perspectives 18-19, 29-30, 75, 173-174; Christ and faith 21-23, 24, 27, 37, 38-39, 173; *coram* 20-24, 25-26, 41, 173; *regnum* 24-26, 27, 33, 172-173; relational 18-19, 28-29, 30, 36, 45-46, 59, 139-140, 173; systematic 27-28, 74-75, 108-109. *See also* Eschatology

Theology 19, 36-37, 45-46, 70, 112; of the cross 43, 45-46, 50-51, 56, 87, 94-95; subject of 19-20, 22, 23, 36-37. *See also* Knowledge of God; Knowledge of man; Reason

Thomas, St. 10

Tillich, P. 15, 45, 113, 153

Tyrants 52, 53-56, 59-60, 61. *See also* Atonement; Jonah; Sin

Ubiquity 39, 128-138. *See also* Christology; *Communicatio idiomatum;* Lord's Supper; Reason; Speculation

Ultimate *see* Schema

Word and Sacrament 124-125, 127, 135-136

Works 71-72, 73-74, 77, 87-88, 98, 109-110, 114-115, 155, 156-157, 172. *See also* Faith; Grace; Law; Person-work

Zwingli, H. 31, 126, 127, 177. *See also* Lord's Supper

Index to *Luther's Works*

Against the Heavenly Prophets in the Matter of Images and Sacraments 128

Antinomian Disputations 12, 13, 68, 69

Assertio omnium articulorum 12, 140

Babylonian Captivity of the Church 88, 89, 102

Bondage of the Will 12, 87, 89, 91, 95, 140, 141, 145-148

Confession Concerning Christ's Supper 12, 128; cf. in general the essays *Ubiquitas Carnalis Christi* 123 and *Larvae Dei* 138.

Dictata super psalterium 85-86, 91

Lectures on Galatians 1519 13, 68, 73, 86-87, 90, 109

Lectures on Galatians 1535 12, 13, 53, 55, 65, 68-69, 73, 90, 92, 96, 97, 149

Lectures on Genesis 13

A Treatise on Good Works 87-88

Lectures on the Epistle to the Hebrews 13, 94 108

Der Prophet Jona Ausgelegt 13, 48, 124-125 135, 145, 149, 176

Operationes in psalmos 12, 46, 87, 89

Lectures on Romans 9, 12, 13, 55-56, 62, 68, 76, 85, 96, 100, 102, 108, 148, 150

The Sacrament of the Body and Blood of Christ—Against the Fanatics 128

That These Words of Christ, "This is my Body," . . . *Still Stand Firm Against the Fanatics* 12, 128, 129; cf. in general the essays *Ubiquitas carnalis Christi* 123 and *Larvae Dei* 138.

Index to Scripture Passages

Gen	3:9	92		5:5	68, 109
Deut.	27:26	90		7	71, 117, 118
Ps.	2	25		8	114
	5:11	87		8:7	50
	22:25	46		8:7-20	93
	45	98		8:19	19, 86, 94, 115
	51	19, 25, 28, 31, 32, 35, 85		9:28	96
Matt.		107	Gal.	1:24	73
Luke		107		2:16-20	73
Acts		107		2:19	55, 68, 109
Rom.	1	85		3:7-23	90
	1:21	48		3:10	90, 97
	2:12-15	67		3:12	90, 91
	2:15	108		3:13 ff.	17, 55
	3:2 f.	85-86		3:17	90, 91
	3:2 ff.	64, 85		3:23	90, 91
	3:4	76, 100		5:14	98
	3:7	85	1 Tim.	1:9	108
	3:12	86	Heb.	3:13	49, 50
	4:7	86		7:12	108
	4:13-21	86		10:34	93
				11:1	83, 93, 95, 96